"When drinking the water, remember the source"
This book is dedicated to my parents

Rebuilding the Ancestral Village

Singaporeans in China

KUAH KHUN ENG
University of Hong Kong

Ashgate

Aldershot • Brookfield USA • Singapore • Sydney

DS
610.25
.C5
K83
2000

Published by
Ashgate Publishing Limited
Gower House
Croft Road
Aldershot
Hants GU11 3HR
England

Ashgate Publishing Company
Old Post Road
Brookfield
Vermont 05036
USA

Ashgate website: http://www.ashgate.com

British Library Cataloguing in Publication Data
Kuah, Khun Eng
    Rebuilding the ancestral village : Singaporeans in China
    1.Singaporeans - China 2.Social values - China
    I.Title
    305'8'951

Library of Congress Catalog Card Number: 99-75458

ISBN 0 7546 1137 X

Printed and bound by Athenaeum Press, Ltd.,
Gateshead, Tyne & Wear.

Contents

Maps

Tables

Diagrams

Photographs

Romanisation

Chinese terms and place names are transliterated by the Hanyu Pinyin system in the text. Some commonly used terms and names by the informants are romanised according to the Fujian dialect and are identified with a [H] immediately following the term. A list of the romanised terms and names and their corresponding Chinese characters is provided in the glossary.

Acknowledgements

In researching this piece of work I have benefited greatly from the assistance given to me by many people. I am grateful to the Department of Sociology, University of Hong Kong, for some financial aid that helped to pay for the research assistants who helped me with the fieldwork and the interviews in Anxi. I am also extremely grateful to the University of Hong Kong for granting me a year of study leave and to the Harvard-Yenching Institute which provided me with the Visiting Scholar fellowship that enabled me to work on the drafts of this manuscript. I am also grateful to various people who had provided me with opportunities to engage in academic dialogue and have shown much interest in this work. I am grateful to my colleagues in the Department of Sociology, to Professor Wang Gungwu who has taken time to read and comment on the manuscript and to Arthur Kleinman and Joan Kleinman who have shown much interest in this work. Various drafts were read at workshops in Taipei, Harvard, Singapore, Australia and the Netherlands and the comments received are gratefully acknowledged here. I am also grateful to John Thorne who edited the initial draft of this manuscript, Eric Tsang for his assistance in the maps and photographs and to Clara Wan for helping with typing the Chinese characters.

While institutional and collegial supports have been important in the shaping of the manuscript, it is to the informants that I owe my greatest debt. I am grateful to the Singapore members and the Anxi villagers for sharing their thoughts and ideas with me. I am grateful to those who have endured my intrusion and suffered numerous rounds of interviews and questionings. In Anxi, I am especially grateful to the villagers and members of the lineage for helping me with all my needs and demands. Without their readiness to assist and their openness to answer all my queries, it would have been very difficult for me to complete this work. Needless to say, any shortcoming remains my sole responsibility.

I also wish to acknowledge the following publishers, with their kind permission, to reproduce part of my articles and chapters for the following chapters found in this book. (1) For chapter 5, "Rebuilding Their Ancestral Villages: The Moral Economy of the Singapore Chinese" in Wang, G.W. and Wong, J. (ed.), 1998, *China's Political Economy*, Singapore: University of Singapore Press and World Scientific, pp. 249-275. (2) For chapter 6, "The Changing Moral Economy of Ancestor Worship in a Chinese Emigrant Village", in *Culture, Medicine and Psychiatry*, vol. 237, 1999, pp.99-132. (3) For chapter 9, "Doing Anthropology within a Transnational Framework: A Study of the Singapore Chinese and Emigrant Village Ties" in Cheung, S. (ed.), 1998, *On South China Track*, Hong Kong: Institute of Asia-Pacific, Chinese University of Hong Kong, pp. 81-109

Finally, let me acknowledge the assistance that my parents and extended family have provided me. They have been very generous with their time and patience. My husband, Matt Pearce has been most encouraging, looking after our newborn daughter which has enabled me to work and complete this book. I am also grateful to him for the final editing of this work.

As the saying goes, "when drinking water, remember the source". I wish to dedicate this book to my parents for all that they have done for us.

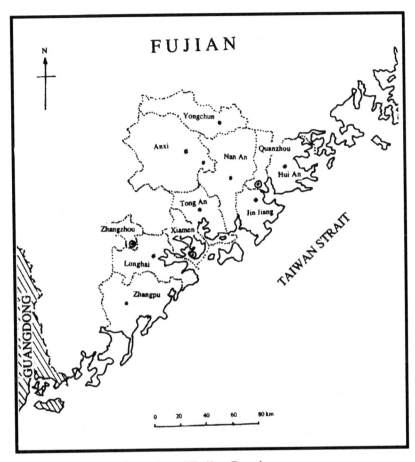

Map 1 Cities and Counties of Fujian Province

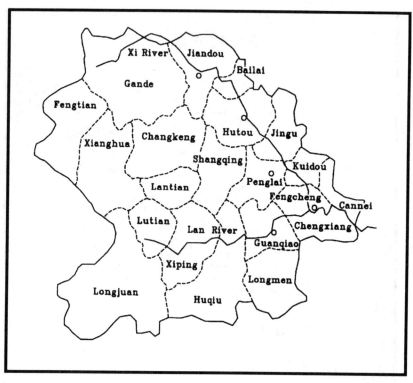

Map 2 Administrative Units of Anxi County, Fujian

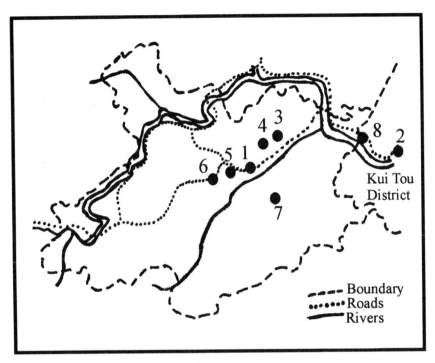

Map 3 Peng Lai District, Anxi County

1 Peng Lai Zhen   4 Lian Meng Village   7 Peng Xi Village

2 Kui Tou Zhen   5 Ling Dong Village   8 Kui Tou Village

3 Lian Zhong Village   6 Ling Nan Village

1 Introduction

Introduction

This is a study of the relationship between two groups of Chinese, the Singapore Chinese and the village counterparts in Anxi County, Fujian. It investigates the Singapore Chinese and the search for cultural roots by tracing their origins to their ancestral home village in Anxi, resulting in the revival of the Chinese lineage. Anxi County is popularly known as the district of emigrant villages, or *qiaoxiang* (僑鄉), from which people emigrated to various parts of the world, especially to Southeast Asia, during the nineteenth and the first half of the twentieth centuries.

Since the early 1990s, there has been much interest in the study of the *qiaoxiang* and of the Chinese in overseas communities. While some literary works have focussed on the attempts of the "Chinese overseas" to trace their roots back to their home villages in China, there has been very little systematic work done on the relationship between the Chinese overseas and their *qiaoxiang* connections.

The central focus of this study is to address the questions of why the Singapore Chinese continue to be interested in their ancestral home villages and why the Singapore Chinese, and especially those locally born, have become involved in the life and in the socio-economic reconstruction of their ancestral villages as well as the reconstruction of their own culture. This study is thus about the creation of a moral economy which resulted in the ancestral villages experiencing general prosperity within the county.

The primary focus of this study is to examine how collective memory serves as a powerful force in pulling the Singapore Chinese back to their ancestral home village. Through this collective memory, the Singapore Chinese are able to revive the Chinese lineage and reinvent socio-cultural and religious roles. The involvement of Singapore Chinese in village activities has resulted in a need to reinvestigate the role of lineage structure in both contemporary Singapore urban and rural village Chinese societies, an issue that will be dealt with. The way in which a sense of moral responsibility has helped them to redefine their roles within a Chinese village milieu will also be discussed. At a broader conceptual level, this study looks beyond the Singapore Chinese-*qiaoxiang* connection and seeks to link it up with Chinese communities elsewhere. It is also a study of the position of the Singapore Chinese and their *qiaoxiang* relations

1

as part of a cultural network and of the transformation of the Chinese lineage from a parochial structure to a transnational network structure.

Establishing a Moral Economy

Why do Singapore Chinese feel morally obligated to assist their ancestral homes? To understand the reasons for their motives and actions we need to explore their understanding, identification and affinity with their ancestral villages and with their specific ancestral homes, *lao-jia* (老家); and also their understanding of their moral duty and the level of their moral consciousness. It is imperative to understand their moral sentiments from an inter-generational perspective in order to understand the continuities and discontinuities between the Singapore Chinese and their *qiaoxiang* kin. At the same time, it is also important for us to understand the Anxi Chinese and their actions in creating an environment that binds the Singapore Chinese to their ancestral villages, thereby establishing a moral economy.

The inter-generational perspective will enable us to understand the differences across generations. It is often the case that the migrants who immigrated from elsewhere to Singapore continue to have strong sentimental ties with their ancestral villages. This has proven to be the case among a majority of the first generation migrants from Anxi. Because of these ties they feel morally obliged to assist their immediate village kin financially and materially. They have also become extremely active in contributing substantially to village infrastructure development and to socio-religious activities. Even during times of political restriction, the Singapore Chinese have managed to send small remittances, medicine and other material goods to their village kin. Also motivating them is their knowledge of what poverty is and of how their ancestral villages have, throughout history, been one of the poorest districts in China. Many of these Singapore Chinese migrants are therefore sympathetic to their village kin and are committed to alleviating their poverty. Some are also committed to eradicating poverty at the county level.

What about the Singapore-born Chinese of Anxi descent? How do they look at the ancestral village and the demands of the moral economy? A common view is that these Singapore-born Chinese have less emotional attachment and interest in their ancestral villages and are hence less likely to assist in village reconstruction or to participate in village activities. This view argues that these Singapore Chinese do not see the ancestral villages as having any important significance except for the fact that their ancestors came from them. It further argues that the ancestral origins of these Chinese are less important to them, and that they therefore want to have very little dealing with their ancestral villages.

In fact, Singapore-born Chinese of Anxi descent have substantial interest in their ancestral villages. A sizeable number of Singapore-born Chinese of Anxi descent have visited their ancestral villages and have participated in various socio-religious activities there. They have also contributed significantly to village infrastructure development. Several factors account for their active participation. The first is the strength of the lineage structure in Singapore in binding the younger members to their primordial kinship networks. The fact that the younger members of the lineage continue to socialise and have links with one another allows the lineage to create a critical group of younger members within itself. They are drawn into participating in village activities by the older members. Another factor is the strength of the family. In most cases, the older members often encourage the younger members to visit, participate in and contribute to village development in Anxi. In recent years, the (Singapore) Anxi Association has also played an instrumental role in encouraging the younger members to participate in the activities of their ancestral villages and Anxi County. Through the use of moral persuasion both the older and younger members of the lineage become involved in village affairs.

At the village level, the Anxi Chinese draw on existing primordial social ties, or *guanxi* (關系), to extract monetary and material benefits from their Singapore kin. They use moral arguments and persuasion to encourage the Singapore Chinese to become more involved in village affairs. These Anxi Chinese, by recalling their kinship ties and insisting on the moral duties of their Singapore kin, have managed to tap into the feelings of sentiment and guilt harboured by the Singapore Chinese. They are thus able to create a moral economy based on a sense of moral responsibility.

At the same time, the Anxi Chinese have publicly displayed the various types of social recognition bestowed on the Singapore kin for contributing to village development. By honouring them for their contributions to their ancestral homes and by pointing out their moral duties to their home villages, the Anxi Chinese have further entrenched the foundations of a moral economy. However, this moral economy is not a harmonious one. It is imbued with tensions, conflict of interests, rivalry and resentment between the two groups of Chinese. Tensions and resentment are most acutely felt by the younger generation of Singapore Chinese who often do not feel belonged to the ancestral village.

Collective Memories and Nostalgic Sentiments

A second major theme that will be explored is the power of the collective memories and nostalgic sentiments that the Singapore Chinese continue to hold for their ancestral homes. This is especially true for the generation of older Chinese who immigrated to Singapore. Their early experiences in villages in China and their memories of them continue to hold place in their hearts. Many have been unable or unwilling to erase these memories and have passed them on to their children, grandchildren and great-grandchildren. These early experiences in their home villages in China have become a sort of collective living memory for them and for their descendants.

According to Le Goff, "memory, the capacity for conserving certain information, refers first of all to a group of psychic functions that allow us to actualise past impressions or information that we represent to ourselves as past" (Le Goff, 1992: 51). There are two main types of collective memories: one is social and historical memory, and the other is artificial memory as found in computers.

What concerns us here is the social and historical memories of groups of people. According to Le Goff, memory is an essential element of any individual or collective identity (Le Goff, 1992: 98). Each society has its own forms of memories. Some tribal societies have no written records but only oral collective memories in the forms of songs and stories. Other societies have their memories written down so that their members and future generations can turn to them for guidance. Through historical development, social and collective memories have undergone changes. Depending on the social conditions and expectations of each historical epoch, the collective memory undergoes change through a process of divinisation, secularisation and rationalisation. The focus, in some societies, on mythology and religious activities has led to the placement of much emphasis on divine ideologies and on religious structures and rituals. Many of these have been written into the collective memory of these societies (Le Goff, 1992: 58-64).

Memory is also a subjective thought-process. At the personal level, it is the events and situations that individuals have experienced that constitute personal memories. These memories are passed on in various ways: through recording in diaries, memoirs, and letters, and through storytelling and other forms of oral transmission. Those that are not recorded in any form are often lost permanently (Watson, R., 1994:8). At another level, there are collective memories. According to Halbwachs, "while the collective memory endures and draws strength from its base in a coherent body of people, it is individuals as group members who remember" (Halbwachs, 1992: 22). Thus, there are as many collective memories as there are groups and institutions in a society (Halbwachs, 1992: 22). These are usually shared experiences of individuals within a group who have "remembered" events: they have not necessarily experienced the actual events but are well versed in the images and imagery of them. These events are often represented in various forms - historical monuments, stories, paintings, rituals, poetry, music, photographs and films (Watson, R., 1994:8).

The remembering of events is never systematic. Memories are not logically presented, nor do individuals intellectualise them in any way. Thus, the representations of this collective memory - whether in visible form as in monuments, paintings, and rituals, or in documented form as in diaries - remain fragmented. Nevertheless, these memories provide images to rely on for a group of people searching for the events that affected the life of their ancestors, their society and their country. To a large degree, collective memories allow individuals to reconstruct their collective past by thinking about what the collective events were like at crucial historical moments. History and historical events are not snapshots and cannot be conceived of as such. It is this fluidity of events and their representations that allow for the flow of images and imagery that is encapsulated as collective memory. Here, the causal relationship between memory and history has been clearly stated. However, while history records the interpretation of memories at various levels - public, private and personal - memories remain on the individual level.

Collective memories are derived from a collection of individual memories grounded in a particular social context. They therefore represent a social memory. Depending on the group of people and the social framework, collective memories are the products of individual understandings and are also subject to personal and varying interpretations that changes through time and space. Thus, it is not uncommon to have several variants of collective memories.

There are historical and social memories, which are important in helping individuals to re-establish themselves in relation to the past and to provide anchorage in their search for self-identity in contemporary society, where the past and the present have become increasingly separated. Memory thus provides the link of continuity from the past to the present and into the future where it helps to shape present actions and reactions to past and present events. Memory also permits individuals or groups to use the existing knowledge based on their recollections to pursue future goals. To the Singapore Chinese from Anxi, what they remember as their ancestral or home villages and of the social events there are important reminders of who they are and where they come from, and which push them to react to the call of help from their ancestral village.

Halbwachs argues that "while the collective memory endures and draws strength from its base in a coherent body of people, it is individuals as group members who remember" (Halbwachs, 1992: 22). It is thus important to locate individual memory within the thought of the relevant social group of people in order that such memories become meaningful and relevant to all within it. According to Le Goff, in many societies without written traditions, there are "memory specialists, memory men". These are "genealogists, guardians of the royal lawbooks, historians of the court, traditionalists" (Le Goff, 1992: 56) whose main preoccupation is to maintain the cohesion of a group of people or a tribe through a continuous reminder of the commonality of these people. Le Goff considers this as "ethnic memory" (Le Goff, 1992: 55). He argues for "the accumulation of elements within memory [as] part of everyday life" of individuals (Le Goff, 1992: 55).

In collective memory, family plays an important role in establishing the framework for the types of memories to be included and for the transmission of such memories to its members. Because certain activities and ideas have been repeatedly transmitted to the members, they became deeply embedded in their minds and are reproduced for future use. Part of this involves the reproduction of the past.

The significance of collective memory lies in the roles it plays within the society. Memories do not only help people to understand certain historical events but also to understand present ones. Collective memories are known as historical facts. These historical facts embody a set of values that the society once upheld. While some of these values are still held by the group involved, others have been discarded. In reinventing collective memories, the group is, at the same time, attempting to revive traditional values in the face of social change.

Memory is also seen as an instrument and an objective of power. As such, a struggle for domination over remembrance and tradition involves the manipulation of memory (Le Goff, 1992: 98). The types of memory that are reconstructed and/or censored are deliberately and consciously chosen in contemporary society. They are used to assert authority and/or to legitimise one's position. To understand how collective memories work for a community or an individual, it is important to position these memories within a relevant social framework. Halbwachs looks at the initial preservation of collective memory as the primary domain of the elite class that has an entrenched tradition and a class hierarchy. The elite was once predominantly from the gentry's class. Since it was the elite version of the collective memory that dominated society, it was also the elite version of social values that was dominant within society. However, when a group of non-elite enter the nobility class, Halbwachs argues that the society needs to re-organise and modify, to some degree, the frameworks of its memory, either by distorting its past or by limiting the field of memory in order to screen out less desirable elements. Often, such a re-organisation is required as the new elite demands that their actions and values become incorporated into the collective memory. It is not uncommon for such societies to forget their remote past and only concentrate on the recent past contiguous with the present.

Additionally, Halbwachs argues that when a certain category of people have been conferred higher prestige and when this is collectively recognised by the society, it is because these people and their activities have contributed most to the entire social body (Halbwachs, 1992: 138). Thus, in such a situation, collective memories in the forms of titles, functions, philanthropic and charitable acts are based on the judgement that society makes of its members (Halbwachs, 1992: 144).

In traditional societies, the titles, functions, philanthropic and charitable acts are often associated with the gentry-elite class and it is this framework to which the society has been exposed. It is also this elite-based framework that is subjected to challenges by new groups. As collective memories involve collective social values of the established elite group, the moral tradition is therefore part of this established social value system. Here, Halbwachs argues that it is the rich who must be responsible for imparting the moral tradition to the poor, for they do not have a moral tradition. However, with changing social order, moral traditions are subjected to challenges from the newly-rich-turned-elite. There is thus a corresponding emergence of a new morality. The new members of the elite comprise an assortment of people ranging from artisans to merchants and others.

Likewise, the modern idea of virtue is elaborated in the wealthy class where each family head that has amassed wealth has done it through his own efforts. To a large extent, Halbwachs equates the scale of wealth with the scale of personal merit. Thus, the possessor of quantities of goods can be evaluated through such an equation. Such a person and his qualities have to endure the scrutiny of his society over a passage of time in order for the society to evaluate his contributions. After a considerable length of time, and if his qualities and contributions can make an imprint on the memory of the society, memories will serve to perpetuate the legacy of such a person or class of persons. To a large degree, in traditional society the conferring of titles recognised, and those with titles embodied, the desirable social qualities and virtues.

What happens with the emergence of new wealth and a new elite? Within the new moral tradition, wealth becomes an important social asset and those with wealth, irrespective of their occupational categories, assume high social status. As members of these new elite do not fit into the traditional framework of success, wealth and money become important yardsticks to measure their achievement. They therefore need to create a new order of tradition that will allow them to be incorporated into the existing social order. At the same time, this tradition must also recognise them as the new successful elite.

Inevitably, the creation of a new tradition comes into conflict with the existing one. The relationship between tradition and morality also comes into question. In the views of Halbwachs, the old tradition continues to be seen as one that corresponds to morality, while the new tradition is associated with immorality or, at best, with utilitarian morality. Utilitarian morality is used by the new elite to justify its commercial activities and the moneymaking process and presupposes the need to sacrifice, perhaps involving an element of altruism.

As changes occur within a society, it is forced to adopt new values and in doing so, it is forced to consult other collective memories and other frameworks of social values in order to establish a new tradition and a new order of social values. Apart from the dominant elite tradition and the elite version of collective memories that the society has been exposed to, alternative collective memories of various groups, not only of the new elite, but also of the various existing social groups - lineage, family and minority groups - begin to become important. These groups begin to exert their presence and demand that their memories and social histories become incorporated into the mainstream societal thought process.

An anthropological discourse of collective memory and nostalgia is therefore important in attempting to understand a group of people - be it an extended family, a lineage or a community - who are seeking to re-explore their cultural roots and identity. As with other scholars, it is possible to see the pursuit of memory as promoting and maintaining cultural formations in all their fullness and complexity. In this respect, Kuchler and Melion (1991: 7) argue that memory is characterised as follows:

(1) it is an actively constructed social and cultural process;
(2) it operates through representations;
(3) the modalities of recollection are historically based and the project of understanding is a historical one; and
(4) forgetting and recollecting are allied mnemonic functions where forgetting is a selective process through which memory achieves social and cultural dimensions

Memory can be tapped and activated through processes of philosophical inquiry but it does not itself generate these processes (Kuchler and Melion, 1992: 3). It is thus significant to understand the ways in which experience shapes and reshapes the collective memory. On the other hand, nostalgia is seen as a response to dissatisfaction with one's immediate situation. Such dissatisfaction provides an individual with a reason to idealise the past and past events. By looking towards the idealised past, one can momentarily disengage oneself from the immediate, less-than-enchanting present (Nosco, 1990: 4). Brought together, collective memories of the past allow individuals or social groups to recreate the past to satisfy their present needs for identity and for interaction.

The past is invoked to provide individuals and social groups with a shared social and collective understanding of the socio-cultural elements that they or their forebears have experienced. This serves as a binding base by means of which they identify themselves as a social group with a unique tradition. The past and tradition thus become important elements that are intertwined. In understanding memory and its recollection, the accuracy and exactness of each event has become a subject of contention by scholars of inquiry, especially those practising psychology and psychiatry. Lengthy works have been written on this issue. However, it is not the objective of this work to discuss the scientific inquiry into memory and of the accuracy of recollection. Rather, we are interested not so much with the "true" but with the process of recollection and with what events, images and representations are being recalled as important memoir experiences, cultural events and social processes. This involves selection. In this way, collective memory is part of social memory (Fentress and Wickham, 1992).

Another aspect that is of concern here is the role of women. Geary (1994) argues for the need to study the "memory of women" who are active in remembering, preserving and transmitting the past. It is through such acts of preservation, structuring and moulding that the past, along with its institutions, is remembered and its dynamics brought to knowledge in the present. Here, women as rememberers and women who are remembered are both important issues. While women as rememberers take a front seat in this area of collective memory; the issue of women who are remembered has paled into insignificance, given the dominance of a patriarchal structure. This is especially true in Chinese society. Thus, records of women who are remembered are scanty, to say the least. It remains to be seen whether, at the level of oral history, the prominence of women is more readily articulated than in the written tradition (Geary, 1994: 51-73).

This issue of the role of women is related to the issue of the professionalisation of the carriers of memory. Oral transmission was and is still an important method of imparting memories to future generations, especially at individual and familial levels. At lineage and other social levels, there is a tendency to establish memory on a permanent basis. Oral transmission has thus given way to written records. Genealogies are official records that serve to formalise present events and preserve them as memories for future generation. Thus, the concern of collective memory is not for the present but for the future. Such texts also maintain a high level of accuracy, which is important for future reference. These documents and records of the past enable us to reconstruct the past and revive the memories that are associated with them, thus providing us with a continuity from the past to the present. In a way, this has allowed for the development of two streams of memories. One is the official version, as represented by genealogies and written records. The other continues to be at the individual and folk levels where memories are passed down through oral transmission. It is possible for both official and unofficial versions to converge. It is also possible for the two to diverge, each giving a different version. The extent of convergence and divergence spells out not only the emphasis that different groups make in consciously remembering, but also the specific material that they want to represent. This selection is very much influenced by the social, cultural, or political environment during the time and at the place when the collective memory was transmitted and documented.

In the daily discourse of individuals, from storytelling to the reproduction of cultural items and rituals, it is the personal version of memory that we are confronted with. What is articulated consists of individual, personal and fragmented accounts of what individuals could remembered, choose to remember and want to remember. They come in the forms of stories, reminiscences and matter-of-fact statements. Usually, they are told to members of the inner kinship network. These are the stories that children, grandchildren and great grandchildren hear from their grandparents. Today, these stories form part of the oral history of the early emigrants who arrived and settled in Singapore.

By exploring this framework of collective memory, it is possible to understand the emotions and attachment of migrants to their ancestral home villages. This framework also helps us to comprehend the eagerness of the first-generation Singapore Chinese in visiting their ancestral homes and ancestral villages as well as their willingness to impart large sums of money and other contributions to help with the reconstruction of their ancestral villages.

Singapore Anxi Chinese and Their Collective Memory

The collective memory of the Singapore Anxi Chinese is tied to their shared understanding of their ancestral home, past experiences and present expectations. The crux of it lies with their desire to perpetuate a cultural identity. To the Singapore Chinese, memories of great difficulties are bittersweet experiences that serve as reminders of their ancestral home. This collective memory, to a certain degree, propels the migrants-turned-citizens to visit their ancestral villages. It also pushes the Singapore Anxi

Chinese to contribute financially to the socio-cultural and economic life of their home villages. The collective memory also has a negative impact on some. It acts as a resistant force, convincing some not to visit the home village.

For these Singapore Chinese, collective memory of their ancestral home is selective. In reconstructing the past events, many recount the great difficulties and poverty that they were in, their fear of the unknown when they set sail for Singapore and their eventual success, however modest, in Singapore. They especially remember the early years and their struggle for survival in the village. It is this memory that they have kept alive and that they choose to pass on to their descendants.

The collective memory of most Singapore migrant Chinese is one of poverty. Early experiences of poverty pushed many migrants to endure great difficulties and to work hard. Today, even as many have become relatively successful and have accumulated modest wealth, these Singapore Chinese continue to work hard. This form of work ethic is now widely studied and debated. Neo-Confucian scholars have argued that such work ethic is attributable to the existence of a Confucian Ethic. These scholars have cited the economic success of Taiwan, South Korea, Hong Kong and Singapore, all of them influenced by Confucian ideology, as proof of the existence of the Confucian Ethic. In the Singapore example, the Singapore State has consciously use various elements found within Confucian ideology for purposes of economic and social engineering.[1]

This collective memory of poverty is also instrumental and has become, in part, a guiding principle for the dealings between the Singapore migrant Chinese and their village counterparts. By recalling the poverty that they have undergone, Singapore migrant Chinese adopt a liberal, humane attitude toward the existing poverty experienced by their village kin in the ancestral home villages. They have become actively involved in providing financial, technical and informational assistance to their ancestral village and county. Initially, they helped members of the immediate family and lineage. Gradually, they became involved in village reconstruction. In recent years, they have become involved in county-level activities. From the early contributions to the members of their immediate kinship circle to involvement in county level activities, these Singapore Chinese have helped transform the emigrant villages from extreme poverty to relative prosperity.

The collective memory of these Singapore Chinese also provides these Chinese with a framework within which to search for their cultural roots. A part of the collective memory involves a repertoire of social customs, rituals and religious elements. Within the Chinese community in Singapore, these social customs, rituals and religious elements have become routinised as part of the communal social fabric. They are enacted on a regular, and for some elements on a daily, basis. When visiting the ancestral village, these Chinese bring along and reproduce their understanding of the social customs, rituals and religious elements.

The collective memory also provides this group of Chinese with a sense of identity. It reminds them of who they are and where they come from. As Singapore citizens living permanently in Singapore, these Chinese continue to have a strong sense of affinity, *ganqing*, (感情) for their ancestral home, *zuxiang* (祖鄉). A strong sense of affinity is imperative to locate their identity within a known and manageable social framework. This social framework is grounded in kinship ties. The collective memory is also significant in the revival of both primordial and secondary social relationships with the ancestral village.

At another level, by recalling collective memory and transmitting it to the younger generation Chinese, collective memory serves to keep alive the experiences of the ancestors for the younger generation. It reminds these younger members of their ancestral villages and of their wider social kinship networks. Among the Singapore Anxi Chinese, the migrant-Chinese have imparted this collective memory through reminiscences, oral stories and actions. Most of these elements of the collective memory are transmitted in a spontaneous and fragmented manner. This collective memory is seen as a social bridge that can link the younger Singapore Chinese to their ancestral villages.

A collective memory of the ancestral village, either through oral transmission, written accounts, or both, is important in a society. It keeps alive the images of the ancestral village and of its members and their socio-cultural, economic and political experiences. Through the collective memory, awareness of the present state of affairs of the ancestral village and of its members and activities is kept alive. The Singapore Chinese are also reminded of their ritual obligation to perform duties to their ancestors and engage in cultural reproduction.

The Ideology of Moral Duty

A third theme to be considered is the role of ideology in shaping the attitudes of the Singapore Chinese towards their ancestral villages and the effect this has on cultural identity. The Singapore Chinese have undergone various phases of change in Singapore. The migrant-Chinese continue to be governed by a sense of moral duty to their ancestral villages. What is this sense of moral duty? Is this sense of moral duty influenced by the Chinese understanding of Confucianism, the Buddhist notion of karma, or other ideologies?

Halbwachs sees the preservation of collective memory as an important moral duty, irrespective of whether it belongs to an individual, family, lineage or a social group. He argues that it is the desire to preserve this memory that leads group members to embark on philanthropic or charitable acts. He sees the act of philanthropy as a tangible outcome to preserve the memory of the giver after his or her death. Philanthropic acts enable future generations to remember his or her name. Philanthropy is thus seen as an act that is aimed for future gratification after the passing away of an individual or a group. The present action is thus a prelude to the preservation of a memory of a person or group in future.

It is also possible to argue, as Weber, that the creation and the giving-away of wealth and the sacrifice of enjoyment are grounded in one's moral duties. According to Weber (1966), these are calls of an inner-worldly asceticism for self-denial and for the solution of the problem of theodicy in one's spiritual development. The creation of wealth is important, but the giving-away of this wealth is a more important act than its creation. This sense of moral duty lies in fulfilling God's calling and the giving-away of wealth is done in the memory of the god itself. In this Christian model of moral duty, Perry (1909) argues for the uncomplicated good nature of human beings as the key to moral duty to a community by individuals. The actions are altruistic, for the individuals desire neither any fame or social reward.

In Confucianism, the moral duty of an individual is governed by the observance of the five moral values. They are humanity, *ren* (仁); righteousness, *yi* (義); rituals, *li* (禮); loyalty, *zhong* (忠); and filial piety, *xiao* (孝). Individuals are expected to perform what are considered as right and moral actions. In the ideal-type situation, a person who has perfected all five moral values is a gentleman, *junzi* (君子). A gentleman has to commit himself totally to the cultivation of these moral values as second nature. For an individual to attain the highest level of moral cultivation, he/she has to routinise moral practices as part of the daily routine. It is also imperative that an individual has full knowledge of the self, of him/herself, in order to achieve moral and spiritual perfection. Here, the most important act is to learn to become human, *ren* (仁). Tu argues that human nature is perfectible and that perfection can be achieved through a continuous process of "inner illumination and self transformation" (Tu, 1985: 19) of a moral and spiritual kind (Tu, 1985: 22). According to Tu, self-knowledge of one's mental state and inner feeling is the key to the process of inner illumination and transformation (ibid.: 19). This self-knowledge will enable an individual to act, to create and to transform his/her self into a perfect self (Tu, 1985: 19-20). It is "an objectless awareness, a realisation of the human possibility of 'intellectual intuition'" (Tu, 1985: 20). One's true or real nature is thus "a self-creating and self-directing process" (Tu, 1985: 20). It is also a liberating process, freeing oneself from the trappings of human desires.

In the book of Mencius, according to Tu, human beings are endowed with moral sense, *xin* (心). This moral sense consists of four basic human feelings. These are commiseration, shame and dislike, deference and compliance, and right and wrong (Tu, 1985: 24). It is these feelings that push the individuals to learn and refine the self (心). The *xin*, in this context, symbolises conscience and consciousness (Tu, 1985: 24). Imbued with these feelings, human beings are able to cultivate and attain perfection. These feelings serve as imperatives for moral cultivation. Thus, Confucian teaching sees altruistic motivation as an important force for the perfection of the self.

Morality and moral actions are to be found in daily social intercourse. The *Book of Filial* Piety, *Xiaojing* (孝經) stresses the moral responsibility of an individual to his or her parents, to family, as well as to other lineage-members, including the dead ancestors. To neglect them is to be unfilial, *buxiao* (不孝); consciously to neglect one's parents or ancestors is to descend to the lowest level of moral responsibility. Thus, a consciousness of the responsibility to one's parents is a moral requirement. Aged parents should be regarded with high esteem. An individual is expected conscientiously to look after the spiritual and material well being of his or her parents. There are two reasons for this, the first reason being that the individual is indebted to his or her parents for the gift of life and the second being that the individual is indebted to his/her parents for raising him/her from infancy to adulthood. This form of indebtedness is incurred irrespective of the treatment the person received during the various stages of growth and development. In the *Xiaojing*, individuals are expected to transcend personal feelings in carrying out filial duty and becoming morally worthy.

The Buddhist notion of karma and merit making shapes the way in which adherents devote themselves to cultivating moral good in order to achieve spiritual enlightenment. The Buddhist notion of one's ability to realise one's self serves to encourage individuals to cultivate their spiritualism, *xiuxin* (修心) through this-worldly asceticism. This is the willingness to sacrifice immediate material enjoyment to prepare for otherworldly spiritual achievement. This includes doing good and depriving oneself of all material and sensual pleasures. The ultimate goal is to attain Buddha-hood.

Within the Mahayana Buddhist tradition, the concept of the bodhisattva reveals the ultimate path towards Buddhist morality. Differing from Theravada Buddhism, which focuses on self-enlightenment,

Mahayana Buddhism stresses mass salvation through the help of the bodhisattva, a perfected being who postpones his or her attainment of nirvana indefinitely in order to help all sentient being along the path of enlightenment. This is a selfless, morally virtuous act that those who have aspired Buddhahood will attempt to emulate. The taking of the bodhisattva vow by the adherents is an important step towards this process of self-realisation.

Buddhism argues that the heart of every individual is capable of doing good deeds. Within the mundane world, doing good is translated into practical selfless actions that are aimed at assisting the welfare of others, in both spiritual and material senses. Good deeds and works of charity are regarded as important social actions. Other key concerns in Buddhism are the notions of karma and merit making. Every individual is subjected to karmic influences. The karma of an individual is dependent upon individual actions accumulated, during both past and present lives. There is both good and bad karma. The main purpose of performing good deeds is related closely to merit making. Among the Singapore Chinese, a key concern in doing good acts is the accumulation of merit and good karma in this life to cancel bad karma previously accumulated.

Another concept is that of the transferability of good merit from one person to another. Individuals can engage in meritorious deeds to help the dead to increase their store of good merits. It is now a common sight to see charity being carried out in the names of the dead in order to ensure that the dead have a sufficient store of merits and good karma, which is essential for ultimate enlightenment. Charity work and good deeds are likewise carried out for the living with the aim of making merit and storing good karma for future use. This is to ensure that in after-life individuals will be relieved of extreme sufferings. Caught in the wheel of rebirth and the knowledge of the possibility of a rebirth into one of the six planes of existence, a store of good karma will enable the dead to move swiftly from the netherworld to the human plane. This is important for it is only when one is reborn on the human plane of existence that there is hope for the ultimate cessation of rebirth. This is the primary reason why believers and practitioners of Buddhism practice good acts and charity.

In Daoism, goodness and compassion are considered to be part of human nature. Daoism sees moral good as the flow of nature. To do what is not good is to be unnatural and against the Dao. Moral good and moral duty is thus an essential part of human nature.

Reinventing A Chinese Culture

A fourth theme that will be investigated in this study consists of the concepts of cultural reinvention and cultural reproduction. Hobsbawn defines "invented tradition" as "a set of practices, normally governed by overtly or tacitly accepted rules and of a ritual or symbolic nature, which seeks to inculcate certain values and norms of behaviour by repetition, which automatically implies continuity with the past" (Hobsbawn and Ranger, 1983: 1). The term "inventing traditions" is taken to mean a "process of formalisation and ritualisation, characterised by reference to the past" (Hobsbawn and Ranger, 1983: 4). The invention of tradition is required under three circumstances. The first situation that requires the invention of a tradition is the need to establish the social cohesion and membership of a group within a real or imagined community. The second situation is the need to legitimise the institutions and authority structures of a given society. The third is to provide a set of values and beliefs for members of a community (Hobsbawn and Ranger, 1983: 8).

In the process of reinventing a culture, the significant elements that a group of people considers as representational of their culture are invented. These include material icons, ritual functions, ritual behaviours and social customs. During the process of reinventing a culture, there are two groups of players. One set is engaged in the decision-making process. Its task is to detail the elements that are to be reinvented. This group comprises the elite and dominant members of the society. They have the resources and the intellectual and cultural depth to engineer the reinvention of selected cultural elements that they see as significant in portraying their culture and their cultural identity. The second set consists of those engaged in the actual process of reinventing these cultural elements and acts. These players lack the resources and administrative skills needed to initiate the process of cultural reinvention, but they are active participants in the reinvented culture. The culture that is reinvented within a society can thus be seen as the idealised and imagined culture of the dominant group. Through time, this invented culture disseminated into the wider community and becomes accepted as the culture. Under such situation, no one within the community questions its origin.

The timing and the socio-political context in which cultural invention takes place are important factors to consider. Success in cultural reinvention can only be realised when the timing is correct and when the political climate is conducive to reproduction. It is important that the members of the group share a collective need for such a reinvention and believe that such action is necessary for the survival of their social collectivity. A conviction of such need will push the members to group together and engage in this process of reinvention. But success can only be achieved if there is no hostile political climate to interfere with cultural reproduction. In many cases, it is important that the state supports such a reinvention. A relaxed and liberal climate will enable the group to engage in the reproduction of cultural elements without fear of reprisal for its members and without the suppression of its cultural practices.

Within a migrant society where there are numerous groups in existence, each group attempts to reinvent its own culture. Within the Singapore Chinese community there are numerous groups based on dialect and territorial affiliations. These smaller groups have brought varieties of cultural elements and have placed varying degrees of significance on the various cultural elements that they have been taught in their ancestral villages. Thus, within the dominant Chinese cultural system there are several sub-cultural systems among Chinese subgroups.

For the Singapore Chinese, the ancestral village provides a physical space to carry out the elaborate socio-religious activities that are no longer fashionable within Singapore society. The functions that are conducted in the ancestral village are either religious activities or have strong religious overtones. Communal religious fairs and ancestor worship have become two important activities, the *raison d'etre* for village visits. These functions are conducted with great elaboration.

In the ancestral village, socio-religious activities were not the central focus of village life until the early 1980s, when economic liberalisation brought about socio-cultural liberation. Traditional practices had not been regarded as significant by the younger generation. Older villagers had also come to accept their inability to carry out many of these activities. Only with the return of Singapore lineage members did attempts at reviving and reproducing certain aspects of socio-religious practices begin.

The reproduction of a culture within the ancestral village milieu can be seen as an outcome of a process of negotiation between the Singapore Chinese and the villagers. When the Singapore Chinese began to visit their ancestral villages they brought along the knowledge and cultural practices that they were familiar with in Singapore. They sought to reproduce these cultural items within the ancestral village context.

Within Chinese villages, many of the cultural practices of the pre-Communist era were considered a waste of precious resources. This is true of religion, which was considered as superstition and was officially banned. In recent years the Communist State has formally recognised the existence of institutional religions, but religious practices continue to be low key affairs. Today, any form of organised religious function continues to receive the close attention of Communist officials. Yet, within the ancestral villages, such functions have received a more liberal treatment. As the villagers revive their socio-religious practices, many are forced to rely on their memories to reconstruct them. At the same time, ritual practices have been consciously constructed to suit the political ideology in order to safeguard the interests of the villagers and not to offend the Communist State.

As a result of the differences in the social environments and political requirements experienced by these two groups of Chinese, there exists a great gulf between them in the understanding and interpretation of cultural and religious practices, so that what we see today in the ancestral village is a tradition negotiated and invented by these two groups of Chinese. It is a tradition based on a shared understanding of what constitute the core elements of the culture and of what can be practised within the existing socio-political framework of the ancestral village setting without arousing official dissatisfaction.

The content of this negotiated culture is geared towards ancestor worship and folk religion. These practices are known to both the Singapore and Anxi Chinese. However, there remain differences in the style, ritual content and elaboration of these activities between the two groups of Chinese. An agreement on practice has been reached, and today we see each lineage conducting ancestor worship and folk religious practices according to their internally agreed upon agendas.

It is possible to argue that an invented tradition has to be seen as an outcome of a process of negotiation between various elements found within the social group of the community at large. What are seen as common and shared cultural elements will be reproduced and accepted by all, while elements that do not have the support of the majority will either be eliminated or confined to subgroups and will be seen as reflecting the particularistic values of those subgroups.

An invented tradition often represents only selected aspects of the existing culture, with, at times, the introduction of elements of foreign culture into it. There are thus often both familiar and unfamiliar elements found within the invented culture. It is also the case that cultural elements undergo various phases of change and adaptation to new situations, resulting in new forms of practice and new interpretations despite the continued use of the old contents. There are also cases of the hybridisation of old and new contents, giving the impression of a changed culture. Under such situations, a quest for cultural authenticity becomes less useful than a study of how groups develop and interpret their cultural practices.

The significance of culture within a society is closely linked to its values and the individuals within it. Bourdieu argues that knowledge of the cultural capital will place those individuals with specialised knowledge in a high position within the society. By learning and possessing such knowledge, an individual can get a position in the social structure that would otherwise be inaccessible to him or her. According to Bourdieu, cultural capital is symbolic capital that acts to enhance the economic status of the individual, group or society that owns this capital (Bourdieu, 1993: 75). Persons in possession of cultural capital will be able to make names for themselves and attain social prestige. Such persons are cultural bankers (Bourdieu, 1993: 75).

During the process of cultural reinvention in ancestral villages, selected members of both Singapore and Anxi Chinese groups are seen as cultural bankers. They possess the knowledge of ancestor worship and religious practices and help to reproduce them. In so doing, the rituals related to ancestor worship and folk religion are once again revived and practised within the village structure. Through these practices, the Singapore and village members of the lineage are brought together in a ritualistic fashion to acknowledge their shared identity.

Chinese Overseas and the China Connection

A study of the Singapore Chinese and their ancestral villages will not be complete without an understanding of their positions within the global history of Chinese overseas. Lately there has been great interest in the study of the global spread of Chinese overseas as well as of their communities and their links with China in general. This has been in part due to the success of the little dragons of Asia (e.g. Hong Kong, Singapore and Taiwan), where large Chinese populations reside.

Two main streams of thoughts have emerged in the search for a way to understand the increasing economic integration between Mainland China, Hong Kong, Taiwan, Macau and the Chinese communities overseas. The first is the "Greater China" thesis[2], *da zhonghua* (大中華) and the other, initiated by Tu, is the "Cultural China"[3] model, *wenhua zhongguo*, (文化中國). Both approaches attempt to explain the continued links between Mainland China; the peripheral areas of Hong Kong, Taiwan and Macau; and the Chinese communities overseas.

Greater China can, according to Harding (1993: 660-686), be seen at three levels: One level is the emergence of a transnational Chinese economy. Here, the main issue is the rapid rate of economic growth and integration of China with Hong Kong, Macau and Taiwan specifically and with other Chinese communities in general. The interlocking relationships and the rapid growth are attributed to economic complementarities and cultural similarities among these regions. This has led to calls for the formation of a single economic bloc of these Chinese communities.

A second level is a globalised Chinese culture. On this level, the "Greater China" thesis assumes that there is increased cultural interaction between people of Chinese descent on an international level. Currently, a large number of Chinese from overseas visit China; they come from Taiwan, Hong Kong, Macau, Southeast Asia and many western countries. In recent years, the number of Chinese from the PRC who visit these Chinese communities overseas has increased. Communication has also intensified through, for example, the use of telecommunication. Likewise, the flow and interaction of both popular and traditional forms of culture between China and the Chinese communities elsewhere is on an increase.

On yet another level, "Greater China" is associated with a reunified Chinese state. Here, the idea is that this "state" should incorporate Mainland China, Hong Kong, Macau, Taiwan, Mongolia, Tibet and Xinjiang. Harding suggests the ways which a reunified Chinese state might be governed. Should it be governed according to a "One Country Two Systems" policy, as the case of Hong Kong, which has once again become part of Mainland China? Or should the "reunified Chinese State" or "Greater China" be governed as a "Chinese Federal Republic"?

A central criticism of the "Greater China" thesis is its failure to account for the status of the Chinese overseas communities scattered throughout the world. Wang Gungwu (1993a: 926-948) has argued that the use of "Greater China" should be context specific. When "Greater China" is used to refer to a transnational economic system, it is important to point out that the "economic integration" refers more to the "South China Economic Periphery" where economies are booming and where there are links among Hong Kong, other South China areas of the PRC, Macau and Taiwan. When "Greater China" implies a political concept, it is the regions that are inside the borders of the PRC that count and are important, not the ones outside. Used in the sense of a "globalised culture", the term includes the cultural values of the Chinese overseas communities, values which have undergone changes due to modern influences and adaptations with which those who live abroad might find it possible to identify (Wang, 1993a: 926).

According to Wang, Chinese overseas cannot be part of Greater China politically: there is a need to take into consideration the demands of the new nation states over their citizens. These demands include political allegiance and absolute national loyalty to the new nation-states. Increasingly, Chinese overseas have adopted nationalist feelings towards their adopted countries. By confirming their loyalty to these nation-states (Wang, 1993a: 940), they gain the trust of their respective national governments. The participation of the overseas Chinese in the economic development of South China has gradually come to be accepted by the national leaders of the countries where the overseas Chinese live. Their actions are not considered to be disloyal to their nations (Wang, 1993a:

940). Wang argues that the acceptance of the Chinese as full-fledged, loyal citizens has led to the possibility of their push for cultural autonomy and for its acceptance by the nation state. Such is now the situation in Singapore, but other countries have yet to fully adopt such an attitude. An example of this is Indonesia, where Indonesian Chinese investments in the PRC continue to be viewed with suspicion by the Indonesian government.

The other main model that attempts to explain the increasing economic and cultural integration between Mainland China and Chinese communities elsewhere is the "Cultural China" model or thesis initiated by Tu Wei-ming. The Cultural China thesis offers three symbolic universes. The first of these refers to Mainland China, Taiwan, Hong Kong and Singapore, which are populated primarily by cultural and ethnic Chinese. To the second universe belong the Chinese communities that form significant political minorities within their adopted countries. Malaysia and the United States are part of this universe. The third symbolic universe consists of individual men and women - mainly scholars, teachers, journalists, industrialists, traders, entrepreneurs and writers - who attempt to understand China and bring their understanding of China to their own linguistic communities (Tu, 1994: 13-14). According to Tu, for this universe membership in the global Chinese culture is defined in terms of cultural understanding and acceptance rather than according to ethnicity.

Tu argues that the increasing influence of the Chinese communities overseas has created a situation where the periphery has become a centre with much power and influence. He writes that "it is unprecedented for the geopolitical centre to remain entrenched while the periphery presents such powerful and persistent economic and cultural challenges" (Tu, 1994: 13). Tu further states that "the centre no longer has the ability, insight or legitimate authority to dictate the agenda for 'Cultural China'" (Tu, 1994: 34).

Lately, the Chinese communities overseas have attracted much attention among scholars who study the Diaspora phenomenon. In a study, a group of scholars call for the study of Chinese overseas as part of "Chinese Transnationalism" (Ong and Nonini, 1997). In another study, a recent collection entitled *Nations and Migrations*, Peter Van der Veer (1997) has explored the "politics of space" as a mediating factor between a displaced population's relation to a homeland and its relation to the nation-state of the displaced population. He has studied Indian populations who live in different places around the world and his research can therefore be classified as concerning a South Asian Diaspora. According to him, it is the "politics of space" that connects Indian populations regardless of where they live. This is a politics by which the migrants or the Diaspora ethnic community contests with the nation-state for a place to live and for a space to express their cultural and ethnic identities. Van der Veer sees space as the alienating property of the nation state and not as a property of the Diaspora. The migrant communities continue to experience marginalised positions and retain marginal spaces.

In his work, this politics of space has grown as a result of two primary factors: British colonialism and the emergence of indigenous Indian culture and religion. Van der Veer argues that it was British colonialism that brought about sensitivity that resulted in a search for an indigenous ideology to compensate for the British ideology. The result was the emergence of an indigenous Indian culture and religion. This has formed the ideological basis for Indians overseas to reproduce their cultural identity.

Not only space but also time is an important factor in the study of the Diaspora. According to Van der Veer, there are two types of time. One is "structural time", for which the starting reference point is the beginning of colonialism. From that point time gradually moves to post-colonial time, and then on to contemporary time and ends with nation-state time. The second type is the so-called "cultural time" which involves moving back in history to the source of an indigenous culture and its religion. The purpose is to answer contemporary cultural and religious needs. In so doing, cultural reproduction becomes the key concern.

How relevant are these models to this study of the Singapore Chinese and their *qiaoxiang* connections? I find that the labels are less important than some ideas that have grown out of these various discourses. An important aspect of the "Greater China" thesis is the concept of a globalised Chinese culture which is important to our understanding of the links between China and Chinese overseas communities. For the "Cultural China" thesis, the strength of the periphery dictating the agenda of mainland China has some merit in the contemporary relationship between China and the Chinese overseas. Likewise the issues of structural and cultural time allow us to understand the significance of memories, social experiences and the acts of cultural reproduction.

In searching for an appropriate framework to understand the social relationship of the Singapore Chinese with their *qiaoxiang* counterparts, I feel that the migration-Diaspora framework is useful for evaluating the emotions and the actions of the community. The migration-Diaspora framework also allows us to look at the various disparate overseas communities from a global-historical perspective.

Therefore, we need to take into consideration the following factors: (i) the migration history; (ii) the changing status of the overseas Chinese from migrant to citizen of the adopted country; and (iii) the formation of the Singapore nation-state, with its citizenship and with the corresponding question of allegiance either to a national entity, to an ethnic entity, or to both.

At the conceptual level, the formation of the Chinese community in Singapore can only be understood as part of the wider global migration history of the Chinese. Globally, the Chinese created physical spaces with which they came to identify. Within these spaces, the Chinese reproduced their socio-cultural and economic structures. As migrants, they maintained links with their ancestral villages through occasional letters and regular remittances.

Early on, Chinese were sojourners to Southeast Asia in search of economic opportunities and employment. Historically, these Chinese sojourners rarely considered settling overseas as an option - they were either temporary traders or labourers. Social and political forces were hostile towards their settling permanently. This, however, did not prevent them from settling down, as many did. They thus became permanent or semi-permanent migrants.

The concept of "sojourning" was traditionally defined as temporary movement to an unfamiliar place. Recently, however, Wang has considered sojourning as not to refer only to a temporary phenomenon but also to one that might last for a lifetime and which might stretch over generations. As a historical phenomenon, such sojourning is taken to mean "that a highly particularistic loyalty towards family and the clan-based village formed the basis of linked space over a great distance. Under these circumstances, it was possible to create small independent groups, which were later supported by the advancement in technology and information. Sojourning for them was based on physical and trading ties with their ancestral homes" (Wang, 1993b: 138).

Today, a telecommunication revolution provides quick information and allows individual Chinese to communicate and travel at ease. This has brought individuals together (Wang, 1993b). The access to modern technology has made it possible to create an intensive network of linkages for Chinese in different countries, irrespective of their geographical locality. What lies between the migrants in overseas communities and their ancestral villages is then the social distance between them.

After the formation of the Singapore nation state, the Chinese in Singapore were given a choice of citizenship. Those who opted to remain permanently, adopted Singapore as their home and assumed Singapore citizenship. The issue of loyalty to China or to Singapore was an important area for the contest of allegiance right till the 1980s. Only in the 1990s has there been an acceptance of a Singapore Chinese identity by the state, a development which has created less suspicion within the nation state and with its geopolitical sensitive neighbours.

This conceptual transition from temporary sojourner to citizen is an important factor to consider in our attempt to study the Singapore Chinese and their *qiaoxiang* connections. It allows us to understand the sentiments that the Singapore Chinese attach to their ancestral homes, as well as their present actions and participation in village reconstruction and cultural reproduction. By understanding this transitional process, the constraints and conflicts of interest arising from their links with the ancestral villages can be further understood.

Contest of Identities

An underlying theme throughout this study is the issue of identity among the Singapore Chinese. Contests of identities occur at various levels. There is a contest of identity between the Singapore and the Anxi Chinese at the lineage level. On the state level, there is a contest between Chinese ethnicity and the national identity. At a global level, there is the contest between Singapore Chinese identity and global Chinese overseas identity.

At the lineage level, the issue of identity is a crucial one. By acknowledging the existence of the ancestral village and participating in village affairs, Singapore Chinese become part of the lineage structure. They become insiders to the activities. Through such acknowledgement, the structural continuity of Anxi Chinese identity is maintained, and inducting the younger generation Singapore Anxi Chinese into the lineage structure becomes crucial. This structural continuity is important and unique in the history of Chinese overseas communities, in many of which a permanent break has already occurred. In the Chinese communities in United States, Australia and Europe, as these communities enter third and fourth generations, permanent breaks have already occurred: most members have very little knowledge of their ancestral villages, and few have active interaction with the lineage members of these villages. In contrast, the Anxi Chinese, by consciously maintaining lineage continuity, ensures that a permanent break does not occur.

The Anxi example thus illustrates the point that migration does not necessarily lead to the cessation of contacts with ancestral villages, and that ultimate integration with adopted countries, as in the nation state, does not have to mean a discontinuity with the ancestral villages from whence the migrants first emigrated.

It is also possible to view the acknowledgement of the ancestral home as a home for the "others". Despite the common origin between the Singapore Anxi and the village members, there continues to be a list of differences between the two groups. Each group looks at the other as both insiders and outsiders, thus spelling out the tensions that exist between them. The contact of the younger Singapore-born Chinese with Anxi lineage members is very recent and their feeling for the ancestral home is a very ambiguous one. The great differences in attitudes and general lifestyle make them feel alien to the village members. Many are inclined to draw a divide between themselves and the Anxi members. The same feelings also exist among the younger Anxi members who feel that the younger Singapore members are arrogant and proud. These Anxi members tend to treat the younger Singapore members as "outsiders" and "others". At the same time, some younger Singapore members do not want to be seen as "insiders". They consciously behave as "outsiders" when in the village.

For the Singapore Chinese, visiting the ancestral village is a return to their cultural roots. At the same time, it serves to reaffirm their Singapore Chinese identity and helps them to locate themselves within the Singapore polity. It is only by going away from the Singapore base to their ancestral base that they come to grips with their new identity. It is a hybrid brand of identity that they now possess.

As citizens of the Singapore nation-state, Singapore Anxi Chinese are very much influenced by the operation of the policies of multi-ethnicity and nation building of the Singapore State. In the change of status from that of migrants to full-fledged citizens of a nation state, the Singapore Chinese have adapted to a change in their identity. They have become Singapore Chinese. This entails more than just a symbolic name change. On arrival in Singapore, the identity of the Chinese migrants was closely tied to the lineage, village and territorial boundary. The migrants were differentiated by their dialect groupings. Their identity was highly primordial and kinship-based. In a nation state, their brand of Chinese identity is constantly subjected to contest with the national identity. Their cultural practices are also subjected to challenges from the forces of modernity.

The creation of a national identity is part of the nation-building process. In Singapore, the state regarded it as a significant policy matter to create a set of common values among the different ethnic groups in Singapore. Anderson (1986) argues for the existence of an imagined community within the nation state, imagined because people imagine themselves to be one national group and one citizenry. The Singapore State has, since independence, conscientiously created a set of shared values among its multi-ethnic population to shape them into adopting the Singapore identity, people who would call themselves "Singaporean". To a large degree, the process of nation building has been successful, and citizens identify themselves as Singaporean.

Among the Singapore Chinese today, there exists a composite

identity. They identify themselves as Singaporean, as part of a Singapore citizenry. But they are also Chinese, and further identify according to their different dialect affiliations. For the Singapore Anxi Chinese, this has meant the invention of a parochial trans-village, trans-national identity - a Singapore Anxi *huaren* identity. Such an identity has three component parts. It is grounded in the primordial place of origin. It is also an identity that takes into consideration the ethnic factor in a pluralistic world to which these Chinese are exposed. Hence, they are Chinese. Finally, they themselves fit into the trans-national framework as a subgroup wholly within the national boundary of the Singapore nation state.

Within a Global Chinese Cultural Network

A final consideration is the study of the globalisation of the Singapore Chinese-China connection. One key factor here is the role played by the lineage structure and other traditional institutions in providing an interconnecting network structure for members scattered throughout the world.

By exploring the lineage structure as a cultural network and resource base, it is possible to map out the linkages among disparate groups of Chinese of the same ancestry or lineage. The Singapore Anxi Chinese and their village counterparts have begun to create a network to help bring together members from all over the world. Through their formal institution, the Anxi Association, they consciously search for members, whom they invite to participate in various activities that the Association organises. Modern informational technology has allowed the association to establish a database of membership and to provide a communication channel for its members. The Association organised the 1st International Anxi Association meeting and invited participation worldwide. Another method of communication, which is under consideration, is the establishment of a homepage through the Internet and World Wide Web.

Chinese social institutions are important organisations for the transmission of this cultural identity. At the immediate level, the family and the lineage structure are the two most significant social institutions that enable such an identity to become operationalised. At a global level, traditional clan, dialect and territorial associations have become significant in transmitting Chinese culture.

The Chinese lineage is instrumental in tapping into the sentiments of these people scattered throughout the global community. Early migration to Singapore and other Southeast Asian countries and later migrations to the English-speaking countries of America, Australia and Canada have created numerous Chinese communities throughout the world. In these countries, Chinese associations based on territorial origin or lineage/surname origin have formed. The lineage association has been an important institution in that it has created a cultural network through bringing lineage members together. Through this role, it has once again become an important social institution in contemporary Chinese society.

Lineage organisation has created a globalised space for members to interact with one another on the social and economic fronts. On the social front, lineage organisations help small groups of Chinese scattered throughout the world to experience a level of cultural familiarity by introducing them to their lineages and to their ancestral homes. This is done through encouraging members to visit their ancestral villages and to participate in their cultural and religious activities. The lineage, thus, provides a platform where cultural continuity may take place. On the economic front, the lineage has also become actively involved. The lineage has become actively involved in both economic development of the ancestral home and, at the same time, it has involved itself and its members in the lucrative China trade. In recent years the lineage and its members have operated businesses in both the ancestral village and in other parts of China. It has also taken on the role of resource base, providing the necessary social connections (*guanxi*) and helping its members to venture into new economic areas not only in China but also in other Southeast Asian countries. In this regard, the lineage has extended its socio-economic space.

The contemporary expanding globalised roles of the Chinese lineage should be conceptualised as a cultural network. With the ancestral village as the conceptual point of origin or source, continuous regional and peripheral interaction takes place within this cultural network through regional and peripheral lineage associations scattered throughout the world. This continuous interaction is essential for the flow of communication and information. Through this flow of information, members become aware of the activities both at the ancestral village source and in the regional centres, and can choose to participate in some or all of them. By belonging to this lineage cultural network, members in various parts of the world are brought together to acknowledge their ancestral village, their ancestral home and ancestors; by participating and involving in socio-religious activities and village development, they renew both their lineage and cultural identities.

Methodology

This research is divided into two parts, the Singapore and Anxi parts. In Singapore, research was conducted at various stages. Participant-observation started since 1991 and was easily conducted as the author herself is part of the Anxi community and of the Ke lineage, and there is much empathy and interest in her work. Non-intrusive participant-observation was conducted into the numerous communal socio-religious activities in Singapore. Conversations among the members were also recorded. Collection of this data was unstructured. This was followed by in-depth interviews which were conducted with selected members, especially with those actively involved in activities in Singapore and also in the development of Anxi. The number of those who accepted in-depth interviews is 20. During the third stage, two sets of questionnaires were issued to a random sample of members (one set for first generation migrants and the second set for those with Anxi ancestry only) in order to provide the quantitative breadth that I wanted for the research. The total number of Singapore Anxi Chinese interviewed for the questionnaire survey is 40. This part of the research was conducted from February to March 1995.

Fieldwork in Anxi did not follow the conventional village-study pattern. It is conducted in the Peng Lai district in Anxi County. Again, it was conducted in a manner that I thought would provide me with the most opportunities to interact and to observe the socio-religious functions and decision-making processes. During the first stage, I usually followed the Singapore Chinese back to Anxi whenever there were major events that they had organised and were returning to participate in. In such cases I was able to participate and observe as a member. The first trip was made in 1988. During the second stage, I visited Anxi as a researcher to conduct interviews with selected members, both those who were involved in the organisation of activities and other villagers. During the third stage, I issued two sets of questionnaires, one to tap the views and attitudes of the villagers and the other to tap the views of the official cadres. The questionnaire survey was conducted with the help of four researchers from Xiamen University. The total number of questionnaire interviews conducted on the villagers was 200. The total number of questionnaire interviews conducted on cadres at various levels was 98. These interviews were conducted in April 1995. In addition to the above, I have collected a large quantity of letters from both Singapore and village Chinese and this has provided me with additional information, particularly concerning their livelihood during earlier periods.

In conducting this research, there are several problems that I have confronted. One is the dichotomy between insiders and outsiders. As a member of the community, I am an insider and so was given access to much information. The members were usually friendly and open to me. In this sense, as an insider, I had a great advantage and conducting research was made much easier. Another advantage is that there has been, on the whole, no desire on the part of informants to "please" me by saying only things that they thought I wanted to hear. Most of the time, while doing research in Singapore and in Anxi, I was considered as an insider, and a high level of trust was lavished on me.

This brings me to a major dilemma that I am confronted with. When there is so much trust lavished on the researcher, there is also the expectation that follows: one is expected to write only the good and not the bad. To a large degree, the interpretation and the presentation of the data reflects the intersubjective view of the researcher and his or her informants. While I consciously attempt to distance myself from informants, it is inevitable that subjectivity can intrude into the analysis.

Outline of the Book

In this research, I attempt to bring together various theoretical understandings to the study of the relationship between Singapore Chinese and the emigrant villages and especially of the continuity between them. Chapter 1 explores the various themes that are conceptually significant to the understanding of this relationship. Chapter 2 examines how the Singapore Chinese attempts to establish a cultural identity within the Singapore polity using their experiences in both village China and Singapore. It is a multiple identity that they have assumed. In order to understand the reasons why the Singapore Chinese become not only interested in visiting their ancestral village but also to become actively involved in village reconstruction, chapter 3 provides some background information and of the state of poverty that Anxi experienced during the early years and even today. Chapter 4 looks at how the Singapore Chinese remembered their ancestral village and how their collective memories and early social experiences have played a large role in their way of looking at village life today, thereby influencing their participation in village development.

Chapter 5 examines the role of the Singapore Chinese in village reconstruction and explains why they are primarily involved in the development of infrastructure in the village and the strategies adopted by the villagers, village and county level cadres to encourage the Singapore Chinese to invest in infrastructure. It also investigates how the Singapore Chinese use their contribution in infrastructure development to bargain for concessions in the areas of cultural reproduction. Chapters 6 and 7 look specifically in the area of cultural reproduction namely ancestor worship and religious revivalism. Chapter 6 investigates the reasons for the significance of ancestor worship to both the Singapore Chinese and the villagers while chapter 7 explores the extent to which religion and religious fairs are being revived in a present-day village environment. Chapter 8 examines the rewriting of the genealogy and how through the genealogy, the two groups reclaimed their own social identity and re-established their lineage links. In an attempt to understand this relationship between the Singapore Chinese and their village kin, it brings to mind an important conceptual issue. This is the issue of how we should conceptualise Chinese lineage given the fact that migration, in both historical and contemporary times, has brought the creation of new Chinese communities that are scattered through the world. This book, to a certain degree, attempts to locate this study within the understanding of the wider Chinese overseas community and to reconceptualise the structure of Chinese lineage in contemporary global context. Building on the arguments and information of the other chapters, Chapter 9 provides a theoretical conceptualisation of the Chinese lineage, arguing for the need to look at Chinese lineage as a cultural network rather than as a social institution. In the concluding chapter, Chapter 10 draws together the various themes and at the same time, explores future directions of the Chinese overseas communities and the formation of their identity.

Notes

1   For a discussion of the use of Confucian ideology for statecraft and economic development, see Kuah, K.E. 1990; Chua, B.H. 1995: 147-168; Wong, J. 1996: 277-293; and Kuo, E.C.Y. 1996:294-309.

2   For a discussion on the debates supporting the "Greater China" phenomenon, see *The China Quarterly*, special issue on Greater China, December 1993, vol. 136.

3   For a discussion on the debates supporting the "Cultural China" phenomenon, see Tu, W.M. (ed.), 1994, The Living Tree: The Changing Meaning of Being Chinese Today, Stanford: Stanford University Press, originally published in Daedalus, as a special issue on "Cultural China", Spring 1991.

2 Constructing a Singapore Chinese Cultural Identity

Introduction

The changing political and moral order has brought about a renewed search for individual identity, be it ethnic or cultural. As migrant communities throughout the world settle into the countries of their adoption and as younger generations become identified with these countries, diaspora experiences are replaced by a sense of affiliation within the boundaries of nation-states. Yet the question remains whether these migrant groups can become fully integrated into the adopted nation states. Violence and tension have become hallmarks of contemporary ethnic politics, and separatism is on the increase. Amidst all these developments, the emergence and maintenance of a Chinese cultural identity in Singapore, and its meaningfulness to the people and the nation state, are now important issues to examine.

"Within the four seas, we are brothers" (四海之内皆兄弟也). This old Chinese saying continues to hold relevance for the Chinese overseas today. The urgency of searching for cultural roots and identity on the part of Chinese in various parts of the world has never been more intense than at the present time. Throughout the world, Chinese community members are becoming more confident of their own communities, irrespective of their minority statuses, as well as more vocal and assertive in their quest for an identity of their own within the national polities of which they are citizens. In very recent days they have also participated in mainstream politics, thereby further elevating the statuses of their communities within the nation-states.

In Singapore, the search for cultural identity has pushed the Chinese to re-evaluate their cultural and religious practices in order to establish a sense of cultural continuity. Despite the fact that the Chinese form the dominant ethnic group in Singapore, comprising 77 per cent of the total population, the pursuit of cultural identity is guarded. Three factors account for this: (1) the heterogeneous character of the Chinese community, (2) the strength of the Singapore state in its role of social engineer, and (3) the issue of multi-ethnic identity. The Singapore State is particularly notable for engineering the development of a Singapore identity that

31

encompasses multiple ethnicity within an acceptable socio-political framework. Calls for lower-level cultural identity during the early years were closely linked to the elements of cultural chauvinism and were actively discouraged by the Singapore State. Today there is a gradual acceptance of the need to develop respective cultural identities for the major ethnic communities.

Creating a Chinese Community in Colonial Singapore

The history of the Chinese who immigrated from the two southern provinces of Guangdong and Fujian to Southeast Asia from the nineteenth through the second half of the twentieth century has been well documented. A later wave of migration, short and intense, occurred in the 1950s and 1960s during the Communist period. Right till the 1960s, many Mainland Chinese continued to move out and to land in Southeast Asia, but since then the new nation-states have imposed entry restrictions, which have, made it difficult for would-be migrants to enter. There were also ethnic tensions and racial riots in Indonesia, Malaysia and Singapore that made these places less attractive. In addition, effective control on emigration imposed by the Communist regime in China after the Cultural Revolution made it even more difficult for Mainland Chinese to emigrate out of China.

In Singapore, as elsewhere, the migrants were mostly from Fujian and Guangdong. Today the Fujian-speaking Chinese form the majority within the Chinese community. There were three categories of migrants: the first, who constituted the majority, arrived under the ticket-credit system; the second were sponsored by their kinsmen. The third, however, were independent migrants who arrived with little money and few direct kinship connections, but with some knowledge of *Nanyang* (roughly, Southeast Asia) and with the knowledge also that they could draw upon the existing social networks that previous migrants had established.

The early migrants were predominantly able-bodied men, who ranged in age from twenty to fifty. They were largely from the peasantry and were armed with few skills, but they had a sense of survival, as well as intelligence and a willingness to perform hard labour. It was only in the early twentieth century that women began to arrive. Their arrival helped to create permanent Chinese settlements.

Wang has categorised these migrants into four categories: traders, coolies, sojourners and re-migrants (Wang, 1991: 3-21). These four groups were represented in early Singapore society, but it was the peasant-turned-trader and the coolie-turned-trader groups, which became the pillars of the economic strength of early Singapore. By 1947 the Chinese population in

Singapore stood at 730,133 and constituted seventy-five per cent of the total population of 940,824. Singapore became a "Chinese community" amidst the Malay majority in the geopolitics of the region during these early years. This is still the case today.

These early migrants were not homogeneous, but were differentiated according to lineage, territorial and linguistic background. There were eight distinguishable Chinese languages, dialects or sub-dialects spoken by the migrants; although the three major ones were, and still are, Fujian, Chaozhou and Cantonese. In 1947, Fujian-speaking Chinese constituted about 40per cent of the total Chinese population; Chaozhou-speaking comprised 21.5 per cent and Cantonese 21.6 per cent; the other languages were Hakka, Hainanese, Hinghoa, Hokchhia and Hokchiu (Freedman, 1957: 12).

The main areas from which these Chinese came included various districts in Guangdong: in and around the port city of Canton, as well as Sze Yap, Mei Hsien and Putian. In Fujian, migrants came from the port city of Xiamen and its environs, and from Chuanzhou, Zhangzhou, Tong Ann, Long Men, Nan Ann and Anxi. These districts, considered the emigrant districts, are today the *qiaoxiang* (僑鄉) - the ancestral villages of the emigrants and their descendants. Since the 1978 reform in China, these *qiaoxiang* have experienced rapid social and economic transformation as a result of the flow of capital into the region and the increase in their human relations with overseas Chinese, and have also become important growth nodes and cultural centres in South China.

A sizeable group of Chinese came from the numerous villages in Anxi County in Fujian. These numbered over 40,000 during the first half of twentieth century, the immediate post-war years, 1945 - 1950, witnessed some 20,000 more Anxi villagers emigrating to Singapore. Today, the total number of Chinese from Anxi is estimated at 185,309, about 10 per cent of the total Chinese population in Singapore. (Anxi Xian Zhi, 1994, v.2: 854).

During the nineteenth and early twentieth centuries, as mentioned, there was an influx of male migrants into colonial Singapore. Very few women emigrated because of political restrictions under the Qing rule and also because it was ideologically incorrect for women of good family background to emigrate. This imbalance created a bachelor society, characterised by a sojourner's mentality, of a transient nature. From the 1920s onwards, there was a change of British colonial policy to encourage more Chinese women to emigrate through a relaxation of the immigration law. Since then women had arrived in greater number.

By 1947, the Chinese male to female ratio had reached a balance. There were 387,883 male to 342,250 female (Freedman, 1957: 25). This change coincided with an increasing political instability in China that pushed women out of the country, and so a substantial number of women immigrated to Singapore to join their husbands. Another result was the emergence of a group of independent women who had immigrated to Singapore to take advantage of the expanding economic opportunities made possible as a result of expanding trade and mercantile activities. The coming of women signalled the formation of conjugal families with children and the creation of domestic hearths which, combined with economic opportunities, contributed to a more stable social structure. At the same time, extended kinship structures, clans, and lineage and dialect associations all created an environment that encouraged permanent settlement within the emerging post-colonial Singapore society, and signalled the passing away of the sojourner's transient community and mentality.

The social institutions that were established by the migrants during the early phases of migration took on extended roles. Now, the utilitarian institutions that catered to the needs of the bachelors gave way to those concerned with families and lineages. The dialect associations also become routinely involved in socio-cultural events. All of these social institutions have become increasingly involved in reproducing elements of culture - daily social routine, social interaction, domesticity, religion, ancestor worship and customary practices - thereby allowing the Chinese to establish a permanent home for themselves in an overseas environment. Thus, from the second half of the twentieth century onwards, *luo-di-shen-gen* (落地生根)[1], planting one's roots in the adopted home, became the norm rather than the exception.

The Migrants' Social Experience

Chinese intending to reside permanently in Singapore were confronted with a variety of rapidly changing political structures and experiences. First, there was the colonial structure. During the nineteenth century and through the first half of the twentieth century, the Chinese migrants had little interaction with the British colonial administrators except through their headmen, or *Kapitans China*. Scholars have argued that the British policies of indirect rule had resulted in the establishment of an "*imperium* in *imperio*", a city-within-a-city, phenomenon. As such, the Chinese were left alone to create their own socio-political structures that perpetuated their own lifestyles and their own rule.

Right up to the eve of decolonisation, the migrants were cushioned from the British administration by their tightly knitted social institutions, which interlocked to form an institutional web impenetrable for outsiders.

These social institutions included clan associations, dialect organisations, secret societies and temples. While each of these had its own distinct identity and function, they were nevertheless interlocked in social networks (社會網絡) involving *guanxi* (關系); within which they shared the same leaders, and jointly organised social and cultural activities representing both their own subgroups and the wider Chinese community.

It was not unknown that, during the earlier years, the secret societies represented the political arm of the Chinese community, with their leaders holding numerous positions in the other social institutions. The roles of the secret societies have been well recorded and their legitimacy in the eyes of the early migrants remained unquestioned. However, their official role, after the Secret Societies Ordinance in 1867, became marginalised as they became associated with the criminal aspects of society. Increasingly, their legitimacy within the Chinese community became more of a liability than an asset, so that, from this period onwards, association with the secret societies could no longer bring about social status, and ordinary people avoided joining them. Concurrently, a separation of leadership between secret societies and other social organisations occurred. Leaders of clan, dialect and temple organisations distanced themselves from the secret societies, playing only marginal roles within them. The de-legitimisation of secret societies thus led to an increase in the strength of other social institutions. However, while at the overt level the separation of leadership and membership of the secret societies from those of other social institutions occurred, in reality some form of interlocking membership continued right till the eve of decolonisation.

In the early days, the clan, dialect and temple organisations were important in galvanising the Chinese together and giving them an identity. Each organisation provided a network from which its members drew economic, social and emotional support when in need. During the nineteenth century, they helped Chinese bachelors locate jobs and provided them with shelter and food. These institutions also organised communal social and religious activities that provided much needed breaks in the otherwise mundane routine life of coolies. The familiarity of cultural practices that were reproduced in the alien colonial environment helped many to cope with the monotonous working life, loneliness and homesickness that came along with an isolated migrant lifestyle.

At a later stage, the clan and dialect associations financed schools that provided education for the children of the migrant families. A good education had always been considered as a privilege of the literati class; in the colonial environment, an English education provided by the colonial administration was restricted to a selected few - i.e. those that were favoured by the colonialists. Among them, only very few - those who called themselves Straits Chinese - formed the privileged group, whose English education eventually allowed them to hold positions within the colonial administration. In the aftermath of decolonisation, English-educated Straits Chinese filled the civil bureaucracy of the new nation state. For the majority of the migrants, however, education remained a lofty ideal. For the few wealthy, home tuition, *si-shu* (私塾) had been the only option for their children to receive an education.

All this changed with the introduction of Chinese vernacular education, which was provided by the clan and dialect organisations: for the first time, a modified form of mass education became a reality. Children of Chinese migrants were sent to schools that followed the curriculum offered in Mainland China. During this period, girls were also encouraged to study in schools, although boys continued to be given preference by their parents. As clan and dialect associations funded the education, expenses for the individual family were kept to a minimum, and those who could not afford it could ask for assistance from the associations.

The evolution of clan- and dialect-based education was attributed to the foresight of the clan and dialect leaders, together with that of several of the lesser scholars who immigrated to Singapore. An example of the former was Tan Kah Kee, who was an important proponent of education and who spent much of his wealth on educational projects both in the *Nanyang* region and in China. Other leaders of education included Lee Kong Chian and Tan Lark See. The availability of a Chinese education constituted the foundation for an emerging Chinese-educated elite group who would become the champions of the Chinese community within the multi-ethnic polity of post-colonial Singapore (Yong, 1968).

From Peasants to Family Business Firms

The Chinese social structures, which permitted the Chinese to become self-sufficient within their self-created world, also assisted greatly in the development of family business firms. The indirect British rule had left much of the conduct of Chinese affairs to Chinese leaders. At the same time, the Chinese also had very little interaction with other ethnic groups: the indigenous Malays and the Indian migrants co-existed with the Chinese, but each group participated only in its own activities. Ethnic interaction among groups was nominal and occurred mainly in the market place, which was thus seen as a common gathering ground for all ethnic groups, where a small amount of social interaction accompanied economic interaction (Furnivall, 1980). It was in the market place that some forms of cross cultural diffusion occurred: the common language there was bazaar Malay, and most Chinese traders and workers managed to speak some form of it.

For the most part, the Chinese were thus cushioned against an unfamiliar political structure and a multi-ethnic population by their own cultural apparatus and institutions. Their social network became important for the development of economic institutions and helped them to become successful traders, entrepreneurs and merchants in early Singapore. They were also good workers, and continued to be considered the best in that part of the world. Many Chinese who started off as coolies took advantage of Chinese social networks and established family business firms. The credit rotation system helped to provide initial capital for the start-up of these small businesses, and other capital was raised from loans given by kinsmen and other business people on the basis of trust, *xin-yong* (信用). Self-help and trust was instrumental in developing a whole generation of small family businesses and helped with the generation and accumulation of wealth within the Chinese community.

The credit rotation system acts as an informal financial system. In most cases, a person who is in need of money would gathered a group of kin, friends or business associates, usually 10 to 12 or 15 for a credit cycle. The leader is know as the credit rotation head, *hui-tou* (匯頭) and he would set the monthly credit limit. During the early years it would be $10 or less. Today, the month credit limit could range from $1,000 to $10,000. Each month, the participants would pay the stated amount minus the interests that the bidder is willing to pay for the bid. The credit rotation head is usually given the first bid. Usually the bidder would pay an interest of 5 to 10 per cent depending on competition for the bid for that month. The participant would need to pay the amount minus that month's interest to the bidder. The last person in the group does not need to bid and gets the full sum, thereby concluding a credit rotation cycle.

In the urban environment, Chinese peasant migrants learned rapidly and adapted to an economic structure very different from that which they had been used to. Their quickness in learning the commercial ethos of the entrepot trade, as well as their willingness to form a wage labouring class, enabled them rapidly to shake off their peasant backgrounds.

In the early years, the majority of the Chinese migrants were labouring coolies and workers in various trades. As some advanced from being labourers at heavy menial tasks in the dockyards to become clerical workers and administrators in trading firms, they exuded a sense of hard work, diligence, trustworthiness and perseverance. They also acquired the knowledge of trade and business, and took advantage of whatever opportunities arose to start family businesses. The transition of Singapore Chinese society from a peasantry to a commercial class was completed with the emergence of a new breed of entrepreneurs and businessmen, who relied more on their hard work and business acumen than on capital. These Chinese were able to make use of little capital to build sizeable businesses during the early years. Some of these businesses have undergone various stages of expansion and have developed into modern conglomerates in contemporary Singapore.

The move from peasant to coolie and eventually to trader or entrepreneur is a deeply emotional story in itself. The economic success of many family businesses was made possible by the existence of the social networks, *guanxi wang* (關系網), supplemented by sworn brotherhood (議兄弟) in the secret societies which operated to bring both kin and non-kin into the fold to reinforce social relationships among members of the Chinese community, so that no one would be left out of a network which allowed migrants to tap into important sources of business skills and financial support. This *guanxi wang* bonded together clan and lineage (surname) associations, dialect associations, trade guilds and Chinese chambers of commerce to allow the migrants to draw on existing knowledge of the markets, resources, trading practices, business networks and capital from these institutions. The relationships among traders and these institutions were both formal and informal, but were never legalistic, although most of the functions of the social institutions did not operate strictly according to the rule of law.

The establishment of a system of credit rotation among Chinese to raise capital for their businesses allowed small traders to handle their own financial needs instead of relying on formal banking and financial institutions. This ability of the Chinese to operate their own credit system led to the rapid rise of small family businesses throughout Singapore during the two decades that followed independence.

The development of the family business firm has become an important economic process within Singapore society. In the agrarian society of village China, the dream was to own a plot of land, and this continues to be a dream even today. However, in a commercial society where trading was the lifeline of the population, the Chinese migrants shifted their priority: owning a family business firm has become an important goal.

Among the forty families that I have interviewed, 75 per cent have some kind of family business, and 25 per cent are workers who work either for these family firms or for other firms. Most of the family firms are small in scale. They range from engineering construction to the wholesale and/or retail of hardware, textiles, fruit and tea. Among the families, only 4 per cent have professional qualifications, and these are in the legal and accounting professions. In most cases the sons, and in some cases the daughters, help with the family businesses.

In terms of educational level among first-generation migrants today, about 90 per cent have only the equivalent of a primary education. Among the second and third generations, over 60 per cent have secondary and post-secondary education and 13 per cent have tertiary education. The rest have some form of technical and vocational training.

As the Chinese have become economically and socially established in Singapore they have gradually come to regard Singapore as their home. Although all are Singapore citizens, their sense of citizenship and identity comes under scrutiny in the newly independent nation-state.

Citizenry and Identity in Post-colonial Singapore

After the end of World War Two, as part of the global dismantling of empires, the process of decolonisation was completed in the Malay Peninsula with British withdrawal and exit from the Malay Federation. The political tumults of the 1950s and 1960s affected the social and economic well being of the region, one result being that Singapore established self-government in 1965.

After independence, the ruling People's Action Party (PAP) under Lee Kuan Yew had several tasks to consider. One was the post-war, post-independence economic reconstruction, and the transformation of Singapore from a predominant entrepot into one of the most modern and successful economic powerhouses of Asia. The party implemented strict political, but liberal economic, policies, a main consideration being to make Singapore a politically stable place in order to attract foreign investments. Much of Singapore's early economic success had been built upon foreign capital, and now multinational and transnational corporations continued to dominate its economic sector. The high level of political stability, complimented by an efficient and non-corrupt civil bureaucracy, has resulted in many MNCs & TNCs making Singapore their regional headquarters.

The ruling party PAP has intruded deeply into the lives of its citizenry. Scholars and critics of Singapore government have alluded to the authoritarian nature of the government and their strict control over the citizenry. The citizens, on the other hand, have looked at the PAP as benign and paternalistic, and accept such strict controls, which range from campaigns to stop people from performing uncivil acts to those encouraging specific personal values, as a trade-off for a stable, disciplined and economically successful society. Life in the new polity has improved, with better housing, better education and a higher standard of living.

Ideologically, the state has successfully encouraged the gradual transformation of a migrant mentality into identification with Singapore; socially, Singaporeans have become "model citizens" of Southeast Asia; economically, they have carved a niche for themselves as competent businesspeople, entrepreneurs and professionals, and as skilful workers. Thus, within Singapore's short history, the migrants have planted their roots in foreign soil.

In independent Singapore, the migrants had to confront the issue of citizenship. For the first time, they had to make the choice between becoming citizens of the newly independent Singapore nation state or retaining the citizenship of their "home" country. They also had the option of choosing permanent residence status. For the majority, the choice was clear: they opted to become Singapore citizens, and the issuing and attaining of the pink identity cards became symbols of the new citizenship status of these migrants. Those who did not opt for citizenship came to regret it years later.

For the Chinese migrants, two factors accounted for their decision to make Singapore their permanent home. The first, "pull" factor, consisted of the economic opportunity and generally high standard of living in Singapore. There was general consensus that the commercial structure of the Singapore city-state provided better opportunities for migrants and their children than the agrarian structure of their former villages. There was also great optimism over the political leadership and its ability to rule Singapore. The other, "push" factor, was the Communist victory in 1949 and the tumultuous years that followed, which convinced many that returning to China could be disastrous not only for themselves but also for their families. By the mid-1960s the Cultural Revolution in China provided further impetus to those who had been indecisive finally to take up Singapore citizenship.

The difficulty of life for the majority during the early years of independence eased as the encouragement of foreign investors and the setting up of factories provided employment. As the male migrants, now with wives and children, began to see themselves as part of the social fabric of the new nation state and no longer as bachelor-sojourners, their initial motives of returning home with fortunes have given way to the better prospect of establishing comfortable homes in Singapore.

In Singapore, the Chinese migrant-citizens have learned to operate within a new political structure, for the first time being confronted with, and participating in, a system based on universal suffrage. Together with members of other ethnic communities, they have had to learn the meaning of concepts of election, citizenship, national identity and nationhood which are alien and contradictory to their understanding of Chinese identity and of China, and have had to wrestle with the policies implemented by the state concerning multi-ethnicity, religious plurality, state run education, housing, reproduction and health.

Not all Chinese with overseas connections wanted, or managed, to leave their home villages in China, of course. Those who were left behind experienced poverty, and many suffered during the Cultural Revolution. Today, many of these are parents, grandparents, uncles, aunts, sisters, brothers and cousins of persons in Singapore - patrilineal and matrilineal kin, or affines.

The Ethnicity Question

One main issue that the Chinese have to confront is the nature of ethnicity - migration to Singapore has led them to re-evaluate their own ethnic and cultural identities in relation to those of the other ethnic groups. The Malays, Indians and the Europeans are visibly different from the Chinese in phenotype, cultural practice and language, and this has led to the establishment of ethnic enclaves.

British town planning law, which consigned each ethnic group to a specific location, encouraged ethnic segregation during the colonial years. The Jackson Plan of 1827 cut up downtown Singapore into several precincts and slotted the ethnic populations into their respective positions. This continued the ethnic segregation mentioned above, whereby interaction occurred primarily in the market, and primarily on economic, rather than more generally social, terms. The dense, institutionalised Chinese social web encouraged self-containment within the Chinese community, and the barriers erected between "us" and "the others" made each group inward looking. Mistrust and unfamiliarity with other cultures became a great psychological barrier preventing group members from venturing out to befriend others.

In post-independence Singapore under the PAP government, the ethnic issue has become a priority. A policy of multiculturalism, implemented to bridge gaps between ethnic groups, together with an integrated education system, has brought about a higher level of interaction and dialogue among the ethnic groups. At a more intimate level, however, Chinese continue to socialise with "their own kind".

The contest for identities is thus a complex one. At one level, the Singapore State has consciously and actively shaped the Singapore identity, moulding its citizenry as Singaporeans. Today, the Singaporean identity is one with which all Singapore citizens identify. This national identity draws on nationalistic and patriotic feelings towards the Singapore nation-state and is closely confined within the geographical boundary of the Singapore State. It is an imagined identity, in that citizens are asked to imagine themselves as one people and one nation.

The state-constructed ethnic framework, commonly known as the CMIO (Chinese, Malay, Indians and Others) model, is to become the guiding *modus operandi* for ethnic relations within Singapore society. Within this framework, "Chinese" is a standardised ethnic category. Contrary to this state-projected image of a homogenised ethnic Chinese group, however, it is recognised that the Chinese community is, in fact, heterogeneous.

The Chinese of Singapore can be categorised in various ways. At one level, it is possible to speak of a Chinese-Chinese group and a Straits Chinese group. Chinese-Chinese are migrants and their descendants by union with other Chinese. Straits Chinese, also known as *Baba-Chinese* or *Peranakan*, are all locally born and are descended from unions between Chinese migrant men and Malay women.

Straits Chinese differ from Chinese-Chinese not only in their ancestral backgrounds but also in linguistic preference, professional skills and cultural practices. Many speak Malay as well as a Chinese dialect, often Fujian. As has been mentioned, during colonial times many Straits Chinese were English-educated and had professional skills that placed them in high positions within the civil bureaucracy or in the private sector. During the early years Straits Chinese women, known as *nonya*[2], dressed in *sarong kebaya* and developed a different cuisine, which is closer to Malay than to Chinese cuisine.

Within the wider Chinese community there are sub-communities within which the Chinese are differentiated by the dialect they speak, the region they come from and the surname groupings they belong to. The Chinese social institutions that exist today reflected this divisions. Thus, there are the dialect associations, *fangyan gonghui* (方言公會), clan or surname associations, *xinshi gonghui* (姓氏公會) and territorial-based associations, *tongxianghui* (同鄉會).

At one level, the Chinese, like other ethnic groups, are trying to create a cultural identity. Many of their cultural practices are mixtures of migrant culture with new additions. What form should this cultural identity take? Where can they draw their inspiration? Will this identity be one based on the short experience found within the Singapore nation-state or should Chinese delve into the historical past and traditions for inspiration?

Among the Singapore Chinese, there is an increasing desire to explore their parochial cultural identities through dialect affiliation, ancestry, immediate lineage and other kinship networks, in order to understand the depth of their own culture. Although the persons actively involved in this search represent only a small subgroup of Singapore Chinese, they are influential in re-orienting the direction of the search for a Chinese cultural tradition and identity (華人文化傳統及認同). They are not content with knowing themselves only as ethnic Chinese or Fujian or Chaozhou Chinese; they are also delving into their ancestral roots to provide themselves with cultural understanding of themselves. What we are witnessing is the continuing growth and/or production of a multiplicity of identities within the Chinese ethnic group to resist the homogenising influence of the Singapore State of turning Singapore Chinese into one uniform Chinese community with Mandarin as the lingua franca of the community.

Today, Singapore Chinese identity is thus of a composite nature. Singapore Chinese see ethnic Chinese identity as comprising several layers, and there is a constant demand for them to establish allegiances to the various groups to which they belong. The first identity is the Singapore Chinese, *Xinjiapo huaren* (新加坡華人), identity, which binds all Singapore Chinese together. This is the preferred identity of the Singapore State that seeks to constantly promote this form of identity through its nation-building process. The second identity comes from associations with ancestral homes in China - thus, Singapore Chinese see themselves as *Singapore Anxi, Tong-Ann or Mei-Hsien Chinese*. A third identity comes from association with a particular dialect. Hence, the commonly used identity terms are *Singapore Fujian, Chaozhou or Cantonese people*.

These parochial regional identities have become significant, as they represent a renewed sense of confidence in the cultural identity of these Chinese. During the 1960s and 1970s the Singapore government had exercised great caution over such representations, for fear of creating ethnic unrest as Chinese ethnicity was then associated with Chinese nationalism and chauvinism. Today, a more mature citizenry has permitted a more relaxed attitude toward ethnic cultures and ethnic cultural representations and; very recently, some government ministers have called for a better understanding of the historical origins of ethnic cultures. The earlier state policy of creating a homogenous ethnic identity within the "CMIO" framework has thus given way to a policy of intra-ethnic diversity. A better understanding of their own culture is thus helping Singapore Chinese to reproduce and reinvent Chinese cultural elements within the Singapore polity, a process which inevitably takes them back to their ancestral villages in rural China. An understanding of the emergence of cultural identity within the Singapore Chinese community will thus have to take into consideration two processes. The first process of cultural reproduction is one that operates among the Chinese dialect groups and the second process that operates between the Singapore Chinese on the one hand and their ancestral villages on the other.

Reproducing Culture: A Model

By becoming Singapore citizens, Chinese have committed to live and work permanently in Singapore and to raise their families there. In fact, they have also committed to reproducing a Chinese culture within Singapore society.

Cultural reproduction is seen as both spontaneous and selective. Cultural elements and rituals are produced through time to fulfil the needs of the group of people concerned, with no systematic planning of what elements to include; through time, these elements and rituals establish themselves as a cultural orthodoxy. In the case of Singapore Chinese, cultural orthodoxy is derived primarily from the former migrants' understandings of their own cultural practices and of what they had been taught in village China. It can be said that the strength of Chinese culture comes from the diversity and regional differences among Chinese as, underlying these diversities, the cultural elements continue to be broadly identified as uniquely Chinese. Thus, at the macro-level, it is possible to speak of a Chinese cultural orthodoxy, while, at the micro-level, each Chinese group has some different practices that are context-specific. Within Singapore, certain cultural elements are selectively reproduced and incorporated for specific purposes both autonomously, by the members of the Chinese population themselves, and by the Singapore State. In the case of the state, the attempt is to encourage the creation of a "made in Singapore" elite version of a standardised Chinese culture.

It is possible to periodise cultural reproduction within the Chinese community. The first period started with the arrival of first group of migrants in the mid-nineteenth century. This stage was characterised by spontaneity: each individual, family, lineage or dialect group practised and reproduced the cultural elements with which they were familiar from village China. This was especially the folk religious practices which, although geared to an agrarian economy, were yet reproduced in urban, commercial Singapore. This was a process of direct cultural reproduction.

In time, however, a second stage of cultural adaptation and cultural incorporation, which lasted into the 1950s, began to involve the discarding of certain cultural elements and the giving of prominence to others. However, in this stage the repertory of cultural elements continued to be selected from the village culturescape.

The third stage occurred in post-independent Singapore and represents a conscious attempt at reproducing selected cultural elements that are "representative" of the wider Chinese community, under which individual interests and regional differences are subsumed. Here, the differences among the dialect and/or lineage groups are streamlined to produce a standardised Chinese culture. The attempt to do this is a response to the demands placed upon Singapore Chinese by the state in its desire to project a unified and homogenous image of Chineseness in relation to the images of the other ethnic groups.[3] This stage may be called cultural representation.

The fourth stage is an attempt to elevate peasant culture into high culture in a manner that is in line with the modern Singapore image. The idea is that Chinese culture, like other cultures, must have interpretative and modernising power, must also be rational in its ritual contents, and must provide a place for each cultural element within the history of Chinese culture. In doing so, Singapore Chinese have to confront the issue of cultural representation: which items should be included as culture and which should be excluded? Nowhere is this clearer than where Chinese religious practices are concerned, in that there is currently a push towards doctrinal religions. This fourth stage may be called the stage of cultural reinvention.

Finally, there has been a move towards cultural diversity within the Chinese community. In recent years, the state has acknowledged the significance of cultural diversity among the sub-ethnic and dialect groups, an acknowledgement that remits in a raised culturescape within the Chinese community. This fifth stage may be called cultural reintegration.

Cultural Dilution

Moving through the different phases of cultural reproduction to cultural reintegration, Chinese culture has witnessed many changes, yet has retained its core elements: this is the Chinese cultural orthodoxy. However, this orthodoxy is subject to intense competition from modern cultural forms, such as those of popular culture, which have assumed greater significance and popularity among the younger Chinese. The result has been a decline in interest in the "orthodox" Chinese culture and Chinese social institutions.

Chinese cultural identity largely revolves around activities organised by the various Chinese social institutions, with participation on a collective basis. These social institutions include families, lineages, clan groupings, dialect associations, Chinese temples and cultural organisations, where activities are often of a socio-religious kind and the languages used are the dialects. Among younger Singapore Chinese, however, some choose to become "less-Chinese" or "modern Chinese" through non-participation in these social and cultural activities, through moving away from Chinese religious practices and adopting Christianity, through disinterest in kinship ties and through a desire to give up speaking Chinese dialects and/or Mandarin in favour of speaking English.

One indicator of interest in social and cultural activities is participation in activities organised by clan, dialect and other kinship-based associations. Through the years, there has been a steep drop in membership in all of these: a look into the composition of such memberships suggests that over 80 per cent of the members of surname and dialect associations are those of first generation Chinese. Participation in activities organised by these associations has been largely by the elderly; hence, they are often known as clubs for "old folks". The types of activities found in these associations reflect the elderly members' interests, such as mah-jong and conversation. Young Chinese are unlikely to participate in such activities, and few young members visit the associations. This has been a worrying trend for the associations and elders: how to encourage the younger Chinese to join as members has become a critical concern for these associations. Some have provided venues for modern forms of entertainment, such as karaoke facilities and rooms, to attract the young. In recent years the associations have also organised free-tuition classes for the children of their members and have allowed their premises to be used for other educational purposes, thereby encouraging the young to visit the associations and to participate in the cultural activities.

Traditionally, the activities organised by the clan associations were predominantly of a religious kind, such as worship of the guardian god, of the heaven, *Tien Gong*, of ancestors, and celebration of the hungry ghosts in the Zhong Yuan Festival (Lunar Seventh Month). Elaborate rituals and food offerings, together with communal feasts, are still common sights at such celebrations. Although mainly elderly men and women attend these religious activities, young male adults have also attended in recent years - in part on behalf of elderly parents, but also as part of emerging social-cum-business networks among themselves. Presently, increasing numbers of daughters and daughters-in-law are seen accompanying their parents to such activities, reflecting the changing status of women in contemporary Singapore.

Among locally born Chinese, there are increasing trends both towards Christianity and away from any religious affiliation. Those following the latter call themselves "free-thinkers". Among the non-proselytising Chinese religions, however, there is no need for individuals to declare their religious beliefs: all individuals within the general community are also assumed to be part of its religious community. Communal religious worship here is separated from personal belief: Singapore Chinese see these religious practices as part of Chinese tradition and culture. Many Chinese members are thus passive participants in their religion, leaving most of the worshipping to their parents and other elderly family members, and it is a common sight to see many young Chinese observing but not participating in the act of worship. The older Chinese sees this lack of active interest on the part of the young as a trend towards cultural dilution.

Another area of concern is the hiatus in family and kinship structures. The extended kinship system, to a large extent, has broken down, as a result of the emigration during the early years, and there are many cases of immediate family members being separated, resulting in a dilution of kinship ties within the immediate family. Neither is the lineage immune to this. Today, what we find among the Chinese is a truncated kinship structure.

Among Singapore-born Chinese, the main concern is with the immediate family. The shift from extended family structure to nuclear family has progressively changed the kinship structure. Distant kin are no longer seen as important and are paid less attention. This applies both to village kin in China and to Singapore kin, among whom many no longer have clear ideas of who their village kin are and find it hard to categorise their relatives according to the Chinese classificatory kinship system. Many have informed me that they only know a small number of kin who share the same surname.

However, "sharing the same surname" now has a different meaning for younger Singapore Chinese than for their parents. To the elders, a person with the same surname is a blood relative, despite any social and/or kinship distance between them; thus, during the migration years, migrants were given assistance by kinsmen. The knowledge that the migrants were "one of us", zi-ji-ren (自己人) was a sufficient incentive for previously arrived Chinese migrants to extend a helping hand. Such was the personalisation of assistance to the early migrants. Today, however, Singapore-born Chinese attach little sentiment to the fact of a shared surname, and do not necessarily consider it to be evidence of any kinship tie. They therefore do not feel obligated to assist people with the same surname. Here we see the ideological conflict between migrant parents and their children, among whom the recognition of kinship relations is now being restricted to immediate kin. To the older Chinese, the locally born Chinese have become socially distant from their cultural upbringing.

In Singapore, among the first generation, kinship relations continue to play an important role in the daily life, and there is interaction among kin, who talk with one another over the telephone or over tea, visit one another and do things together. But this is less true among the younger Chinese, whose kinship ties stretch no farther than to second or third cousins. Although there is a general acknowledgement of the existence of a kin community, there are fewer contacts among those of the younger generation than there are among their parents. A common lament among parents is that after their deaths, kinship relation, *qin-qing* (親情), will be lost if no attempts are made to preserve these kinship ties. For the time being, only contacts among the first generation bring the younger generations together for various purposes, albeit obliquely.

Due to the twists of fortune, the family business firm has now indirectly brought locally-born Singapore kin together, the kinship ties that helped parents to start family business firms during the early years playing different roles today. It is the sons who will inherit family businesses, and occupational specialisation during the early years meant that many of those within the same lineage engaged in similar trades, thereby effectively facilitating the continuation of social and kinship relations among younger Chinese.

Most Anxi Chinese in Singapore started in the rags business, collecting and selling second-hand goods. Later, they branched out into hardware. Today, those involved in hardware have broadened their scope to deal not only in metalwork but also in machinery, construction, sanitary wares and building materials. Many of these firms started as small retail businesses catering to local needs, while others were wholesale importers and exporters. Presently, most are also involved in manufacturing. They have branched into other fields and expanded to become medium-sized firms or even large corporate groups. Another group of Anxi Singapore Chinese are involved in finance and banking.

Being in the same trades has provided opportunities for younger Singapore Chinese to interact with one another and has helped to maintain kinship relations among members of the second and third generations, continuing to provide opportunities for interaction not only in the business but also in the social arena. This is a reversal of the situation that the coolie migrants first experienced, i.e. where kinship ties led the way to business ties. Thus, through business interaction, some have now rediscovered the significance of kinship ties in contemporary Singapore. The integration of their social networks, *guanxi wang* and economic networks, *jin-ji-wang* (經濟網) has become an asset in their attempts at business globalisation, and in particular for gaining access to the China market. At the altruistic level, the rediscovery of the kinship relations also leads to a discovery of one's cultural identity.

Another factor that influences the promotion of cultural identity is the state-sponsored official promotion of the idea that Mandarin is the *lingua franca* of the Chinese, binding all Chinese dialect groups together. This attempt at standardising Chinese language has led schools to discourage students from using dialects in school. Many Singapore-born parents also encourage their children to use Mandarin at home, seeing this as providing them with a head start in their education. This has reduced proficiency in the dialects among some of the third and fourth generation Chinese.

Added to this has been the introduction of English education in schools where bi-lingualism places emphasis only on English and Mandarin. The Singapore State promotes English as a tool for economic success and Mandarin is seen as an important cultural idiom to bind all Singapore Chinese together. However, familiarity with Chinese dialects continues to be viewed as an important base for the formation of territorial-based Chinese cultural identity by the older Chinese members, especially the first generation migrants. Very recently, Singapore has begun to relax its official policy on Mandarin and dialects phrases have began appearing in the government-controlled broadcasting channels.

Towards the Future

As we move towards the twenty-first century, a confident Chinese community is now re-evaluating its status within the wider Singapore community. As its members entrench themselves as citizens of Singapore, they become more aware of the complexities of identities. They do not only carry one identity with them, but several identities. To them, "being a Chinese" is only one identity, at a broad level; it has to be situated within a social context in order that its meanings become clear both to themselves and to others. Thus there are other identities: Singapore Chinese, Singaporean, Fujian Chinese, Singapore Anxi Chinese, etc; which reflect identification with the nation, with the other ethnicities, with other Chinese dialect groups, and with their places of origin. All these point to a desire to search and construct an overall Chinese cultural identity through relationships of identities with "others". Thus the identities of these others have become important local points for identifying similarities and differences both between groups of Singapore Chinese and between them and other, non-Chinese groups, at intra-ethnic, inter-ethnic and state levels.

In the eyes of the first generation Chinese, their children, grandchildren and future generations have gradually lost interest in Chinese social institutions and have very little knowledge of Chinese cultural practices. This is most evident in the declining membership of the clan and dialect associations which, as mentioned above, now consists predominantly of first-generation migrants. There is also the declining interest in orthodox religious practices and other social rituals and the declining emphasis on family and lineage, such that elderly persons are sometimes seen more as a burden than as seniors rich in wisdom,[4] while Singapore-born Chinese are seen as having little interest in, or knowledge of, their ancestors and their ancestral homes. These latter perceptions of the younger generations by the first generation Chinese have led them to refer to the younger as "babaised", *fan* (M), and *huang* (番) - i.e., uncivilised and detribalised. However, this trend towards "babaisation" is considered reversible through the reintroduction of the younger Chinese to Chinese culture and the re-establishment of "their" cultural identity.

The task here is thus to reproduce Chinese culture and to re-establish the traditional moral order that will result in the re-discovery of cultural identity. To the proponents of cultural reproduction, such a process can only be successful if the young Singapore Chinese are introduced to their sources of origin. These proponents believe that, as the Confucian saying goes, "when drinking water, think of its source" (飲水思源). This is the key to "becoming Chinese", *huaren hua* (華人化), and undoing the "non-Chineseness" of "Chinese" people.

The older, especially China-born, Chinese, feel that they have a moral obligation to prevent the decline of their cultural identity, and thus feel an urgency to prevent the younger generations from becoming *fan ren* (番人). As one elder commented, "we have to lead the young ones in the search for an identity. They would not be able to find the way. So it is up to us with the seniors to lead the way to our roots [and cultural identity]". To them, this can be done by introducing young Chinese to their ancestral villages and ancestral houses. They thus encourage and lead their children and grandchildren back to visit their ancestral villages and encourage them to participate in village ancestor worship and religious activities as well as getting them involved in village reconstruction.

The Quest for Kinship and Lineage Continuity

The search for ancestral identity is coterminous with a quest for lineage continuity. One informant commented that "our link with the Anxi relatives is like a very thin thread. Once broken, it is very difficult to mend". This is how the Singapore Chinese elders see their link with the ancestral village: to them, the tie is tenuous and needs to be strengthened in order that kinship and lineage continuity with the ancestral village can be maintained. The only way they know is to encourage their descendants to explore this source of origin, to kindle in them the sentiments for their ancestral home villages which they, the elders, have.

Today this quest for self-identity is an extremely emotional affair. Many of the China-born Singapore Chinese are now in their sixties, seventies and eighties, although a smaller number are in their forties. These elders regard their responsibility to preserve kinship ties with their village counterparts as a matter of great urgency: in the Confucian tradition, the failure to bring together two branches of a lineage and to rekindle kinship relations constitutes an unfilial act, and those who thus fail are held responsible for the destruction of the lineage and the kinship ties.

Left alone, the Singapore and Anxi branches of a lineage would face ultimate separation when the older generations pass away. There would be no incentive for younger generations to revive such ties: younger Singapore Chinese today already perceive it to be disadvantageous to maintain them. Maintaining kinship ties with kin whom one has never met is an extremely difficult task. This lack in Singapore-born Chinese of sentimental attachment to their ancestral villages has driven their parents and other forebears to visit their ancestral villages and to help with village reconstruction. For the younger, however, the different socio-political environment and a set of negative collective memories that they have been brought up with have tarnished the images of the ancestral village and of village kin. They do not have first hand experience of village life as their forebears did, and many have not visited their ancestral villages: only in recent years have some ventured to do so. For them, the memories and stories of the ancestral village told to them have been of underdevelopment, regional poverty, greed and lack of consideration of village kin. Such memories and stories have led them to harbour strong negative sentiments of their ancestral home and of their relatives: they not only have little emotional attachment to their ancestral homes but many have consciously chosen to have little or no dealing with their village kin and ancestral villages. Thus, the challenge for older generations is to create an environment that would reverse such negative attitudes and to encourage the Singapore-born Chinese to embrace their roots and ancestry.

For Singapore-born Anxi Chinese, visiting Anxi is one important way of understanding and raising consciousness concerning the ancestral village, one way to rekindle kinship ties between two groups of Anxi Chinese. The elders are concerned that their children and future descendants have knowledge of Anxi. One said, "although we have been naturalised in another country, we should not forget our origin. In fact, we should know more of our origin. This is important for our children. They (children and grandchildren) should know more about their ancestors and their achievement. It is important to encourage them to visit Anxi and let them understand their ancestral village and the existence of their village kin. We have the responsibility to introduce the ancestral village to them. But what happens after that depends on themselves". Another said, "I will encourage my children and grandchildren to return home for a visit.

Whether they want to go or not is their choice. But I will definitely encourage them to do so". A third said, "the young ones should know Anxi because it is their roots. They should at least know of this. If we do not have a lineage and culture, then other people will not respect us. We would be like a pack of loose sand without a centrifugal force to bind us together".

Some feel that one way to encourage the younger Chinese to take an interest in the ancestral village is to become very active in village life. One said, "it is important to maintain contacts in Anxi. That is why we visit and participate in the activities there. We also invest in village reconstruction. This is one way to arouse their interest in the ancestral village". Another feels that "to arouse their interests, we should show them photos and videotapes of the village so that they have an idea of what the village is like". This sentiment is shared by another who said, "I have taken many photos and collected information for my children, including maps and videos. It is very important for my children and grandchildren to know their home village. This is because their global outlook has led them to become more preoccupied with the outside world than with their home village. I have also brought them back to the village and will encourage them to go again. But I will not force them. It is pointless to coerce them to go. Rather, persuasion will be a more effective method". The urgency of showing the ancestral village is encapsulated in this comment: "it is important for the young ones to know their home village and their ancestors. But if they do not want to go back, we could not possibly force them to go. But we need to encourage them as often as possible. To arouse their interests, we should bring them back to Anxi and see their reaction. If they come back with some interest, then there is hope that they might maintain some contacts with the ancestral village in the future. Otherwise, it is finished. When we die, it will end with us. It will have to be a go-slow approach. We will first encourage them to go back and have a look. The second step will be to encourage them to participate in the activities there. Gradually, they might develop some sentiments towards the village and their village kin".

While it is easy to lead children and grandchildren back to the village, it requires more effort to make them interested in village activities and to help with village reconstruction. The elders can only hope that their enthusiasm and interest will become an influencing factor in helping the young Chinese to look at their ancestral village in a more positive manner, instead of relying on the negative memories and sentiments of the earlier years. This is a difficult task. Today, some Singapore-born Chinese have expressed some interest and have participated in village activities. The elders feel that such participation has ignited, to a certain degree, the kinship flame among the younger generations, which will allow for lineage continuity. One said, "very few Singapore-born Chinese recognise their ancestral home. Most of them are English-educated. It takes patience to arouse their interest. But we are gradually getting round and a few have shown some interest". But the frustration continues: another said, "I have encouraged them to go and have tried to tell them about their home village. But they are not very enthusiastic. It is very hard to force them to go if they do not want to".

Some feel that another way to encourage younger generations to become interested in the ancestral village is to participate in various activities organised by the lineage and clan associations in Singapore. Another informant suggested that the Singapore Anxi Association should organise more activities both in Singapore and in Anxi, and that locally born Chinese is encouraged to join in the activities. It is also important to consider the genealogy as an important source for the understanding of cultural roots: another informant suggested, "To arouse their interests, let them explore the genealogy. Explain to them their ancestors and their origin. Then, bring them back to the village for a visit. The genealogy will help them to understand their origin and will serve as a stepping stone to their participation in the cultural and religious activities. It might also encourage them to join Anxi Association". Most feel that it would be easier to educate younger generations about their ancestral villages at a young age.

Locating self-identity in Singapore is especially important. One informant commented that "they [younger generations] need to know their ancestral village. This is their root. It is important that they are able to answer who their ancestors are when asked by outsiders. If they do not know, then they would be telling the rest of the world that they have forgotten their ancestors and signal broken ties with their relatives. It will also tell the world that they have lost their focus. Under such circumstance, they will not be able to locate their identity. It will be embarrassing for them and for us as parents. It also means that we will have failed in our duties as parents". Furthermore, "the need to know one's identity is especially important in Singapore. One only need to look at the history of race relations in this part of the world to tell us that if we do not recognise our own identity, then we would be subsumed by other ethnic groups. Our geopolitical racial relationship is very complex. There is social comfort and security in knowing the importance of being Chinese".

The attitude of Singapore-born Chinese towards Anxi is exemplified in their comments. One said, "I am born in Singapore and do not have a clear picture and understanding of Anxi. I do not expect much from my children. I know of Anxi from my parents and have made several visits to the village. If my children want to know about Anxi, I will tell them. I do not actively tell them about Anxi nor do I encourage them to participate actively in the activities. But I am not opposed to them wanting to know more about or visiting Anxi. It all depends on my children. If they are interested in Anxi, we will give them all the support. Otherwise, I will not bother". Another echoes a more negative view: "for those born in Singapore, like myself, a third generation "baba", we should not and would not push for such recognition. It will be very hard to interest us about Anxi. Personally, I feel that those with a Chinese education might think more of their cultural roots, but for those who are English-educated, including myself, we look more to Singapore as our home".

As for the third and fourth generation Chinese, a large majority see themselves as having only the Singapore Chinese identity. Most of these are in the twenties and thirties. One said, "I considered myself as *Xin-jia-po-ren*. Singapore is my permanent home". Others said that "we are *Xin-jia-po-huaren*. We should be more concerned with the activities and future of Singapore and not that of Anxi. Anxi exists only for sentimental reasons".

However, to some extent, visiting the ancestral home village by Singapore-born Chinese has brought about several consequences. First, it has helped deepen their understanding of rural China and of their ancestral homes in particular. They have come to understand the relative poverty and the lack of economic and material goods in the village. In this sense, some have developed a measure of sympathy that was otherwise lacking in them - a softening of their attitudes towards their village kin. They have also come to accept that Anxi is their ancestral home, even though some acknowledge this fact reluctantly. Secondly, their contact has led them to re-evaluate their identity. They have come to accept that their ancestry is rooted in rural China and have become aware of the physical locality and the social kinship network that is embedded within the locality and ancestral village structure.

Thirdly, this contact has also made them aware of the similarities and the great divide between their village kin and themselves. While, at one level, they have been made aware of the composition of their families, lineages and ancestral community, at another level they have become keenly aware of the differences between them. Such differences mark the boundary between insiders and outsiders. Singapore-born Chinese feel that they are both insiders and outsiders in their ancestral home villages: as insiders, they are part of the kinship and lineage network, and are expected to discharge moral duties and ritual obligations as insiders; as outsiders, they differ greatly from their village counterparts in appearance, eating habits, attitudes, actions, linguistic skills and ideology. By contrasting themselves to their village kin, they contribute to the construction of their cultural identities.

The cultural identity of these younger Singapore-born Anxi Chinese is a composite one. It has elements of Chinese-ness embedded within their ancestral home and home village structure. At the same time, other elements of Chinese-ness are localised, entrenched within the Singapore Chinese community and specifically the Singapore Anxi community. Their identity is also under the over-arching influence of the nation-state, and of the wider society of Singapore. The final product is a Singapore Chinese identity with specific cultural orientations that are characteristics of the Anxi Chinese community. It is this composite, which make the Singapore Anxi Chinese different from that of their village counterparts.

An Emerging Local Singapore Chinese Root - *Luo-di-shen-gan*

Whether they are first generation migrants or locally born Singaporeans, about 90 per cent of those interviewed told me that they would not consider returning to Anxi after their retirement. Of the first generation, some told me that upon retirement they might travel between Singapore and Anxi and stay for an extended period of two to three months in Anxi; however, they foresaw several difficulties of relocating back in Anxi. They feel that they would have to start a new lifestyle and readapt to village life. While this is a romantic idea, they have no illusion of the difficulties, given the relatively underdeveloped nature of the village. Moreover, their immediate families - spouses, siblings, children and grandchildren - are now in Singapore and it would be hard to leave them behind. Furthermore, their prevailing social networks of relatives and friends have sustained them through the last four to five decades of difficulties and agonising moments, when they experienced and endured poverty and hardship before achieving eventual success, and they would find it hard to move away from their social networks. A fourth factor concerns the Singapore nation that they have come to regard as their home. They feel that Singapore has treated them well and they could not just pack and go, as they have developed great emotional attachments to Singapore.

While searching for their cultural roots, it is evident that the Singapore Chinese regard themselves as Singapore citizens of Chinese ethnicity. They also identify themselves as Singapore Anxi *huaren*, or Singapore Anxi *ren*. This multiplicity of identities can be explained according to their self-understanding. At the nation-state level, their identity is inevitably tied to their understanding of nationhood and citizenry, and the political boundary and political responsibilities associated with being a citizen of Singapore spell out their present status. This is one that they are proud of: being a Singapore citizen indicates social prestige, wealth, progress, urbanity and sophistication - a coveted status out of the reach of their village kin. The Singapore Anxi Chinese understand this because their positions have allowed them to structure their social relationships with their village kin and to negotiate for dominant positions vis-à-vis their village counterparts. Yet they call themselves Singapore Anxi *huaren* as a way of identifying their specific origin, claiming that "since our ancestors are from Anxi, we are therefore Anxi *huaren*". Logic dictates that assuming both identities is not only desirable but also necessary. Assuming the Anxi identity does not contradict their understanding of the political culture of Singapore, since being a Singapore Chinese conveys one's present political identity, a matter of status within the boundary of a nation-state, while being an Anxi *huaren* informs of one's ancestral origin and cultural affiliation. One informant said, "We are Chinese but we are Singapore citizens. We need to understand that we are now Singapore citizens as we have already forgone our Chinese citizenship. We should understand this. At the same time, we should not forget our ancestors". Finally, there is the Singapore Fujian Chinese identity. The fact that the Anxi people are all Fujian-speaking and Fujian is the most widely spoken dialect in Singapore has placed them in a dominant position within the wider Chinese community. Thus, to claim a Singapore Fujian identity is also to claim an established dominant status.

Thus, within the social and political discourse of the Chinese community, this group of Chinese assume four identities: Singaporean, Singapore Chinese, Singapore Fujian-speaker and Singapore Anxi Chinese. This is how one identified himself: "I am a *Xin-jia-po-ren*, a Singapore citizen. My ancestry is Anxi. I regard Singapore as my permanent place of residence. I am also a Singapore Fujian person". Others also echo this: "I am Singapore-born and a Singapore-*ren* (person). My blood origin is Anxi. I feel that I am half Anxi-*ren* and half *xin-jia-po-ren*". While they may have multiple identities, they are selective of the identities they used and tailored them according to the social occasions, depending on whether they are with other Chinese in Singapore or overseas or with the non-Chinese people.

This multiple identity of the Anxi Singapore Chinese permits us to understand the extent to which identity is being created and negotiated within a different social and political environment. For this group of Chinese, the necessary to fulfil their quest for their own cultural identity and the need to display a uniform Chinese identity in the Singapore nation-state. As the full cycle of migration and settlement occurred, the migrants and their descendants have come to accept the process of planting their roots in the Singapore soil and to establish identities that would best represent them in various socio-political situations. This multiple identity is the result that incorporates an emerging Singapore Chinese cultural identity.

Notes

1   In 1992, a conference titled "Luo-Di-Shen-Gen" was held at the University of California, Berkeley, which discussed the status of Chinese overseas during the nineteenth and twentieth centuries.

2   Straits Chinese men are called *baba* while the women are known as *nonya*. Because of their unique cooking, often carried out by the women, this form of cooking is termed as *nonya* cuisine.

3   It is to be noted here that the Malays and Indians are not homogenous ethnic groups either, as within each group there are numerous sub-groups, which display a great variety of dialects. Also encouraged by the state, they are similarly embarking on a process of cultural standardization in a quest to portray ethnically unified images.

4   In 1994, the Singapore Government introduced the "Maintenance of Elderly Parents" Act in an attempt to prevent adult children from neglecting their parents. This act requires adult children to provide financial assistance, set at S$500 a month, to their parents.

3 The Ancestral Village in Anxi County

Introduction

Having settled permanently in Singapore and assumed a Singapore Chinese identity, they are now searching for their cultural root. The search for cultural root brings this group of Singapore Chinese to their ancestral village in Peng Lai district in Anxi County. Peng Lai district comprises 31 administrative villages. However, among the local villagers, their district continues to be divided into several precincts named according to the natural terrain found in the region. For example, the area around the source of the river where the villagers reside is commonly known as the creek head, *xi-tou* [M], *kway-tou* [H] (溪頭); the area around the end of the river is known as creek tail or *xi-wei* [M], *kway-ber* (溪尾) A third area around the forest area is known as the behind the tree, *xia-shu-wei* [M], *ae-chiu-ber* [H] (下樹尾) . When asked, the majority of the villagers did not have much idea of the formal name of the villages that they lived in. In any case, they are also not concerned with these administrative names. Only the village cadres have expressed some knowledge of the names of these numerous villages that are found in Peng Lai district. Most villagers will say that they are from Peng Lai and if pushed further, they would answer the precinct name according to the natural terrain. As Peng Lai is the most commonly known name to all, the villagers and the Singapore Chinese, this will be the name used throughout this work.

Within Peng Lai district, there are nine surname groups. All the villages are of a mixed surname composition although in most precincts, it is usually the case that one surname group will dominate the district. Many of these villagers are connected to one another by surname and marriage.

Among the Singapore Chinese of Anxi descent, their knowledge of the ancestral village varies greatly among the generations. The first generation has a clear concept of their ancestral village while the second and subsequent generations have a hasty understanding of it. Among the first generation migrants, they are able to name the village precinct that they came from. However, among the second and subsequent generations, it is most common for them to inform others that they are from the Anxi district. Some are now able to say that they are from Peng Lai district.

58

Beyond this broad territorial classification, almost all are unable to locate their specific ancestral village by name.

Today, the Anxi County is still considered one of the poorest districts in the whole of China. *Qiaoxiang*, with overseas Chinese capital, now are considered potential growth nodes by the government that would bring about development in the county. This chapter will explore the reasons why the county was and is still today considered as one of the poorest regions in China. It will also explore the measures taken by the central, provincial and county government to eradicate poverty and the success of their efforts. It will examine how the Singapore Chinese, in part through the encouragement of the government officials, provide material and financial resources to help eradicate poverty and making the emigrant villages, *qiaoxiang* into prosperous villages and towns in South China.

Where is Anxi?

The Anxi district is located in the south-east region of Fujian, between longitude 117 degrees and 36' and 118 degrees and 17' east and latitude 24 degrees and 50' and 25 degrees and 26' north. It has an area of 3057.28 square metres. In 1990, it comprises 5 towns, 19 counties, 10 government operated farms, forest, tea plantation, 14 people's committees, 426 village committees, 50 people's committees, 6401 village committees. It contains 186,215 households and a total population of 916,204. Of these, 865,075 are engaged in farming activities.

Topographically, the region is mountainous with numerous mountainous ranges rising 1600 metres above sea level. The region can be divided into inner Anxi where the terrain is more rugged while outer Anxi, which has relatively undulating landscape, average 300 to 400 metres above sea level. Outer Anxi has broad plains, valleys and river basins, with average temperature of 19.5 - 21.3 degrees C and an average annual rainfall of 1600 millilitres. Inner Anxi has an average height of 600-700 metres, mostly mountainous ranges, average temperature ranges from 17-18 degrees C, and annual rainfall of 1800 millilitres. The climate is sub-tropical and monsoonal although the four seasons can be easily distinguishable. The region is served by two main rivers, River Xi and Lan and their tributaries criss-crossed the terrain.

During the early years, half of the region is covered mainly with pine forest. However, since the 1950s, especially after the central government policies of conquering and transforming the wilderness to productive agricultural land, the forested region has declined dramatically. Despite this, today, only about 10 per cent of the total land area continues to be arable. The agricultural land suffers from infertile soil which is poor in nutrient and acidic in nature, making farming unproductive. Furthermore, the land suffers from chronic erosion as a result of seasonal monsoon rain that led to swelling of rapid mountain streams (Lyons, 1994: 3-4).

Peng Lai District

Peng Lai district is situated in the eastern part of Anxi, 25 degrees and 08' East and 118 degrees and 05' North. It is 16 km away from the county town centre (Xian-Chen). It occupies an area of 122.38 square kilometres. The district comprises 31 villages. In 1984, the emerging market town was officially recognised and is known as Peng Lai Township, Peng Lai Zhen. In 1992, it had a residence committee, 30 village committees, 14,438 households, with a total population of 67,812. The population density is 556 per sq. km. In 1996, the population has increased to 74,462.[1]

Development in Anxi

The development in Anxi can be divided into two main periods. The first started since communism and ran until 1978. The second begins with Deng Xiaoping's 1978 Reform. Deng's famous phrase of "it does not matter whether it is a black or white cat, it is a good cat if it catches mice" ushers in a new period of rapid development and coincides with the new open door policy. Elsewhere in China, the creation of the special economic zones along the coastal region has greatly impacted on the interior. The opening of the Xiamen Economic Zone has brought about changes in all the counties in Fujian including Anxi. Furthermore, since the 1978 Reform, there have also been new central and provincial policies targeting at the Chinese overseas, encouraging them to invest not only in China but also, more specifically, in their ancestral villages.

    The development of Anxi from the 1950s to early 1980 was very much influenced by the central government policies and the priorities of the Fujian provincial government. Right from the beginning, the rural economy was expected to be self-sufficient with little or no central funding given to its agricultural development. Furthermore, the region was expected to finance its own basic infrastructure development. The result was that during this period, a long term policy of "comprehensive harnessing of mountains, rivers, and farmlands" was implemented at the local level where large numbers of rural labourers were recruited from the collectives to provide labour for all the various projects that were essential to increase agricultural output (Lyons, 1994: 18). During the period 1950-1984, 14,100 water-control projects were undertaken. This included the construction of 541 reservoirs and 158 pumping stations (Lyons, 1994: 18). This increased the irrigated land to 228,000 *mu* in 1980 that was about 55 per cent of the county's irrigated farmland. Apart from irrigation, multiple cropping and increased use of fertilisers had also increased the production yield. However, such increases in yield were also affected by the political climate of the time. The Great Leap Forward and the Cultural Revolution have caused long lasting damage to its economy where the already scarce resources were directed towards these two failed programmes.

From the 1950s to 1978, Anxi remained essentially an agrarian economy with collective farming. Since 1958, agricultural land was organised into communes. As late as 1980, there continued to be 15 communes divided into 240 brigades and 2500 production units (Lyons, 1994: 18). A breakdown of the agricultural production shows that the region continued to focus on a self-sufficient economy where the ratio of the grain crop production (mainly rice, wheat and sweet potatoes) to cash crops (peanuts, sugar cane and tobacco) was 20:1 in terms of sown area. About 91 per cent of the total land area were devoted to the production of grain (Lyons, 1994: 21). Tea and fruit orchards also occupied a small acreage, with 100,000 *mu* devoted to tea plantation and 20,000-30,000 *mu* devoted to fruit orchards (oranges, longan, litchi, plums and persimmon) (Lyons, 1994: 21).

Despite the full concentration of grain production to attain self-sufficiency, Anxi's grain production remained low even by provincial standard. In 1980, grain production stood at 9 per cent below the provincial level. In terms of yield per *mu*, it was 5 per cent below Fujian's average. This was attributed to the intensive double cropping and the irrigation that was in place. The same was also true for their cash crops and tea and fruit production, which also fell below the provincial level. By its own standard, the production yield had already improved considerably as a result of double cropping made possible as a result of the availability of irrigation.

Apart from agricultural production, Anxi was also left to cope with its basic infrastructure development with little aid from the central or provincial governments. During this period, basic infrastructure investment that included rail and road construction, education, health and welfare remained below a pitiful 20 Rmb per capita annually until the late 1970s (Lyons, 1994: 15). Prior to collectivisation, the county had a surplus but since the late 1960s, it had a deficit as a result of remittances to the provincial government. In return, it had to receive subsidies from the provincial government.

During this period, government resources were directed towards government funded investment such as the relatively large water control projects including some hydro electric stations, government-owned tea and tree farms and other projects that were deemed as essential for the general development of the country (Lyons, 1994: 16). One main reason for this general neglect of rural development is that the central government spending was aimed at building urban industry and securing the welfare of the city people (Lyons, 1994: 17). A second reason was attributed to the provincial government's "inland development strategy" where the provincial government directed resources to certain areas which it saw as potential growth corridors. Thus, resources were directed to the area along the railroad running north south, from Nanping to Longyan in the centre of the province (Lyons, 1994: 17). Thus, those cities along the route would benefit from industrialisation and development. Anxi, which is off the route, suffered as a result of this policy.

The second phase of development started with the Deng's economic reform of 1978. The 1978 Reform could be seen as a watershed for the transformation of the Chinese economy and this open door policy also permits the interior region to open up and develop new economic approaches and links with the outside world. During this period, there was fundamental change to the agrarian economy. Instead of encouraging agrarian self-sufficiency, encouragement was given to non-agricultural development and to eradicate poverty in Anxi.

To encourage non-agricultural development, there was a reduction in the governmental control and directives and to encourage external investments into the region through various incentives. The Fujian provincial government developed a two front strategy; one focussed on the mountains, i.e. the mountainous interior and the other on the coastal areas. This strategy was to develop specialised districts and production bases according to the resources of the region (Lyons, 1994: 42-43). Using this strategy, areas that were under tea and fruit production would be encouraged to concentrate on their production. Furthermore, priority would be given to these regions to upgrade their production by providing financial assistance to purchase better quality seeds and to expand on their processing industry, thereby making their products competitive in both domestic and international markets.

Prior to the 1978 Reform, Anxi had only 64 industrial enterprises operated by various levels of government or the communes. These industrial enterprises were scattered primarily in the county towns. The labour force working in the industrial sector accounted for only 11 per cent of the total labour force in 1978 (Lyons, 1994: 21). Since the reform, the provincial government has also actively pursued foreign investors and capital through a series of preferential policies. Special regulations to ensure protection of investors' property and legal rights were given to the Chinese overseas investors, especially for the Taiwanese investors. For example, in the coastal cities of Fujian, special enterprise zones were established for the Taiwanese investors in the Haicang and Xinlin investment districts (Lyons, 1994: 45). This has resulted in investments from Taiwan, which set up a total of 1203 enterprises, totalling US$1.6 billion in 1991 (Lyons, 1994: 45).

The reform policies have also affected the economic restructuring to a certain degree. In the early 1980s, Anxi began to develop small sized processing plants. In 1984, it received its first foreign investment (Lyons, 1994: 45). In 1985, it became part of the newly established Minan (Southern Fujian) Open Area, together with eleven other counties and cities in Jiangjiang, Longxi and Xiamen prefectures. Enterprises in this Open Area enjoyed preferential treatment such as tax rebates of import duties on equipment and a reduced tax rates on profits by the foreign owned enterprises (Lyons, 1994: 45). In 1987 and 1988, three towns in Anxi namely Hutou, Guanqiao and Jiandou were designated as key satellite industrial bases by the provincial government to boost industrial development of the county which will help to focus on their resources and extend their economic linkages with other bigger industrial bases and Xiamen city (Lyons, 1994: 48). Peng Lai town is yet considered as too small for economies of scale to occur and was thus not designated as a key satellite industrial base.

Another area that the provincial and local governments focussed on is the tourist trade. Various areas of Fujian, which were promoted as historic and religious sites, have been well received. As a result of this, the number of tourists jumped from 16,000 in 1987 to 146,000 in 1988 and exceeding 200,000 in each year that followed (Lyons, 1994: 45). In line with the tourist promotion efforts, Anxi too promoted itself as an important religious site, claiming the presence of the Qing-Shui-Yan as its most important temple for the Chinese overseas. Since then, it has a steady stream of visitors visiting the temple. They came primarily from Taiwan, Singapore and Malaysia. However, for the majority of tourists, they came to Anxi with the primary aim of visiting their ancestral village and homes. In Peng Lai district, 99 per cent of the visitors were there to visit their ancestral home.

The Village Economy in the 1990s

The primary economic activity in Anxi was, and still is, farming. However, the mountainous terrain makes farming an arduous task, and efforts put into agricultural activities were not highly productive. Because of the numerous mountain ranges and small amount of flat land, most farming has been carried out on terraces cut into the steep slopes. In some places, the width of these terraces is no more than a foot. Even walking through the terraced fields can be hazardous, let alone sowing and planting in them. Despite this harshness of the terrain, the peasants have continued to farm.

In Anxi, both subsistence farming and cash cropping are important. Wet rice cultivation is the main subsistence activity. The region produces two crops of rice annually for home consumption, but this production is insufficient for the large and growing population, and rice has to be imported to supplement local production. Since the reform of 1979, farming has been operating under the joint family responsibility system, and a market economy has led to a three- to four-fold increase in the price of rice. Despite this, villagers continue to eat rice three times a day as their staple although, in recent years, there has been some change in food habits, and wheat products, including noodles and buns, have gained in popularity. Apart from rice, vegetable gardening and pig and poultry rearing are part of the subsistence economy, and vegetables, pork and poultry are now sold in the market place which is held once a week on market day. During the market day, the place is set abuzz with noise while villagers buying and selling goods. During other days, a small group of farmers bring their unsold or freshly picked vegetables to sell along the street around the market place. In 1994 when the building for a permanent market has been completed, the hawkers who have successfully applied for a license and given a stall to operate have been able to sell vegetables and other produce on a daily basis. However, the villagers continue to patronise the open market for fresh produce where the price is lower and out of their routine habit. In general, over the last few years, there has been a rise in the prices of the market produce. Despite this price hike, the rise in the standard of living has meant that more people than before are able to afford meat and poultry, and most families can now afford some form of meat several meals a week.

Since the reform, greater emphasis has been placed on cash cropping for export. Anxi in general and Peng Lai district in particular, the emphasis is on tea and fruit growing where tea plantation and fruit orchards have continued to be the two most important revenue-earning crops. Taking the cue from the provincial government, the local government has placed much emphasis on specialising in these two produces. The undulating landscape, cool temperate climate, and sufficient rainfall make Anxi one of China's important tea-planting districts. In 1990, the total area under tea plantation was 142,270 *mu* and the area actually harvested was 127,490 *mu*. Production of tea-leaves in the same year yielded 7,023 tons, giving an average of 55 kg per *mu* (Anxi Xian Zhi, 1994, vol. 1:173).

Since the reform, the local government and the people's co-operatives have attempted to increase the acreage of tea production. Various hybridisation programmes have been introduced to produce higher-grade tea. Prior to reform, the main bulk of the tea leaves produced was sent out to the cities for processing and packaging, but now the Anxi County government is planning to build facilities for processing and packaging of the finished product within Anxi. In Peng Lai district, there have also been discussions concerning the building of tea processing and packaging factories to solve the unemployment problems. To do this, officials have courted outside capital - for the most part, Chinese overseas capital - by using their *guanxi* network as a starting point to activate the moral economy. Their efforts have already resulted in attracting Chinese overseas capital into the region.

New hybridisation techniques and improved work ethics towards crop production have brought an improvement in production yield. Compared with 1978, agricultural production had tripled by 1990. Total production in 1990 was worth 138.17 million Rmb. Since 1978, grain productions had increased by 14.23 per cent. The pig population during the same period grew to 285,204 pigs. The major increases in production were in forestry, animal husbandry, fishery and grain production. The total income of each farming household went from 267 Rmb in 1985 to 546 Rmb in 1990 (Anxi Xian Zhi, v.1: 173).

While production has increased steadily, the amount of land devoted to agriculture has progressively decreased, as a result of land being put to non-agricultural uses such as roads, dykes, houses, shops and factories. As agricultural production has now taken a secondary role and replaced by commercial and non-agricultural practices, this trend has worried both local and central governments. In Peng Lai district, as the district assumes a township status, much effort has been used to restructure its economy from agrarian-based to commercial and retailing. The result has been massive conversion of agricultural land for these purposes. There were many incidents where the local government permitted the sale of agricultural land for commercial uses to outsiders. At other times, farmland was simply converted to commercial use by the villagers themselves when they have sufficient capital to start up a business. In 1990, the total area under cultivation stood only at 8.64 per cent of the total land area. Most paddy cultivation is now being pushed to the mountainous region. Today, terrace cultivation constitutes 67.15 per cent of cultivable land (Anxi Xian Zhi, vol.1: 174).

Today, the landscape of Peng Lai district is one with a relatively well developed town and in its surrounding areas, there are small plots of agricultural land, some devoted to rice growing while others devoted to vegetables. For the farming households, they also reared pigs and poultry as important supplements to increase their revenue. Incomes of agricultural households have become much lower than those of wage earning labourers or enterprise households, getihu (個體戶) who are engaged in retail trade or other commercial activities.

Both men and women originally shared in farming, but as men move out of Anxi County and Peng Lai District to the cities in search of employment, an increasing number of plots are worked by women. In 1990, only 28 per cent of the Anxi population were engaged in agricultural production (Anxi Xian Zhi, vol.1: 175). As the organisation of agricultural production shifted from collectivisation to the joint family responsibility system, 1990 saw a total of 175,316 agricultural production household units, with a total farming population of 865, 075 (Anxi Xian Zhi, vol.1: 75).

Local animal husbandry consists of pig, buffalo and rabbit rearing. Pig rearing is probably the most important activity among individual farming households, as the profit margin on pork is much higher than for the other animals, and pig production has increased six-fold over the last fifty years. In 1990, the number of pigs reared totalled 285,204. Water buffaloes are kept for cultivation purposes; cows are kept for their milk, but rarely for their meat. The total number of buffalo and female dairy cattle in 1990 stood at 59,141. The rearing of rabbits for meat and hides has become increasingly important to the farmers, and in recent years the import of a variety of kinds of rabbits from overseas has made this an important primary production. In most households, rearing of poultry is an important side activity. Ducks and chicken are the two most important types of poultry, and are reared for both meat and eggs. Total production stood at 1,756,034 in 1990.

Anxi is one of the most important tea-producing regions in China. Anxi tea is associated with well-known labels such as *Oolong* and *Tieguanyin*. Tea production is found in both inner and outer Anxi, and Peng Lai District. In 1990, total acreage under tea production in Anxi was 142,270 *mu* and total production was 7023.2 tonnes; in that year, Peng Lai District had 8,730 *mu* under tea production, of which 8,432 *mu* were harvested, a total of 394.2 tonnes. The average per *mu* was 46.75 tonnes, which was below the average of 55.09 tonnes when comparing to the neighbouring districts in 1990. Most of the tealeaves produced were sent to the cities for processing; inferior grades were left behind and processed within the district for local consumption. The number of tea processing factories in Anxi in 1990 totalled 280, of which 9 were state-operated, 161 were operated by co-operatives, and 110 were privately owned.

Fruit orchards have also become more important in recent years, catering to the emerging export trade. Tangerines and longans are the two most important fruits grown for export: others include bananas, pomelos, sugar cane, peaches, plums and pears. In 1990, total acreage devoted to fruit orchards was 112,447 *mu*; total production was 4566.7 tonnes. In Peng Lai District, the total area under fruit production was 3,517 *mu* and total production was 423.4 tonnes.

The average income per person in 1990 was 546 Rmb, which represented a substantial improvement from the average income of 23.9 Rmb per person in 1960. However, this pales into insignificance when compared to the earnings of *getihu* or truck operators, whose earning totalled 2,000 - 3,000 Rmb or more a month. The average farm size per person in 1990 stood at 1.42 *mu*, farms classified as "wealthy" averaged 1.6 *mu*, and those wealthy farmers who were partial landowners owned an average of 1.68 *mu*. The "average" farmers owned 1.54 *mu* each, while poor farmers owned 1.35 *mu*. Those who employed workers to work on their farms had an average farm size of 1.53 *mu*. Tenanted farms were the largest, with an average farm size of 2 *mu* (Anxi Xian Zhi, vol.1: 180).

By 1996, it has increased to 2181.88 Rmb.[2] This could be attributed to a shift from grain production to market gardening, rearing of pigs and poultry as well as cash crop production. At the same time, it also reflected on the shift of economic activities of the household members where many members are now engaged in some form of industrial production or enterprise activities as in retailing and service.

Eradicating Poverty

A second goal of the 1978 Reform was to eradicate poverty and raise the standard of living of the peasants in the whole of China. The central government launched an anti-poverty campaign in 1985 to solve the problems of basic subsistence of people living under poverty. It hoped that by 1990, 90 per cent of those below the poverty line would be alleviated to a descent standard of living. Thus, 300 counties were designated as national poverty keypoints. In Fujian province, 14 counties including Anxi became the designated poverty keypoints (Lyons, 1994: 49). One main strategy in this campaign is to provide low interest loans to these counties with a national allocation budget of 1 billion Rmb. In addition, these poverty-stricken counties were given grain allocation and other commodities to pay workers in lieu of money who worked on infrastructure projects. They were also used by the provincial and lower level governments to exchange for raw materials for infrastructure projects (Lyons, 1994: 49).

To counter poverty, the Fujian provincial government, apart from the national designated 14 poverty keypoints, also designated 3 other counties and 200 poverty township in its anti-poverty campaign. It implemented the "3/5/8" strategy where it aimed to solve the basic needs of the majority of the poor households within three years, i.e. from 1986-88; to solve the problems of local budget deficits within five years and encourage rapid growth in poor areas, turning deficit into surplus and start contributing to provincial treasury within 8 years (Lyons, 1994: 49-50). It attempted this by focussing on four areas. First, there is investment in human capital to eradicate illiteracy and boost technical skills for the farming households. Second, encouraging commercialisation and commodity production where farming households are encouraged to diversify their production, especially into cash cropping and to engage in market economy. Third, it wanted to restructure the local economy and this is done by correcting the farming problems such as land degradation and erosion on the one hand and introducing value added industry to better harness local resources and produce. Fourth, it argues for infrastructure development and promoting those sectors that are cost effective with rapid and high returns to stimulate further demands and production (Lyons, 1994: 50).

An anti-poverty bureaucracy was set up at the provincial level that was involved in policy promulgation, implementation and on-site inspection. The bureaucracy was also expected to provide technical expertise and train villagers in the desired skills and to set up linkages among the poor districts to facilitate the campaign.

In Anxi, the local government implemented three policies to eradicate poverty. The first was to implement development by providing capital, technical and commercial knowledge to the poverty-stricken households. The second was to provide preferential treatment to mountain districts to promote growth in these areas by harnessing local forest resources. The third was to open the county to trade and investment (Lyons, 1994: 52). In 1987, its strategy of "taking grain as the foundation and forests as the base, using teas for escaping poverty, and fruits for becoming prosperous" resulted in massive destruction of the forested area and creating environmental problems (Lyons, 1994: 52). Furthermore, this did not solve the unemployment problem of surplus labour. In early 1990s, it revised its tactic and pushed for a "strategy for escaping from poverty and for overall development" (Lyons, 1994: 52).

In the agricultural area, local officials were organised to assist the farmers with new techniques of farming while provisions of fertilisers and other farming essentials were given to the farmers to help raise the production yield. At the same time, training classes were organised for farmers to learn new techniques and methods. There was also encouragement to improve irrigation and to use mechanical plows and fertilisers for cultivation (Lyons, 1994: 59-62). The result was that from 1980 to 1992, grain production increased by 13 per cent (Lyons, 1994: 62).

To encourage diversification and commercialisation, the local government adopted a strategy called "one product per village, one industry per township" with the aim of harnessing local product as cash crop and local resources to feed the industry that could become a commercially viable export industry. Thus, villagers were encouraged to focus on the production of one leading local product such as one kind of fruit or tea.

For the county as a whole, tea production was highly encouraged. It encouraged upgrading the existing tea production by introducing more varieties and higher-grade seeds. The county also set up a "Oolong Tea Research Institute" and a "Oolong Quality Control Centre" to improve and standardise the quality of tea produced in the county. It also embarked on an aggressive promotion campaign to promote its tea around China and in overseas markets. During the earlier years, tea was mainly processed in the designated state-run tea factory. They continued to be important tea processing plants. However, by 1987, village run plants were permitted to operate and in that year, 50 village run plants took advantage of the relaxed policies and began processing tea in the villages. By 1990s, several hundred village-run plants had been established (Lyons, 1994: 63).

Fruit production was also encouraged. The county government has designated that each village should devote 100 *mu* for a collective orchard and each household should maintain a private orchard of 1 *mu*. Those who complied with this demand were given preferential treatment where large plots of hilly lands were leased to individuals and partnership for long term fruit orchard. The result was that by 1992, about 82,200 *mu* of land was devoted to fruit orchards that were devoted for export purposes. One main fruit exported was persimmon (Lyons, 1994: 64). In the Anxi County, in 1992, cash crop production accounted for 19.22 million Rmb. By 1996, agricultural production has increased less spectacularly to 83.08 million Rmb.[3]

There was also encouragement to develop township and village enterprises. There was rapid development of these enterprises. However, most of these were privately owned and not state or county operated. Many were involved in small production that ranges from processing of agricultural products to producing building materials, chemicals and consumer goods such as shoes and garments. By the 1990s, the number of township and village enterprises have grown to over 1,000 but all of these enterprises were operated on a very small scale basis with an average of about 5 workers and an average annual income of not exceeding 26,000

Rmb (Lyons, 1994: 65). In Peng Lai town, the township enterprises employed somewhere between ten to twenty workers and its annual revenue reached over 50,000 to 100,000 Rmb in 1995. By 1990 only 7 foreign invested township and village enterprises were in operation.

The county government also encouraged foreign investment into the region. It instituted a series of ten preferential policies for foreign and joint-venture investments. It also appealed to Chinese overseas to invest in their ancestral villages. It especially encouraged basic infrastructure development, export-oriented industries and general agricultural development (Lyons, 1994: 68). By 1991, there were a total of 38 foreign invested enterprises. Of them, there were 14 garment industries. Others included enterprises involved in the making of umbrellas, silk flowers, rattan products and chemical products including recording tapes and hair shampoo. A small numbers were involved in production of consumer goods. Of them, 25 were equity joint ventures, two were co-operative ventures and eleven wholly foreign owned. Most of these enterprises were found in the county seat of Fengcheng and other larger towns such as Hutou, Peng Lai, Kuidou, Xiping, Jingu and Shangqing (Lyons, 1994: 69-70). The average investment capital for these enterprises averaged US$280,000. Only a handful of them have investment capital over US$1 million. They came primarily from Taiwan and Hong Kong (Lyons, 1994: 70). By 1990, these enterprises have employed over 10,000 workers (Lyons, 1994: 71).

In 1990, Peng Lai had 11 joint venture enterprises involved in plastics, garments and tea processing. These joint ventures were set up with capital from the overseas Chinese. One way to encourage further investment into the region was to honour the contributions of these overseas Chinese publicly (Lyons, 1994: 73). At the same time, the local government also allied closely with the overseas Chinese social institutions namely the territorial-based home village associations, *tongxianghui* like the Anxi Association to promote further investments in Anxi.

In 1992, industrial production for Anxi County accounted for 23.3 million Rmb and enterprise activities accounted for 38.52 million Rmb. By 1996, industrial production and enterprise activities have increased several folds to 146.18 million Rmb and 210.46 million Rmb respectively.[4]

Another measure taken to eradicate poverty in Anxi is to develop basic infrastructure such as road and railway in the region. Since 1980, there was a plan to build a railway from Zhangping to Quangzhou with 115 km running through Anxi. The construction of several highways, telecommunications and power plants were also in the pipeline (Lyons 1994: 74). Apart from these major constructions that were state-sponsored, many of the feeder roads, bridges and power plants were all built with money from the overseas Chinese. In Peng Lai district, numerous local roads were constructed. From 1992 to 1996, a total of 36.3 km of sealed surface road was constructed costing about 5.3 million RMB.[5]

Despite of these measures taken to eradicate poverty, Anxi remains one of the poorest regions in China today. This is one main reason why the Singapore Chinese continue to feel that they need to assist their ancestral village kin in redevelopment.

Opting Out of an Agrarian Economy

While agricultural activity is an important economic pursuit in this landlocked and mountainous region, many of the peasants opt out of it whenever there is an opportunity, as the work is hard and the income from it is low. This negative attitude towards agriculture has been further reinforced by the devaluation of agricultural pursuits in the eyes of central, provincial and local governments on the one hand and the Singapore kin who are bias towards commerce and trading. At any rate, there is simply insufficient land to feed the growing population.

Subsistence farming brought little or no wealth to a family, and farmers found it hard to provide sufficiently for their families from their meagre incomes. Even with the market reform and the freedom to decide what crops to grow, agricultural incomes continue to lag behind those of other occupations. The most lucrative form of agriculture is market gardening, and fresh vegetables and produce are now sold daily in the market place; however, although prices of such produce are now governed by demand, profits remain low, in comparison to those earned from other occupations. It is thus not surprising that many young villagers are deserting farming for other kinds of jobs. To them, farming is a dead-end job, with farmers confined to the village and with no prospect of social mobility and no possibility for wealth accumulation. Such an attitude is shared by Singapore kin, many of whom have not only not encouraged their kin to go into farming but have actively persuaded their kin to give up market gardening in favour of the trading and service industries. Given this disdain for agriculture, Singapore Chinese have not contributed significantly to improving agriculture.

Thus, today, many villagers with Singapore connections have opted out of agricultural production. Those with farmland have several choices: some lease their land to other farmers; others engage farm labourers to work for them; and a third group trade their land to the district government for sums of money which are then used to buy shophouses in Peng Lai town, in which case the land, especially that near the market town, is put to commercial use. Yet another group have built modern style houses for themselves on agricultural land.

The impact of the shrinking agricultural areas has been felt in recent years. The district must import more of its daily needs, and this has resulted in price inflation for all products, the prices of basic essentials like rice, oil, and vegetables having gone up four to five-fold.

Luxury items like cigarettes and beer have also suffered a price hike, although this has been caused by increased consumption of these items. Villagers have complained loudly about this inflation but have been helpless to stop it. They have blamed it on the reform, on massive consumption by Singapore Chinese when they visit, and on the increasing number of wealthy Anxi villagers with ostentatious lifestyles.

To a certain extent, those with wealthy Singapore kin have been cushioned from the rising cost of living, while those without overseas connection have felt that life has become tougher within the village milieu. Irrespective of this, however, many have felt that the changes have been good, having brought wealth to some and opportunities to others. The very poor without overseas connection now have the opportunity to become tenant farmers and earn a reasonable living. Sometimes, the wealthier households with farmland and no one to work on it simply lease the land to the landless farmers without charge. This has allowed the landless farmers to move beyond subsistence farming and earn an extra income from the surplus produce.

The reform and rekindling of kinship ties with their Singapore kin have enabled Anxi villagers to have bigger dreams and to turn them into reality. Many now have the opportunities to move out of the villages and live in Xian Chen, or in bigger cities such as Xiamen. For a long time, they had kept their heads down and had gone on with a life that was dictated to them, with little to dream about and no vision beyond the village boundary, fighting only to survive unscathed. Now, situations have improved, and in dreaming of life beyond the village their life energies once again flow, making them ready to face new challenges.

Notes

1   Figure provided by Anxi County Administrative Office.
2   Figures provided by Anxi County Administrative Office.
3   Figures provided by Anxi County Administrative Office.
4   Figures provided by Anxi County Administrative Office.
5   Figures provided by Anxi County Administrative Office.

4 Negotiating Collective Memories and Social Experiences

Introduction

Since the nineteenth century, emigrants have moved out of Fujian to Nanyang and elsewhere in search of better economic opportunities and a large number moved to Malaya and Singapore and settled there. After World War Two, another 20,000 Anxi villagers immigrated to Singapore. Today, the total number of emigrants from Anxi to Singapore totalled 185,309 that are about 10 per cent of the Chinese population. Of these Anxi migrants, 41,075 came from the Peng Lai district (Anxi Xian Zhi, vol.2: 854). The primary reason for this emigration trend is, as outlined above, extreme poverty in the villages.

Today, it is precisely this same reason - poverty in Anxi - that lures back the Singapore Anxi Chinese to visit their ancestral villages and assist with the rebuilding of their ancestral homes. Several reasons accounted for this desire to help with village reconstruction. Most of them remembered their ancestral village, experienced the poverty and continued to witness poverty in the villages when they first returned for a visit in the late 1960s and early 1970s. Many feel their fortune and guilt at the same time about their relatively comfortable status in Singapore and their helplessness to assist during the early years. After the 1978 Reform, the changing political climate in both China and Singapore have enabled them to re-evaluate their situation and their relationship with their Anxi kin. They are now in a position to assist as a result of their prosperous status in comparison with their village kin and feel the compelling need to provide assistance to their village kin and the village in general.

This chapter will explore how collective memories serve as an important power and moral capital that will constantly nag at the Singapore Anxi Chinese and tug at their conscience. These memories do not go away and provide them with little peace of mind, challenging their emotions and sentiments until they have done something for their ancestral village. However, the same set of memories also served to obstruct the Singapore-born Chinese from visiting their ancestral village. The result was the tension at the inter-generational level between the China-born and the Singapore-born Chinese on the one hand and tensions between the Singapore Anxi Chinese and their village kin on the other.

The Flow of Collective Memories

The collective memories and sentiments of the first-generation Singapore Anxi Chinese are tied to their shared understanding of their ancestral home, their past, their present and their desire to perpetuate their cultural identity. To these Singapore Chinese, such memories are bittersweet experiences, which, on the one hand, propel them to return to their ancestral village and contribute much to the socio-cultural and economic life there; and, on the other, act as a resistance to their return. This rollercoaster of emotions is expressed in a variety of ways that will be discussed later.

For these Singapore Chinese, the collective memories of their ancestral home are selective ones. In reconstructing past events, many recount the great difficulties and poverty that they have faced, their fear of the unknown when they set sail for Singapore, and their eventual success, however modest, in Singapore. They especially remember the early years and their struggle for survival in the village. It is these memories that they have kept alive and that they choose to pass on to their descendants.

The memory of poverty and great difficulties not only pushed these migrants out of the village but also pushed them to work hard and overcome the difficulties of the early years. This is the refugee mentality and the spirit of survival. Today, even with success and wealth, some of these Singapore Chinese continue to work hard. It is also this memory that has become, in part, the guiding principle for the migrants in providing assistance and involving themselves in the reconstruction of their ancestral villages in the hope of helping to eradicate poverty among their kins-people. Projects, which began with the aim of helping the immediate family members and lineage, have now gradually shifted towards helping the wider community in the social, education and welfare arenas. In shifting their contributions from the immediate kin to the wider community, the migrants attempt to make clear distinctions between private needs and public demands.

Nostalgia and sentiments for their ancestral homes play an important role in luring first generation migrants to visit their home villages. This strong sense of belonging is imperative for their socio-psychological well-being, for it allows them to locate themselves within a known and manageable social framework, which, grounded in kinship ties, facilitates the revival of relationships and lost primordial kinship ties. It has also allowed them to measure their self-worth and tó fulfil their moral duties, which include providing a bridge to link the younger Singapore Chinese to their ancestral home, as discussed in Chapter 2.

Memories of the past and present, of the ancestral home, transmitted orally or in written form, are important for keeping alive images of home villages, people and experiences, which can then be related to children, grandchildren and other kin in routine conversation. By doing this, the older members have had some success in making the younger Singapore Chinese more aware of the plight of their ancestral village. These memories are not only kept alive and circulated within the kinship circle.

In keeping alive the memories of their home villages the Singapore Chinese are reminded of ritual obligations and of their initial failures to carry them out both in Singapore and also in their ancestral villages, at a time when the Communist regime prevented even their village kin from carrying out religious rituals and ancestor worship on their behalf. As the political pressure has now eased, the Singapore Chinese hope once again to re-establish links with their Anxi kin and revives and reproduces these rituals for communal ancestor worship and religious ceremonies.

Maintaining Links from the 1960s-1978

The last major wave of migration to Singapore began in the 1950s, when many young men and women in their teens, twenties and thirties emigrated and joined their families in Singapore. During this period, the established nature of the Chinese community, with its numerous social networks, enabled the newcomers to adapt to the new environment with relative ease. Independent migrants, too, could tap into the existing networks. This was also a period when wives and daughters joined their husbands and fathers, a period of great reunion for the immediate family.

However, family life was difficult. Most *sinkhehs* (new guests) gained employment as workers where wages were low and lived in crammed housing with sparse amenities. It was common for several households, usually of related kin, to share one house.[1] While the men were at work, often for ten hours or more a day, the women were left to cope with a limited budget, a shared kitchen, a growing family and very limited physical space. Most households then consisted only of a single room in the house. There was mutual assistance among these families: women informants have told me that there were many occasions when the lack of money forced the women to help each other with food and cash.

From the 1960s to 1978, despite hardship, many families continued to maintain some sort of links with their village kin. One method used to maintain links and gather information among village kin is through sending gifts and letters. Families were known to send money and parcels back to their home villages in Anxi on a regular basis. My mother would go through our wardrobe, selectively pick out some of our old clothing and, together with some new clothing, fabrics, foodstuffs and medicated oils, bundle it into a parcel. It would then be sent to the village, either by post or via returning relatives.

Though they were on very tight budgets and often did not have enough for their immediate families, many continued to send small remittances to their immediate Anxi kin. This was motivated by their knowledge of the great poverty in Anxi. These letters, in addition to conversations, have allowed us to create the images of village life during the early period. The letters written by villagers to their Singapore kin had one common trait: the difficulties of making ends meet in a poverty-stricken village - i.e., the difficulties faced during the collective years; difficulties of scarce resources such as food, clothing and medicine; difficulties of large families, bad weather, and poor harvests. Most households were then barely subsisting, and many letters sent to Singapore kin asked for various forms of supplies. The most frequently requested items included foodstuffs, clothing and medicine; large items included bicycles and sewing machines.

Maintaining contacts was not an easy task. Those left behind in the village were often semi-literate or illiterate, and most letters were written by village letter-writers that charged a fee for the service. Thus most letters received were identical in style, with limited variation in contents. Most villagers did not write regularly; the standard was for villagers to write two or three letters a year to their Singapore kin and to receive the same number in return: additional letters were dispatched to Singapore only if there were important matters to report, such as the death or impending marriage of close kin. Letters from Anxi villagers often consisted of inquiries concerning health and family well being, in addition to accounts of the difficulties faced at that time. Special needs would generally be implied rather than stated openly, and readers were expected to infer what they were from suggestions, and to act accordingly.

For the Singapore Chinese, sending a letter was not a straightforward affair. It was expected that a remittance, and occasionally gifts, would be included. For this reason, letters were usually sent off during Lunar New Year to help with the festivities of the occasion. This was the norm then and now.

Receiving a Singapore letter was an exciting affair for the villagers concerned, as letters were often accompanied by gifts of various sorts -

money, clothing, medicine, foodstuffs, bicycles, sewing machines and so forth. Because of this link between letter and gifts, it became increasingly difficult merely to send a letter of inquiry, as the expectations dictated that a letter would not be sent without accompanying gifts. This made it extremely difficult for the majority of the Singapore Anxi Chinese to keep up with regular letters, and reduced the incidence of communication with their Anxi relatives. Thus, receiving a "China letter", *tang-shan-xin* (唐山信) created a plethora of imagery and of wants that the Singapore kin found hard to satisfy at times, and there was very little joy in receiving *tang-shan-shin*, as the China letter has come to be synonymous with wants and requests from village kin. A common attitude towards receiving a China letter is that "it is expected, they will ask for things. Why bother to receive them?" Others commented, "here it comes again, they are asking for money again".   After a prolonged period, some simply stopped responding to their village kin, which led to mutual ill feelings. One of the most common expressions from village kin is represented by the comment, "What is the use of having overseas Chinese kin, *qiao-qing*, they don't even bother to maintain contacts with us. We have received no benefits from them. They don't send us anything. It is better not to have them as *qiao-qing*".

Correspondence and gift giving were made more difficult during the Cultural Revolution and the immediate years that followed. The fear of persecution by those with capitalist *qiao-qing* connections meant that few letters were send to their Singapore kin; likewise, there was a drop in the number of letters and gifts to village kin from Singapore. Although parcels of old clothing were sent to those in dire need, almost no new clothing was sent to the village, although a few stashed several pieces of new clothing in bundles of old ones, or new clothes were deliberately made to look like worn ones, one common method being to patch new clothes with small pieces of old linen. Such small parcels were sent by post to village kin, but many were not confident that the parcels would reach their village kin intact, as there were much suspicion that part of the gifts would be pilfered or confiscated by people in authority.

Many Singapore Chinese remembered this as a very difficult period for their village kin. There was great political upheaval and uncertainty in the villages. Overseas connections were politically suspect. Most Singapore Chinese did not know how to respond to the changes that were occurring. Since even very limited correspondence or contact could jeopardise village kin, many stopped writing. For those who continued, letter writing became an art of abstraction with few words: letters of this period contained only a few sentences, or at most a paragraph; most contained only words of greeting and inquiry of health and general well-being, and were otherwise devoid of sentiment or emotion. Such precautionary measures were necessary, as it was common for letters to be opened and read by postal officers before being sent on to Singapore or forwarded to the villagers. The general attitude, then, was that no news was good news, although receiving any letter remained a sufficient sign that village kin continued to survive. After awhile, everyone in Singapore knew the harshness of life in the villages, and people became very apt at reading into the silence of the absence of letters, such that Singapore Chinese could understand the broad picture, although it remained impossible for them to reconstruct all the details.

During the course of this research, I was told that many letters sent by Singapore Chinese to their village kin were simply destroyed, although recent letters were kept. On the other hand, I managed a sizeable collection of letters sent by villagers to their Singapore kin. Only during later years did more sentiment and emotion appear in the letters. After the reform years, things returned to normal and steady communication was once again the norm, when two or three times a year, each side would write. By the 1980s, face-to-face contact had become more common, as more *qiao-qing* visited Anxi, and communication by letter was reduced to a secondary importance.

Today, long-distance telephone conversations have taken the place of letters - a far cry from even the mid-1980s, when telephone calls had to be made at the village post office. Today, the village not only has facilities for long distance telephone calls, but those households which can afford one install long-distance telephone lines, to facilitate communication with their Singapore *qiao-qing*. But while Singapore Chinese now rely substantially on telephone communication with their village kin in the event of matters needing immediate attention, this is not the case for village kin, for whom the cost of making a long distance call is huge. Instead, they continue to send letters two to three times annually. Apart from being more economical, letters, being tangible, continue to be regarded as an important testimony of communication between the two groups. This is fortunate for researchers, as, if telecommunication had been the norm during the last century, much important information would not have been recorded.

Early Trips to Ancestral Village

A second method to maintain ties is to visit the ancestral village in person. This was an extremely difficult method but some people did managed to go on trips and visited their ancestral village. The main reason was political, both in Singapore and in Communist China. In Singapore, the cold war was still raging and the Singapore government imposed severe restrictions on communications and travel to and from China. Those below the age of 45 would not be given exit permit by the Singapore immigration authority to visit China. Likewise, getting a Chinese visa to visit China was also subjected to various restrictions. Only those who have reached the age of 45 could legitimately apply for an exit permit and a social visit visa, to embark on a long and arduous trip to visit their ancestral home.

From the 1950s through 1970s, and despite the difficulties of travelling to China, a small number of Singapore Anxi Chinese managed to visit their home villages. Early travel was hindered by transportation problems, as there was no direct flight to Xiamen: those who travelled by air had to transit in Hong Kong and then make their way by sea to Shantou (Swatow), and/or travel overland to their home villages. Others made the journey from Singapore to Shantou or Xiamen by sea - a long, tedious and rough journey.

During these early years, there were only a few travel agencies that specialised in trips to China and people wanting to travel to China would generally book through them. The agencies would arrange for exit permits, visas to China, ticketing and all other related matters, including the handling of crates of personal effects when travelling by sea. Passenger ships plied from Singapore to Shantou (Swatow) (汕頭), Xiamen (Amoy) (厦門) and Quanzhou (Chuanchiu) (泉州) on a regular basis, usually once a month. Many visitors travelled by sea, and not on an individual basis, but commonly in small groups of related kin, one of whom would initiate the journey and then invite others to join them, so that a group of ten or more would keep each other company and provide moral and physical support when the need arose. Each passenger was allowed a crate of personal effects - hence the attraction of sea travels, as airlines permitted only 20 kg of baggage.

During these years, more women than men travelled to their home villages, part of the reason being the lengthy time period required for the trip. The journey by sea would take several days, and usually two to three weeks would be required for the visit, such that the whole journey often lasted a month. It was difficult for working men to travel for such extended periods, and those men who did so travelled by air and were usually in the village for only one or two weeks. Many male travellers were retired elderly men who had more time to spend in the villages.

After they had booked travel by sea, the preparation process began. Women of the household mainly did preparation for the journey. Besides packing for personal use, most travellers would prepare one or two wooden crates of goods to be distributed, and there would be much agonising over the items to be included, as it was extremely difficult to know the exact needs of village kin. There was some knowledge of conditions in home villages, however, often provided by the few whom had visited earlier. From what they knew and what they thought their kin needed, women prepared the most essential items. Although these decisions were mostly made by women, often some discussion with husbands was necessary - in their words, they "discussed and informed" their husbands of their decisions - as the approval of husbands was needed in order to be given money to purchase the items. During these early years there was very little surplus money within the household, and in many cases it was the men who controlled the purse, although women had some si-fang-qian (private room money) (私房錢): money given by husbands to satisfy personal needs, plus savings from women's marketing expenses. This money was also used to purchase gifts for the journeys.

Common items to be taken included new and old clothing, fabrics, foodstuffs (biscuits, cooking oil, dried meat), medicines (medicated oil, various types of vitamin pills, cod liver oil pills, western medicine for headaches, flu and cold, Chinese medicine including ginseng), bicycles and sewing machines. Although there was also an occasional motor-scooter or other more expensive item packed into the crate, the Singapore Chinese were cautious not to over-pack the crate with too many such luxury items out of fear that they might be taken away by customs officers when the crates were opened for inspection at Shantou or other port of disembarkation. According to the travellers, they mostly packed necessities, especially clothing and medicine. They told me that the villagers had very little clothing, some only one or two new suits a year that would hardly kept them warm during the winter months. Medicine and vitamins were non-existent in the villages, and it was common to pack several kilograms of vitamin pills and cod liver oil capsules. Cod liver oil was considered a very good health supplement much sought after by the village kin, and during this period pharmaceutical houses sold them in big packages for this purpose. Locally produced medicated balm, such as "Tiger Balm", "Pak Fai Yew" and "Hu Piah Yew", were most sought after, and visitors would generally take several dozens of them to distribute to their relatives. Traditional Chinese medicines such as ginseng, herbal roots, and animal extracts and products were expensive and would be purchased, in smaller quantities, for immediate family members. These would be packed in hand luggage. A limited amount of gold jewellery was also taken, including rings, ear rings and gold chains. Some of these, to be given away on arrival, were worn as personal items to avoid customs declaration. Inexpensive watches were taken for the men. Most people would also carry a limited amount of cash, but this was to be distributed to more distant kin, as it was general knowledge that cash was less important than material goods at this time. Villagers said, "during the early years, it was pointless to have money because there was nothing one could buy with it. All material things were rationed to us. So, it was better for our relatives to bring us material goods".

Although these Singapore travellers packed as much as they could into the crates, somehow there was never enough, for everyone wanted a share of the goods. During this time, somewhat mysteriously, the kinship circle expanded: everyone who came to visit the Singapore guests claimed that they knew, or were related to, someone in the immediate family, and it became very difficult to reject these distant relatives and neighbours who came to call; and so each would be treated to a meal and a small amount of cash, about five Rmb.

In 1974, my mother made her first trip back to her home village, twenty-four years after she first set sail for Singapore. There was much excitement in her, and this became contagious among the children. Two weeks prior to her departure, my father had instructed his company workers to assemble a wooden crate about one cubic metre in volume. Inside this, my mother packed new and old clothing, fabrics, and large tins of cooking oil, biscuits, grains, shoes, medical products, a sewing machine and a bicycle. My siblings and I took turns to flatten the fabric so that we could create extra space and pile in more things. My mother also took small jewellery items, such as gold rings and earrings, for the women, and inexpensive watches for the men.

Although my mother had only packed one crate of goods to be distributed to all our Anxi relatives, some of our other Singapore female kin prepared two or three crates. Together they took the crateloads of goods to our village kin, forgoing taking the aeroplane and instead journeying by sea, thus enduring a week of sea sickness and extreme discomfort. When the vessel arrived in Swatow (Shantou) they disembarked and, after collecting their crates, journeyed to the village. It was an arduous journey. Although conditions on board the ship had improved compared to those encountered during their maiden trip to Singapore, they were not ideal: the food was poor, and over-crowding was the norm. Despite these, the women endured the difficulties and braved the journey back to their home village, where they visited their village kins.

My mother stayed with my aunt (father's elder sister) and her family. She had thought that, after the crate was opened, she would be able to distribute small amounts of the contents to each household related to my father or her. As my father has only two elder sisters (one deceased now) and my mother has two elder brothers and one younger sister, in her mind there were only five households closest to her with which she considered herself to have true ties, and a large share of the goods would go to them. Ties to others were more distant, and they would be given an item each, while those who visited her but with whom she had no blood or other close ties would be treated to a meal.

However, she was awakened to reality when her understanding of the order of kinship relations prove to have little bearing on events: when her crate was opened, there was a mad rush for all the goods that mother had brought back. Despite the fullness of the crate, there was hardly enough to be distributed to all, and those who were more daring simply grabbed more. Although my mother tried to stop them, it was a futile exercise: the goods were too much of a temptation for civil behaviour. My mother had underestimated the boldness of some relatives, or maybe she had underestimated the extent of the material poverty and deprivation of the village kin. She could not stop her nephews and nieces from taking things from the crate. The result was that the material goods that she had painstakingly planned and placed in the crate for the various kin were taken away from her. The kinship order had collapsed in front of her. She was disappointed and disillusioned. When a similar event happened at the household of her husband's elder sister's family, the helplessness she felt must have been hard for her to bear. The oppression of being a junior member within the extended family structure had dictated that she hold her tongue and swallow the bitterness and frustration that emerged from within, as there was nothing she could do. It was a painful and pitiful sight to see the looting of one's treasure, yet be helpless to do anything about it.

In her words:

My relatives met me at the port of Amoy. My husband had earlier written and informed them of my trip. So, my brothers, sister-in-law and nephews waited at the port for me. Then they hired a van that brought us to our village. We had to stay for a day in Amoy to unload the cargo. Once we had the crate, we set off for the village. It took us a full day from Amoy to reach Anxi.

I was taken to my sister-in-law's home. The condition of the house was not very good. They had not yet renovated the house as they awaited my husband to send them money to help with the rebuilding. At that time, although there was a guesthouse for overseas Chinese, it was not appropriate for us, especially women, to stay there on our own. All of us stayed with our relatives. I was no exception. Further, the main idea behind the trip was to rekindle our relationship with our relatives. Staying elsewhere would not have been the right thing to do.

When we arrived at the home, even before I could have a little rest, my nephews started opening the crate. They did not ask my permission nor did they ask whom the goods were intended for. They assumed that it belonged to them. When the crate was opened, they took out everything and those they wanted, leaving very little behind. I was not consulted over whether the goods were for them or not. At that time, as I was still suffering from motion sickness and fatigue, I did not have the energy to tell them not to take all the goods that were in the crate. So, they had the lion share of it. My siblings had very little. Fortunately, I had also placed some clothing and medicines in my personal suitcase and they had no access to this. It was locked and I did not let them opened it. I was able to control the distribution of the little I was left with.

Suddenly everyone in the village became related to you. They told me that they knew my parents and grandparents. It was difficult to ignore them. I would give a small amount of cash. At that time, I would give five Rmb to each person. I tried not to give them the clothing and goods that I brought back for my close relatives. But it was very hard to ignore some, especially the very old ones. They came and asked for an extra shirt to keep them warm. But most would come asking for medicine. There was nothing in the village and they would say, "Could you please give me a bottle of 'tiger balm' or 'hu-piaw- yew'? I often feel dizzy and I feel good after inhaling this medicine". Others would say, "Could I have some ginseng from you? My health is bad and ginseng would provide the tonic that my body needs". It was hard. How could I reject them? Many a time I found myself dividing these into small portions and giving to them. But, no matter how much I brought back, there would never be enough to give to everyone.

When my mother returned to Singapore after a month's visit, she was exhausted and disappointed. She tried to be empathetic, and talked much about poverty in the village. But there was little doubt of the disappointment she had experienced with some of her kin, and it would be another ten years before she set foot in her home village again.

Dividing the goods to be distributed proved to be a more difficult task than expected for the Singaporeans. What was supposed to be a straightforward distribution was complicated by the need to display a sense of diplomacy, generosity, compassion, good kinship and neighbourly ties. As the kinship circle had inevitably widened, it was not possible to include all, yet one had no choice but to take into consideration all these "extra people" that appeared on one's doorstep in order not to be branded as *bu-hui-zuo-ren* (不會做人), one who does not know how to be a person and behave with propriety - a "miser" or "mean person".

My mother's experience was not a unique one. Throughout our kinship circle, both women and men had been trading their experiences visiting their home village. The stories were of poverty, great difficulties, fear, sadness, greed and resignation. The picture, by all accounts, was not a cheerful one. Another informant, Kay considered herself more fortunate:

I was met by my husband's brother's family in Amoy and stayed with them for a whole month. His family members had better upbringing.

When we arrived at their place, they asked me to have a wash and a little rest. They served me some tea and food.

The crate that I brought was left in the house. But no one opened it as other relatives of mine had experienced. They were polite and inquired about my journey and my family. It was only on the second day, after I have rested, that I asked my brother-in-law to open the crate. When the crate was opened, none of his children rushed and asked for things although they were in the house. My brother-in-law and sister-in-law helped me to unpack the various goods from the crate. I was able to control the situation and told them of my distribution plan. They did not ask for anything more than what I have given them. It made the task a lot more pleasant. Because they did not ask for anything, I felt that I had to give them more. Anyway, if you stayed at someone's place, it was expected that they would receive more from you although they did not say it. Also, they were our closest relatives and they were so polite. So, I did not mind giving them more than the others did.

Then there was also the poor living condition that they experienced. The negative views which the Singapore Chinese returnees held was reinforced by the lack of amenities and the difficulties that these Singapore kin faced in the home village. Poor housing, inadequate heating during the winter months, poor food and unhygienic sanitary conditions made their visits unpleasant. Living in orderly and stable Singapore for two to three decades had made village life seem exceptionally harsh to them, and for some the culture shock was more than they could handle; others found the adjustment difficult even though it was only a short stay. Informant Bee retraced her encounters with the reality of village life:

I knew that the conditions in the village would be very bad. But I did not expect it to be so primitive. The house was old but it was liveable. What I did not expect was the toilet facilities. It was very bad. They had to go to the communal latrine, mao-wu (茅屋) which was basically a hut made of dried leaves. The mao-wu had several holes dug out to contain the human dung. The smell was very bad even when one walked passed it. I did not know how they could use it. But I just could not. This was the worst shock I had when I visited the village. Fortunately for us, we had our own latrine outside the house. So, at least, I did not need to go to the communal latrine.

The village was even worse than the "kampong" in Singapore during the early years. It was dirty and smelly. The smell from the poultry and pigs was unbearable most of the time. But there was nothing one could do. Also, the place was very dusty and it was difficult to feel clean.

The food was also very bad. The villagers did not know how to cook good food and it was tasteless. Fortunately, I brought some chilli sauce so that I could flavour the food with it. I would prefer to cook my own food but it was difficult for me to venture into the kitchen. The women kin would not allow me to do so. But I went into the kitchen several times and taught them how to cook with spices so that the food would taste better.

The stay was not very easy although I tried my best to adapt to the place and not complain about it. But conditions have improved substantially today compared to the first trip I made in 1974.

Negative Representations

The action of the village kin was seen as uncivil and barbaric behaviour. There was little that they saw that they liked. However, these women who visited their ancestral village rationalised such behaviour as attributes to the great hardship and poverty that these village kin had undergone since the Communist rule. Life had been hard and there was great material poverty. The villagers simply had nothing and they lived poorly, mostly in broken down sheds and huts. There was insufficient food and clothing and children were not given an education. It was this image that elicited from them great sympathy and sadness. It was this form of representation that pushed them to want to further assist their village kin in whatever small ways they could.

These initial encounters with their long separated kin left a deep impression on these visitors. To a certain degree each encounter was different. But, it was this set of negative representations that they brought home to Singapore that became commonly known among the Singapore Anxi Chinese. Upon returning to Singapore, they exchanged information and provided advice to other intending travellers. The knowledge of the village kin were told and retold in the following manner and were to become an important part of the repertoire of their memory and representation of their ancestral village. These were passed down to their descendants: and remained in circulation today.

These village people were very greedy. They were like bandits and demanded everything off you. They wanted not only the goods that you brought with you, but also the clothing, jewellery and money that you had with you. When they came to visit you, you were expected to play host. You were expected to cook and feed them and if you were a man, you would be expected to throw a feast for all villagers. So, the household that you were staying with would be very busy. They had to cook continuously and served those who came to pay you a visit. Besides, you would also be expected to give them something before they left for their home. Some might ask you for specific items especially the medicinal products. Others would just talk and talk with you until you gave them a small amount of money.

These imageries became a standard way of portraying the villagers in Anxi. They became stereotyped as "greedy", "bandit-like", "demanding", "inconsiderate" and other negative phrases. A whole generation of Singapore Chinese was brought up with these images. First, the letter correspondence and second, during the trips to their home villages where their village kin made insatiable demands. Affection of their village kin and ancestral home soon turned into disappointment, frustration and resentment. What the Singapore Chinese had envisaged before their return trip had turned into a stressful and unpleasant experience. This created tension between them and their village kin. The sentiments of warmth and kindred spirit that they harboured were shattered with the social reality that they had encountered. It was this collision of the imagined village life and the actual reality that shocked the visiting Singapore Chinese, resulting in much disappointment and ill feelings among them. Despite this, they continued to visit their ancestral home in later years.

Thus, for Singapore-born Chinese, the archetypal village kinsperson is utilitarian: his or her friendliness is measured by the amount of gifts and money given to him/her. He/she is demanding and greedy, and thinks that the *qiao-qing* owes him/her a living. He/she may be subtle, but is outright in demanding material goods and money from the *qiao-qing*. He/she is lazy and does not bother to work for a living, but sits around and does nothing except talk with other villagers, drink tea and smoke.

The archetypal village is one with undeveloped road system and limited accessibility. There are little or no modern amenities, such as piped water, air conditioning, or electricity. There is also no proper sanitation. The village is very undeveloped - with few schools, bridges, roads, or hospitals to cater for the local needs. There are also no entertainment facilities such as cinemas, karaoke bars and skating rinks. There is also a lack of economic facilities - few factories and shops, the main activity being farming.

It is often the case that habit dies hard, and perception and attitudes are even harder to change. As individuals and groups visited their home village and brought back similar stories, and as their experiences were told and retold over and over again to their children and grandchildren, the resulting static pictures of village life and village kin reflected the conditions of the 1950s and 1960s. At present, despite some attitudinal changes, this set of negative images continues to influence the outlook of the Singapore-born Chinese, and, to a large extent, continues to shape their relationship with the village kin.

It was these stories of our ancestral village, and of China in general, that we, the children, were brought up with and we were supposed to feel a sense of sympathy for these village kin. While the first generation

Singapore Anxi Chinese have developed a sense of sympathy, some members of the younger generation have developed strong feelings of resentment towards them, and it was not surprising that some chose not to be part of this kinship matrix but to become outsiders. This resentment was a powerful and irrational force that served to turn many away from visiting their ancestral home. When sympathy drew others back to the village at future dates and when some, seeing the underdeveloped conditions and material poverty that surrounded the households, willingly provided assistance to village redevelopment, their early memories had yet marred their sentiments, so that they depersonalised their contributions: instead of providing assistance to immediate kin, they engaged in charitable and philanthropic activities, contributing to public projects and helping with general village reconstruction of roads, schools, hospitals, and temples that benefited the community as a whole rather than selected kin. Many villagers, especially those who had gained little from their Singapore kin, found it hard to understand the logic of this, and among them there is much ill-feeling. Such Singapore kin, often seen as "outsiders" by their village kin, are "overseas comrades", qiao-bao, (僑胞) to the official cadres, who have sought to attract overseas Chinese capital.

Renegotiating Kinship Sentiments Since the 1978 Open Door Reform

A new era - the 1978 Deng Xiaoping's Open Door Era - marks a new watershed in Chinese history. They also usher in a new beginning in the history of qiaoxiang relations. The reforms affected the socio-cultural and economic life of the villages, and especially of the emigrant villages, where changes have been dramatic. In Anxi, the policy changes were greeted with excitement and renewed energy and led to renewed efforts to encourage Chinese overseas to help with national reconstruction in China. Two new official policy initiatives towards the Overseas Chinese were brought about. The first was to lure overseas Chinese capital for investment purposes; the second was to encourage overseas Chinese to help with village reconstruction in rural areas, especially in the emigrant districts.

The new Chinese policy coincided with attempts by the Singapore government to encourage the globalisation of local firms, so that the Open Door Policy was looked upon by the Singapore government as a great opportunity for both the Singapore State and the Singapore Chinese to expand their economic interests in China. China represents a vast untapped market, and the Singapore Chinese are considered to be in a good position to embark on economic expansionism because it is perceived that their social and economic networks are already in existence. There has been a normalisation of diplomatic ties with China and an increase in the number of Singapore Chinese travelling there for both social and economic reasons. It is not surprising that both the Chinese and Singapore governments, each with its own agenda, have been encouraging these Chinese to become involved in China.

The 1980s also witnessed a change in the kinship matrix between the Singapore Chinese and their ancestral villages. This is most evident among the Singapore Anxi Chinese, and especially among the Singapore-born Chinese of Anxi ancestry. A rise in the standard of living, increased wealth and a quest for cultural identity has resulted in a more confident Chinese community in Singapore. Among the Singapore Anxi Chinese, there is also a re-evaluation of their relationship with their ancestral villages. Also, the warming of political relationship between China and Singapore has meant less travel restrictions for those who wanted to travel to China and Singapore respectively. Singaporeans could travel easily to China for social and business visits while Chinese could now travel readily to Singapore for social and business visits. The result is that there is an increased flow of visits and an intensification of social links among the Singapore Anxi and village Chinese from this period onwards.

Since the 1980s, an increasing number of elderly China-born men and women, together with their Singapore-born children, have taken advantage of these policy changes and made visits to their ancestral homes, zu-jia, (祖家). This is the case with the Singapore Anxi Chinese. Because of their recent migration history, many Singapore Anxi Chinese families have a generation depth of only three to four generations. A substantial number of the Singapore-born second and third generations have now accompanied their parents on visits to their ancestral homes. Visiting their ancestral villages did not come naturally and they had to be coaxed into making the trip. While most made their trips reluctantly, they nevertheless developed some sentiments towards the village after their visits.

How did the Singapore Anxi Chinese view their ancestral village and the village kin? To what extent did they feel for their ancestral home and their kin? These are questions that beg our attention here. In our survey, we are interested in knowing the degree of awareness and feelings the Singapore Chinese have on their ancestral village. Likewise, we are also interested in how the villagers viewed their Singapore kin.

We found that all the Singapore Anxi Chinese were aware of their ancestral origins in Anxi, and 60 per cent said that Anxi has some sentiments towards the place. These are their responses:

> Anxi has some meaning for me because I know I am from there. It is where my roots, gen-yuan, (根源) are. It is a place where our ancestors

and parents were from; I went back to search for my roots. There are sentimental and lineage ties and kindred spirit, *qin-qing,* (親情).

However, about 27 per cent stated that although they know of their ancestral home, they did not have any sentiment towards their ancestral village. These are their responses:

I myself do not understand China (Anxi), so how can I feel for it? Anxi has not much meaning as I do not have any impression of the place and therefore, I treat it as another place like America or Britain.

A third group, 13.3 per cent, has weak sentiments towards Anxi. They responded in the following manner:

I don't have much sentiment compared with my father. But I still care a little about our home village and our relatives there, but I have maintained some distance and reservation. It is not very good to become too close and attached to the place.

The survey also shows that those in the higher age groups (majority first generation, but with a small number of second generation) have stronger emotional attachment to the ancestral village. The Singapore-born descendants, on the other hand, feel that they need to know something of their ancestral village but need not necessarily have the strong sentiments as their elders. Many of them have more negative feelings towards Anxi as a result of the negative representations that they have been brought up with. Furthermore, the visit and experience in the ancestral visit makes it less likely for them to like the place. The youngest age group has ambivalent but positive feelings.

It is possible to chart the level of emotional attachment and sentiment through an analysis of intergenerational differences. If the above reactions are placed in a three-generation framework, we can better understand why the different generations respond differently to their ancestral home village.

The first factor concerns the search for cultural roots. For the first-generation, China-born migrants, Anxi is their birthplace and ancestral place of origin. Hence, they have strong emotional ties to it. They seek to recreate and re-establish their cultural roots and identity for their children and grandchildren. The second generation, on the other hand, has been brought up with many negative images and memories, which they find hard to ignore. While there have been attempts at creating positive images of home village and village kin, these have yet to become fully accepted. It will take time and many more trips to the village before they are ready to undo the negative feelings and image that have been deeply etched in their memory. Third and fourth generations have been brought up with more information, and have witnessed the active participation of their grandparents in village activities in Anxi. While they do not know much about the ancestral village, neither do they harbour as much alienation as their parents do.

Thus it is possible to chart feelings and emotions for the Anxi home village in relation to knowledge of the place and the extent to which persons are influenced by parents and grandparents: those for whom Anxi has some sentiments have some knowledge of the place and of village kin and their visits to the ancestral village in recent years have given them a clearer image of village life. Most have expressed sympathy with the plight of their village kin and a willingness to assist in the rebuilding of the village.

Among those who have strong sentiments, over half (55 per cent) have a reasonable knowledge of their village kin and are aware of close living relatives in the village. They can spell out the relationships between these relatives and their own families and are able to classify their kin according to the classificatory Chinese kinship system.[2] Others can only manage to classify the village kin as paternal or maternal uncles or aunts or cousins.

Table 4.1 Strength of Sentiments in relation to Knowledge of Kinship

Knowledge of Anxi Kin	Strong sentiments	No sentiments	Weak sentiments
Intimate knowledge	10	4	3
Some knowledge	7	3	1
Little/no knowledge	1	1	0
TOTAL N=30	**18**	**8**	**4**

It is possible to conclude that those with a degree of understanding of the ancestral village are more likely to attach a relatively strong sentiment to the place while those with less knowledge have less sentimental attachment to it. This is especially so for those who have made several visits to the ancestral village and who are able to deconstruct the negative representations of the village life and the village kin.

Singapore-born Anxi Chinese are aware that their parents and/or grandparents have sent remittances and have helped their village kin in various ways. Among second-generation members, some have given money and helped their village kin. These second-generation Anxi Chinese have expressed their awareness of contributions sent in the following ways:

I know that my father and uncles have send money to Anxi but I did not asked my father in person about this. Personally, I think if they can afford to send some money to the village kin, why not? This is especially needed if the relatives in Anxi are really poor. This was especially so in the 1950s. My father had also send foodstuffs, e.g. flour, cooking oil and others to the ancestral village. But if they are wealthy and comfortable, then there is no need.

My parents send money home because it is a tradition and a virtue and out of brotherly love and concern.

While there were those who were supportive of their parents providing some form of monetary and material aids to their village kin, there were also others who disapprove of their parents and Singapore kin sending money to the village kin. They have argued that such assistance would breed laziness and dependence. One informant expressed the following:

There are two effects of sending money home. One is the negative aspect and the other is the positive side. During my first trip home, some were really poor, so it was good that we helped them a little. On the other hand, it created a sense of laziness and dependence. They think that if they do not have money, their Singapore relatives will send them more. Although it is understandable that there is little job opportunity in Anxi, sending them money will only lead to less incentive to create jobs for themselves. So, it is better to establish cottage industries and create employment opportunities for them instead of giving them money.

The money their parents send to the village kin varies quite significantly, in both amount and regularity. There is only a very small number of Singapore kin who send remittances on a monthly basis: the majority remit two to three times a year, usually on special occasions such as Spring and Qing Ming Festivals. The amount remitted is usually small, from S$100-200.

As exemplified in the statements quoted above, Singapore-born Anxi Chinese have more reservations in giving remittances, generally agreeing that the village kin are much poorer than themselves and feeling obligated to assist, but worrying about over-assistance.

Voices from Anxi Villagers

After twenty or thirty or more years of not meeting their siblings, parents or other immediate Singapore kin, there is great expectation when Anxi villagers hear news of a home visit of siblings, parents and other blood relatives. The wait has been long and there is great excitement. In the words of one: "They (brothers by blood) went away when we were all young and unmarried.   Now we are all middle-aged, with children and even grandchildren of our own. It is good to see them again. Our children have not met them before. It will be good for them to meet their uncles and their families. After all, we are still a family".

In the emigrant village of Peng Lai, most villagers know of their Singapore kin. Most of the younger generation of Anxi villagers, in fact, are better versed than their Singapore counterparts on their kinship ties and can accurately classify their Singapore kin. They have been conscientiously told by their parents and grandparents of the Singapore kin and express great excitement when meeting their uncles, aunts, cousins and other Singapore kin when the latter visit the village.

There is, in fact, a range of emotions when the two groups of Chinese meet after long years of separation. Some express satisfaction with the Singapore kin, others are dissatisfied. A small group is openly disappointed with the attitudes of the Singapore kin. These are their responses.

> The Singapore kin did not contribute sufficiently, materially and financially, to help our social situation. Our Singapore relatives were wealthy but "heartless". They were barbaric and detribalised, *fan* [M], huang [H], arrogant, self-centred, mean and miserly. The Singapore women were too lady-like and waited to be served.

Not unlike the Singapore Chinese, who have constructed images of their village kin, the villagers, too, have negative representations and generalisations of the Singapore Chinese. To them, the Singapore Chinese are uncivilised, arrogant, mean and reluctant to help out. Singapore women are seen as women of leisure and "too lady-like".

Many villagers, however, are very generous with their praise of their Singapore kin. These have been very pleased with the generosity of their kin, who have provided assistance to their immediate family needs, from helping with the construction of their old houses, to helping to educate their children, providing expenses for marriages and buying electronic goods for the household. Others have expressed gratitude for the enormous contributions that these Singapore members have made to village schools, roads, temples, hospitals and other infrastructure institutions and facilities.

It is possible to look at the social relationships between villagers and Singapore kin according to degrees of closeness and intimacy. At the one end of the spectrum, some villagers have very close and intimate relationships and enjoy being in contact with their Singapore kin; at the other end are those having little or no contact with their Singapore kin and no special feelings for them. Most fall between these extremes: having some contact with their Singapore kin and having received some remittances and assistance for their various needs, they are generally satisfied with the relationship. They use this phrase to sum up their feelings: Below those above us, above those below us, *bi-shang-bu-zu, bi-xia-you-yi* (比上不足,比下有餘).

Maintaining contact is of central importance to the villagers, so that they can receive material and financial assistance from their Singapore kin. Although letters and oral messages from visiting relatives and occasionally parcels remain the common mode of communication, the low level of literacy continues to make letter writing a tedious process. Regular communication on a monthly basis is confined to a small group, most communicating only two or three times a year. One informant describes how he and his relatives correspond: "Usually they send messages through visiting relatives, inquiring about us or entrusting us to perform various tasks on their behalf. If there is something urgent, they might telephone us and we will phone them too. Letter writing is very troublesome. We usually have to ask people to write for us". Another informant says, "My mother and eleven brothers and sisters are in Singapore. We have regular contacts and a normal relationship. But I rarely write because I am illiterate and all my brothers and sisters are English-educated and do not read Chinese".

General attitudes of villagers towards Singapore kin vary. It is possible to divide them into two categories: the positive and the negative attitudes. The first is the positive one.

We have a close relationship with our Singapore relatives. Our relatives in Singapore include our father's brothers, their 3 sons and their family. They have visited us regularly, especially after the reform. Contacts are normally through letters and oral messages. We also talked regularly on the phone. They often send us gift parcels through visiting relatives".

The second attitude is a negative one:

We have three uncles in Singapore. We used to write letters to them. But only one uncle replied. He only wrote once a year and send us S$50 each time. After the death of our uncles, their children did not write at all. Two years ago, two of our cousins came and visited our village. They stayed at the Overseas Chinese guesthouse in the village. They did not attempt to contact us. We knew of their coming and so we went to visit them. They were very distant. They gave us S$100 and that is all. They did not even bother to come and visit our place or offer any assistance to us. Instead, they were contributing large sums of money to schools and for road works. And they got on very well with the village cadres and the officials of the provincial government. I think they are very snobbish. They look to people with power and look down upon us relatives because we are poor. It is an embarrassment to have this kind of relatives. Sometimes, it is better not to have than to have them. It makes me very sad knowing that they are not willing to acknowledge their kin.

Most villagers consider relationships between themselves and their Singapore kin to be a reasonably good one. However, some felt that their relations had weakened progressively over the years and between generations, saying that, after the death of the first generation kins, contact with the Singapore born generation has decreased to a minimum, the Singapore-born Chinese rarely writing or sending money anymore. One said, "I was an adopted child of the family. When my father was alive, there were contacts through letters and oral messages from visiting relatives. He would also send gift parcels for me and my family. After his death, there was no contacts between my Singapore relatives and me". Another said, "I have three elder brothers in Singapore. When our mother was alive, there were regular contacts and they would send money to support us. Now that she is dead, there is very little contact".

Some feel that the Singapore Chinese are more concerned about their immediate families and life in Singapore and have less concern for their village kin. One informant said, "There is still a little contact; it is not broken yet," although "even if you write, they can't even be bothered to reply". Some villagers who had visited Singapore told me that "the Singapore Chinese are very whimsical about us". They said that some of them had much regard for us and would be very happy when they received Anxi letters, but others were not. Some would "not bother to read our letters and would throw them into the bin without opening them. Since last year, I stopped writing. The previous year, I wrote but there was no reply. So I think, they must have thrown my letter away without reading it. Why should I write if this is the case?" Another informant has this to say: "My husband's younger brother and his family live in Singapore. But there is very little contact between us. It is very hard for us to send letters to them because we do not know their addresses and names. We have to ask our relatives to take the letters to them. But they seldom reply. We rarely receive phone calls and gift parcels". Yet another explained the difficulties in maintaining the relationship: "My Singapore kin include my father's three brothers and their families, my father's second wife and their children, my half-brothers and half-sisters. Previously, there were some contacts. At the moment, only the elder brother maintains contact with us. Most of my half-brothers and half-sisters do not want to have any contact with us. They do not even want to recognise us. Even when our village relatives visited Singapore, they did not wholeheartedly receive them. Originally, my elder half-brother said that he would sponsor me for a visit to Singapore in 1993. When 1993 arrived and I asked him again, he did not reply to my letter. I continue to write to him occasionally. In recent years, I have received no reply, so I stopped writing."

Others are said to have turned *fan, huang* [H]: they are said to be uncivilised and have become detribalised and no longer interested in getting to know their home village anymore. Some have made it known publicly that they are no longer interested in maintaining ties with their villager kin and want to have nothing to do with the ancestral village. They neither write nor communicate in other forms, nor will they provide financial assistance to their village kin. Such an attitude, to the villagers, is both un-Chinese and unfilial. This is why they have become *huang*.

Communication implies two-way traffic. In most cases, contact is reciprocal between villagers and Singaporeans, normal communication being two to three letters a year in each direction, anything extra being a bonus. However, mutual reciprocity is not always the case. Some villagers find maintaining ties with their overseas relatives to be an extremely tedious task: it is very hard for these villagers to continue writing without receiving replies, as they have to face being snubbed by their better-off Singapore relatives, some of whom look upon them not only as poor kindred but, at times, no better than "bandits". It is this negative attitude that Anxi villagers resent most. Another possibility is the Singaporeans' refusal to recognise the villagers as their kin. Although the villagers feel this to be a wrong attitude, there is nothing they can do to change it. Part of the reason for this inaction is the lack of opportunity to explain to the Singaporeans their plight, dream and vision.

Visiting Singapore

Since the 1978 reform, an increasing number of Anxi villagers have visited Singapore; of villager-informants who visited, over 30 per cent of them did so from the mid-1980s onwards. This has been possible because of the relaxation of travel restrictions by both the Chinese and Singapore governments.

The easiest way for a villager to visit Singapore is to ask a Singapore kinsperson to sponsor the visit. Such visits are most commonly proposed by "having a word" with close relatives who visit the village, often beginning in the following manner: "I am already so old and have not been out of the country. It would be very nice to go overseas and see the world. I have heard so much about Singapore. It would be good to see what it is like. Would you sponsor me to visit Singapore?" Some relatives respond by saying "I will see what I can do", while others give no indication of their decision. It is not uncommon for village kin to remind their Singapore kin several times before gaining a positive response, perhaps a few months later. They then apply for a passport and exit visa from the immigration authority in the county town, Xian Chen (縣城) and wait several months before receiving them, upon which they inform their Singapore kin. From the Singapore end, the relative will then arrange for the necessary documentation, buy an air ticket and entrust a visiting relative to take it to the village; or he may avail himself of the services of one of the travel agencies in Singapore that prepare such documentation and arrange for the tickets to be sent, which has made it easier and more attractive for Singaporeans to sponsor relatives for visits. Their Singapore kin regarding the time and date of departure and the time they will need to arrive at Xiamen airport, and are told that they would be met at the airport in Singapore gives villagers specific instructions. Singapore relatives also send motion-sickness pills to those who are known to suffer from motion sickness and instruct them to take them prior to boarding the flight.

After receiving the documentation and air ticket, the villagers prepare to journey to Singapore. This is a serious affair. To impress their Singapore kin, many bring local produce to Singapore, most commonly Chinese tea. Many bring several kilograms, to be distributed to numerous kin; wealthier villagers buy export quality pre-packaged tea.

It has become a norm for the Singapore Chinese to sponsor their middle-aged and elderly village relatives for at least one visit. These relatives normally stay for the maximum period granted by the visa, usually two or three months. Some have visited more than once.

During the first few years, when social visits from the villagers first became possible, Singapore Chinese made great efforts to ensure that their village kin got the best treatment and enjoyed their stay. They were eager to ensure that the villagers returned home with good impressions of them and the Singapore way of life. At that time, "China guests", *tang-shan-ke* (唐山客) were a novelty for the Singaporeans, and especially for the younger generations, so that, when a visitor or visitors arrived, members of the lineage were informed, and the visitors' immediate families housed them and treated them as honoured guests, taking them sightseeing and so forth. Other Singapore relatives would also take them out for meals, sightseeing and shopping, and would present them with gifts, or at any rate give them *hong bao*, customary red packets of money (common sums were fifty or a hundred dollars). Anxi relatives would also visit the homes of various kin. During this initial period, Singapore kin were obliging and drove the villagers to visit all the relatives they wished to see. It was all in good spirits, and everyone was enthusiastic about the visits of their *tang-shan-ke*. During these first few years, villagers might return home with much money, gold jewellery, expensive watches, electronic goods, clothing and other items, not uncommonly amounting to a value of several thousand Singapore dollars or more, in cash and in kind.

As time went by, however, such enthusiasm began to wane, as more and more visitors have been able to come to Singapore. It has begun to seem a time-consuming affair to pick up the guests from the airport, entertain them, and take them sightseeing and shopping. It has also become a very expensive affair for some, which have to finance the trips as well as to give substantial sums for various purposes. Finally, it has become an embarrassment to have the visitors go on a circuit of house calling when it is obvious that their primary motive is to collect *hong bao* (紅包). A matter of too much in too short a period, the "*tang-shan-ke* fatigue" set in sooner than expected: what had been exciting and welcoming becomes tedious, and the *tang-shan-ke* turned into a source of embarrassment.

At present, however, *tang-shan-ke* continue to arrive in substantial numbers, although they become more house-bound and are not taken to all their relatives. Indeed, many Singapore sponsors no longer see the need to inform their other relatives of the arrival of these visitors. Although they are taken for some sightseeing, meals and shopping, most of the time is spent with their immediate relatives. Despite requests to visit other relatives, Singaporeans now exercise tighter control over who they visit, the visitors usually being taken to the homes of their closest relatives but not to those of others. Some of the visitors are not very happy about this restriction and complain that they do not meet all the relatives they know, thus defeating their purpose in visiting Singapore. Others, confined to the home as they are, with nothing much to do, get bored.

On the whole, most visitors are proud to have made a trip to Singapore. They are pleased to have met their Singapore kin and to have "seen the world". Many like the orderliness, efficiency and modernity of Singapore. To them, such a visit is an opportunity that they had never dreamed could become a reality: even setting foot out of the village is a difficult affair for some, let alone making an overseas visit. Making such a visit is also a reflection of their social status within the village and lineage structure and points up their link with Chinese overseas - a formidable force in China today.

Visits to Singapore are not only made by elderly villagers. Today, an increasing number of young villagers are searching for ways to visit Singapore. For those in their twenties, thirties and forties, a visit to

Singapore is a lucrative adventure. However, the chance of these young villagers being sponsored by their Singapore kin is less than for their elderly parents, since, among Singapore Chinese, there is greater sympathy for the older villagers. Few are willing to sponsor the younger ones.

Those who want to visit Singapore on their own have to apply for their own visas and buy their own air tickets. They generally apply to travel as tourists, but approval is given readily if arranged by a travel agency. As for sponsored applicants, it often takes two or three months or longer for their application to be approved by both the Singapore and the county immigration departments. They generally have to borrow money for air tickets and the expenses incurred in applying for exit permits. While making these arrangements, they inform their Singapore relatives of the intended visit and the tentative date of arrival. When everything is finalised, they phone their closest relative of their impending arrival, expecting that they will be picked up from the airport and provided with accommodation.

For this group of visitors, the primary motive is to find a job in Singapore. In the beginning, many failed to understand that visitor's visas do not entitle them to work. On arrival, they expected their Singapore kin to recommend them to employers. More recently, they continue to go to Singapore in search of "temporary" jobs, expecting their uncles and other relatives to provide them; if jobs are not arranged for them, they sometimes try to work in an illegal capacity. This has created much dissatisfaction and annoyance in their Singapore kin. It has now become a standard practice for those with family businesses to give "employment" to their village kin in order "to occupy them so that they do not go out and work illegally". They are thus given odd jobs to do in the family business and are paid an "allowance" for the duration of the period they stay in Singapore. In the words of a Singapore kin, "at least they need not go and work illegally and get into trouble with the authority. Also, they will earn more than enough to cover the expenses that they have incurred for the trip. They will also learn that the work ethos here is different from that in Anxi and that they cannot expect free things in life. They will also not go back empty-handed". Singapore kin who own no business will try to arrange for some kind of temporary job with the firms of other relatives or friends. Some of the local-born also feel a sense of obligation to these Anxi kin and are resigned to the fact that, once they arrive in Singapore, there is nothing they can do but to help them at least to recuperate the expenses that they have incurred in making the trip.

The imposition on the Anxi Singaporeans and the expectation of a job has created much tension between the two groups. To the Singapore kin, the visitors have unreasonable expectations as they do not understand Singapore labour law. It is especially annoying that they are now coming on their own and there is no means of stopping them and that they have to provide them with accommodation, whether they like it or not, as they simply cannot let them sleep on the streets.

To the Anxi kin, a visit to Singapore is expected to provide them with a window of opportunity, within which they hope to earn enough capital to start a small business or build a house for themselves and their family in their village. However, they find that the trip does not live up to their expectations. Some do not earn as much as they have expected, especially as they can not stay beyond the visa limit. The unwillingness of their kin to extend their visas adds to their frustrations, so that some feel their kin are not so friendly, but are rather mean and selfish: "They only take care of themselves and their family but not the village kin". Some feel they are not well treated as, unlike earlier visitors, they are not piled with as much money or as many gifts and are not treated to banquets and much sightseeing. Being young and literate, they had expected to be able to make their way round the island instead of being chauffeured around. Much of this expectation arose because of the information that they got from the village kin who, on their earlier visits, were being pampered with gifts and were shown around in Singapore. Thus, not being showered with gifts and shown around, in their understanding, implied they are not being welcomed by the Singapore kin.

Towards a Compromise

Contacts between the two groups of kin have brought about fulfilment for some and burdens for others. Among the Singapore kin, fulfilment has gradually given way to burden and fatigue. In recent years, the increased contacts between the groups have, at times, brought simmering tensions to the surface, resulting in much loss of face for both parties. One reason for the increased tension has to do with the stereotyped images of both Singaporeans and villagers; another lies with the role expectations that each group has of the other.

Village kins continue to be labelled as "lazy", "demanding", "dependent", "bandit-like", "greedy", "beggar-like", "unreliable", and "ignorant" by the Singaporean Chinese. In contrast, Singapore kin are seen as "*huang*" and "misers" with compassion.

Villagers continue to affirm the stereotype images of Singaporeans listed above. They feel that the younger generation Singapore Chinese has become "*huang*". One said, "They (nephews and nieces) are very polite and will greet me. One or two might have a little conversation with me. But most will not. They talk among themselves in Mandarin or English. They hardly speak in Fujian dialect". Another lamented, "The grandchildren could not even communicate with him in the Fujian dialect. All these young ones are so good in English, but they can't speak our own language. What do you think? They have become *huang*".

Of the younger generation of Singapore Chinese who have visited Anxi, some returned to Singapore more convinced than ever that their village kin are a group of lazy villagers, interested only in talking and smoking. One said, "They spend all their time sipping tea, talking and smoking. It is OK if the old ones do this. But look at the young ones, they are all the same". Another commented, "It is not that we do not understand that there are not much opportunities for them. But they have to be willing to go and look for opportunities. You cannot just sit and sip tea and expect opportunity to knock on your door". A third said, "They just refuse to think for themselves and expect us to do everything for them". Yet another commented, "They do not take initiative on their own, if we tell them to do something, they will do it. Otherwise, they would just sit and wait. This is why it is very difficult to entrust them to do something for us. Many times they would not even do the task well".

Attempts are now underway to eliminate the negative images that each party has of the other. To the Singapore Chinese, one important reason for sponsoring their village kin to Singapore is, as one said, "to let them see and understand that we have to work very hard for what we have and that life is not as easy as what they think it is". Another said, "It is important for them to understand that we too have our family here to look after. It is not possible for us to look after every single relative in Anxi". "Even though we care for our Anxi relatives, it is not possible for us to cater to every demand that they have asked for. Besides, they will also have to understand that they cannot expect charity all the time. They have to work for it. By bringing them here, they can see how hard we all work".

After visiting Singapore, in fact, some villagers have returned to the village with a new perspective of what their Singapore kin are like. They have told me that life is not easy in Singapore. One said, "They have to go out early in the morning, 7 or 8 am, and only return at 6 or 7 p.m. It is also a hard life for them". Another said, "Although they earn so much money, the cost of living is also very high in Singapore. They need a lot of money to maintain their house, their family, to buy food, etc. After all this, they are left with very little money. Although they seem to have all the material things in life - television, videocassette recorder, nice flat, nice clothing - they also have to work very hard for them".

The younger village kin, of course, resent being labelled as "lazy", "demanding", "dependent" and "greedy", and argue that this is unfair. They feel that there is much misunderstanding between them and their Singapore relatives, and that their Singapore kin fail to see the differences between an agrarian and a capitalist economy. They work very hard as farmers, especially during the sowing, transplanting and harvesting seasons. At other times of the year, they rear poultry and pigs, and some also perform odd jobs during the off-season. Despite this, many continue to live in poverty. Thus, to label them "lazy" is unjust. They argue that although they are poor, they do not ask anything from their Singapore relatives and depend on themselves, so how can they be called "demanding" and "greedy"? Finally, they feel that, although there is a small group of villagers who have been untrustworthy with money and responsibility and have simply taken money and failed to perform the work properly, thus earning a bad name for all villagers, their Singapore relatives should not use one label for all.

Most villagers feel that the only way to erase the negative labels that Singaporeans place on them is to demonstrate their diligence and their trustworthiness in the various socio-religious and economic tasks entrusted to them by their Singapore kin. They also feel that their younger Singapore kin should be educated about the difficulties which they, the villagers, face, so that they can better understand village life; and that regular communication between the two groups will bring about better mutual understanding. Besides better mutual communication, the villagers are confident that the economic reforms can help to transform the relationship from one of dependence to one of mutual co-operation.

The desire of the villagers to eradicate the negative image of themselves is complemented by attempts by the Singaporeans to find positive images among the Anxi villagers. Their increased contacts with their village kin and some understanding of the village structure have recently made some Singapore Chinese more aware of the restrictions of village life and village economy. They have now begun to see the social realities and complexities that surround village life instead of being influenced by the collective memories of the 1950s and 1960s. The imagery of the villagers as being "lazy", "demanding" and "greedy" has gradually given way to positive images of "hardworking" and "resourceful" villagers. The numbers of young villagers have become *getihu* and engaged in private enterprises have also helped transform the old image.

The 1980s and 1990s have witnessed rapid changes in village life, with the emergence of a new generation of villagers whose attitude differs from that of their parents and grandparents. Today, the changing environment and the economic dynamism in Anxi County are accompanied by the rise of a group of modern-minded village individuals whose modern approach to businesses and social activities has helped to deconstruct the negative image held by the Singapore kin.

The Singapore Chinese have also come to realise the limited opportunities of a village economic structure. There is little job opportunity and insufficient resources for development. They are also beginning to understand the political economy of the region and the failure of both the regional and central governments to develop Anxi, and are gradually accepting the proposals of district and local cadres, who seek Chinese overseas capital for village reconstruction.

The poverty of the 1950s to 1970s has, in fact, given way to new opportunities as a result of the opening to the outside and the relaxation of internal restrictions, and the villagers are no longer confined to their traditional economic and social roles. They are now able to take on more active roles without awaiting instructions from the provincial or central government. On the economic front, an increasing number of private businesses and an emergence of rudimentary enterprises can be found in the villages. The number of *getihu* is permanently changing an originally peasant region into a lively, commercialised one. At the individual level, this has meant that villagers are able to move out of their established social roles, a transformation that has resulted in renewed confidence about the villagers in the eyes of others and the confidence of the villagers about themselves.

In Singapore, there are now attempts to revise their understanding of the ancestral village and its villagers. Coming into contact with the villagers and visiting Anxi has affected the way they look at their village kin: they are no longer strangers. Singaporeans are beginning to understand that the village kin can be pleasant socially and can be trained to perform skilled work, and that they are not ideologically dogmatic. They want to excel, to become successful and to attain material comfort. Some work hard to achieve this when opportunity arises. As such, some are prepared to move out of Anxi to Xiamen City, Singapore, Hong Kong and other places to work. They are also prepared to take risks, quit the iron rice bowl job in the government and become *getihu*. In short, the village kin can become dynamic people when the political situation allows them to do so and when they have the opportunities to express themselves. Given this re-evaluation of their village kin, the Singapore Chinese are now more prepared to assist in village reconstruction.

The role of the Singapore kin in the transformation of village life and economy cannot be underestimated. Much overseas Chinese capital has been injected into these emigrant villages, making possible recent rapid changes. The capital used for infrastructure development and individual businesses has turned once-quiet villages into prosperous emigrant villages, *qiaoxiang*. In Fujian, it was the extreme poverty of these villages that pushed so many villagers to emigrate for a better livelihood in a foreign environment. Today, these same villages are again in the limelight. This time, it is their material wealth and cultural richness that have attracted attention and have become the envy of the region. These have been made possible because of their *guanxi* network which is derived from the continuous ties with the Chinese communities in Singapore and elsewhere.

Notes

1 Kaye did a sociological study of families in Singapore during this period and concluded that there was much over-crowding, with as many as five or six households were living in a two-storey shophouse. See Kaye, B., 1960, *Upper Nankin Street: Singapore*, Singapore: University of Malaya Press.

2 Many are able to identify their father's brothers as *tang-shu* (堂叔), father's elder brothers as *bo-fu* (伯父), paternal uncles as *shu-bo* (叔伯), elder paternal aunts as *bo-mu*, mother's sister as *mu-yi* (母姨) or *yi-mu* (姨母), father's brothers' sons as *tang-xiong-di* (堂兄弟), fathers brother's daughters as *tang-jie-mei* (堂姐妹), and mother's brothers' sons and daughters as *biao-xiong-di* (表兄弟) and *biao-jie-mei* (表兄弟).

5   The Moral Economy of Rebuilding the Ancestral Village

Introduction

The emigrant villages, *qiaoxiang*, of Fujian and Guangdong have been the recipients of wealth and assistance from their overseas Chinese relatives since the 1978 Reform. Indeed, it is also a policy of the central government to encourage not only remittances but also contributions from overseas Chinese, *qiao-bao* for village infrastructure and economic reconstruction.

Among the Singapore Chinese, there has also been a revival of interests in their ancestral villages. The Singapore government has been instrumental in encouraging some Singapore Chinese to invest in China. However, it has very little effect on their decision to invest or contribute to their ancestral village development. A different set of reasons, not based on economic rationalism, affected these Chinese in their contribution to help develop their ancestral village. The question of interest here is "why do the Singapore Chinese feel morally obligated to assist their ancestral home"? This chapter will explore the extent to which the Singapore Chinese are locked into a set of social relationships within a moral economy that constantly pushes them to assist in village rebuilding. It argues that there are two sets of factors involved in the formation of a moral economy.

The 1978 Reform and Village Reconstruction

After the 1978 Reform, a more liberal political climate between China and Singapore has enabled an increasing number of Singapore Chinese to make regular social visits to their ancestral villages. The Singapore Chinese have also become increasingly involved in village reconstruction. They give mostly financial assistance, but also technical support to help with village development. There are four main areas of basic infrastructure development that they are involved in: (1) building of the old house, *lao-jia*; (2) construction of roads, bridges and power plants; (3) development of education and welfare facilities, mainly schools and hospitals; and (4) establishing petting trading and retailing.

(1) Remittances and the Building of Old Home, Lao-jia

Extending a helping hand to one's ancestral village and lineage is not a new act. The early emigrants were known to have sent regular remittances to their family and home villages. Today, the number of Singapore Chinese visiting their ancestral village and financing the rebuilding of the *lao-jia* has led to a boom in construction industry.

It is estimated that remittances sent back to Fujian during the 1930s amounted to 500 to 700 million Rmb annually from the Straits Settlement. Remittances to the interior regions of Fujian (including Yongchun, Hui-An, Anxi, Lung An and Tung An) amounted to more than 10 million Rmb. Most of these remittances were sent through the ports of Xiamen (Amoy) or Fuzhou (Foochow) (Hicks, 1993:152).[1] It is estimated that overseas Chinese remittances to Anxi in 1938 amounted to slightly over 3.6 million Rmb (Hicks, 1993: 265). Most of these remittances were sent by post, although small amounts were also carried back by returning Chinese (in 1938, a total of 265,386 Rmb) (Hicks, 1993: 273). Greater total remittances back to China were probably made during the 1930s than during any other period; since then, there has been a gradual decline.

After 1949, remittances to Anxi from Singapore declined to just over 1.5 million Rmb in 1954; in 1960, they dropped to just over 1 million Rmb. The years before and after the 1978 reform saw a jump in remittances to Anxi: in 1976 they totalled 3.53 million Rmb, and the amount continued to increase steadily for the next few years, reaching a new high of 7 million Rmb in 1983. Since then, remittances have declined substantially, in 1984 amounting to over 5.4 million Rmb but by 1990 falling to 2.1 million Rmb (Chen, 1994: 97).[2]

Most remittances sent to the home villages from the late seventies through the first half of the eighties were for personal uses, and primarily to rebuild old family houses, *lao-jia* (老家) or second, modern homes *xin-jia*[3] (新家). This has transformed the essentially rural landscape into a modernised one where, instead of mud or wooden houses, stone and brick houses are now common sights. In addition to the traditional housing style with its central courtyard, we now have three- to four- storey buildings surrounded by paddy fields.

In my survey, I found that most villagers received some form of monetary assistance to help rebuild and renovate their old house. Of the 203 respondents, 75 per cent (152 in number) said that they or their parents received some financial assistance from their overseas kin, qiao-qing to help with the building, rebuilding or renovating of the house. In the last few years, several millions RMB have been remitted for building both the *lao-jia* and the *xin-jia*.

They are helped in the following way. They usually write to their related Singapore kin, telling them of the condition of the *lao-jia* and the state of repairs required. In Singapore, upon receiving such letters, the Singapore kin, in most cases, would send some money for such purposes. Sometimes, the rebuilding process might take a few years, with bits and pieces added on to the old house. The amount sent ranges from several thousands to several tens or hundreds of thousands.

How do the villagers convince their Singapore kin of the importance of rebuilding the *lao-jia*? They devise several strategies. The first strategy is to approach the visiting kin and bring them to witness the conditions of the *lao-jia*. One said, "when they are in the village, we will bring them to the *lao-jia* and let them see the poor condition of it. Most of our Singapore kin are sympathetic to our living conditions and would give us some money to rebuild it". The second strategy is to approach only those older and immediate family members who have more empathy and greater sentiments for the ancestral village. For example, one said, "it would have been easier for us to open our mouths and ask our parents or brothers or sisters to help us. But we found it embarrassing asking our grandparents or uncles as they are either too old or not so close to us". A third strategy is to stagger the demands and rebuild the old house in stages. They told me that "we realize that some of our Singapore kin are not very wealthy. They are not the fat kin, *fei-qiao* (肥僑) but are thin kin, *sou-qiao* (瘦僑). So, to lessen their financial burden and to ensure that the *lao-jia* is being rebuilt, we ask for a smaller sum each time, over a period of time. We found it easier to open our mouths this way".

Why is the *lao-jia* so important and why does it need to be rebuilt? What is the symbolic meaning behind it? Most villagers consider the *lao-jia* as the house of their ancestors and this is why it should not be allowed to collapse. To the Singapore Chinese, the *lao-jia* provides them with a physical space where they can locate their cultural roots and recollect their nostalgic feelings of village life, albeit a harsh one. It is also a way of re-establishing their filial piety towards their ancestors and to remember their source of origin, *yin-shui-shi-yuan* (when drinking from the fountain, one remembers its source).

At another level, it concerns the "face" and the need to preserve their feng-shui site. A villager said, "we encouraged our Singapore kin to renovate the old house. I told him that it would cost 500,000 Rmb. My grandmother here brought up their father and their father originally built this house. This is their source or origin and if they let the house go into disrepair, they would also lose much face in the village and in Singapore if our kin know that they have deliberately allowed the *lao-jia* to collapse. It would also be very bad for their and our descendants as the collapse of the *lao-jia* will bring about bad feng-shui to all the living".

There is also sentimental reason attached to the rebuilding. Many qiao-qing who lived there during their childhood years feel sentimental about it and rebuilding it is a matter of sentiment and nostalgia for village life. In many instances, the Singapore Chinese were commented upon by others as when they return to visit their ancestral village, "there is a road that leads to no home", *you lu wu wu* (有路無屋).

Some Singapore kin give only minimal assistance. While some were happy over whatever assistance they had been given, others were less than happy. A village woman said, "He [paternal brother] contributed about Singapore dollars S$1,000 towards the building of the house some 7 to 8 years ago. There is no possibility that they will help us with the house, although we hoped they would. They have been in Singapore for too long and have turned into *fanren*". Others were more understanding and forgiving of their Singapore kin.

Those who did not receive any assistance with building the house expressed their dissatisfaction, sadness and at times, disillusionment over their Singapore kin. One farmer said, concerning paternal uncles and cousins in Singapore, with whom he has had little contact, "...[they] did not help build the house. They should have helped us but did not bother. All of them are now Singapore citizens. We do not know their addresses. They have left the home village for too long. Even those in their fifties did not even come back once".

The younger villagers felt that it was very difficult to ask their Singapore uncles or cousins to help them build a new house or purchase a modern apartment, partly because most of their Singapore kin had already helped their parents with a house and many, although they hoped for help, felt embarrassed to ask for more. One 35-year-old female housewife said, "They [Singapore relatives] have helped the elders to build houses. I hoped that they would help us to build ours. But they have contributed only very little".

Most *lao-jia* that have been repaired or rebuilt or have had new wings added reflect both the new and the old. This blending of the new and old makes the house and landscape an interesting one. There are several *lao-jia* that have been pulled down and new ones built on the site. These are referred to by the seemingly contradictory term "*xin lao-jia*" (新老家), or "new old house". In this case the term *lao-jia* does not refer to the physical attributes of the house, but is more of a social concept referring to the house of a particular household, whose involvement with the specific location stretches back to the first generation which had inhabited the place. It has thus become the source of origin of a particular family, and it is the ancestors that are important. The *lao-jia* thus remains an important physical element in the landscape reminding individuals of their immediate family background and their association with their ancestral home.

Today, there are many renovated *lao-jia*. But many are left vacant with few people living in them. This is because many have moved to live in new modernized houses. In general, most of the occupiers of *lao-jia* are elderly people who have lived in the house for several decades and do not want to move out of it. They attach great sentiment to it. They also prefer the style and the spacious central courtyard where they can sit and relax with other elderly people during their visits.

For the wealthy households, apart from the *lao-jia*, they also build a new house, *xin-jia*. For the younger villagers, they often request their Singapore kin to build or buy a new house. There are now a sizeable number of villagers living in luxurious three to four story type of modern housing equipped with modern amenities. One happy 36 year old housewife said, "our Singapore uncle sent us money to build this 4-storey building which cost 400,000 - 500,000 Rmb. We are very happy and satisfied with it. This house is very comfortable".

The rebuilding of the *lao-jia* has transformed a rural landscape into a modernized one where instead of mud or wooden houses, stone and brick houses are now common sights. Apart from traditional style housing with a central courtyard, modern-style three- to four-storey buildings surrounded by paddy fields are now ubiquitous scenes.

There are four types of housing distinguishable in the villages. The traditional house with a courtyard in the middle was previously the most sought after type of housing. Each family aspired to build a traditional house although most did not manage to and the wealthier families largely inhabited them. Many of them were the *lao-jia* of emigrants who sent remittances to help rebuild them. Within the villages, such traditional houses are scattered about, and it is mostly elderly people who continue to live in them, as the style is now considered old-fashioned by younger villagers, who prefer modern apartment living. There have been many efforts made by heads of household to modernise *lao-jia*, especially if the Singapore kin choose to reside in them during their stays in Anxi. In these it is common to find that modern mosaic or tile flooring has replaced cement. Modern bathrooms, toilets, piped well-water, air conditioning and a modern kitchen together with gas cookers are considered by the Singapore visitors and younger villagers as essential. Most homes now have electricity, although power limitations often provide inadequate lighting and there is often insufficient power to perform various domestic tasks simultaneously. In the last few years another power station has been built and such problems have lessened, although, because of the relatively high cost of electricity, villagers continue to use other forms of power as well as electricity, as the cost of electricity is much higher than firewood and charcoal.

The openness of the traditional *lao-jia* makes it very difficult to keep dust out of the house; because of this, it is often regarded as "dirty" or "unclean" by the Singapore Chinese. The open central courtyard in the middle provides ample ventilation, but unlike a modern house which shuts out the dust with closed doors and windows, this is not possible for the traditional style *lao-jia:* household members close their room doors, but the living area remains open all the time. Furthermore, female members of most households rear poultry for eggs and meat, and chickens are left to roam around the gardens and, often, into the house as well. Because of the stench around and within the house, many Singapore Chinese are reluctant to stay there when they visit.

Anthropologically speaking, the traditional style family house is one of the friendliest types of housing, conducive to interaction among family members. The central courtyard serves as a common place for interaction among the members, while the bedrooms provide privacy for couples and their children. Its spaciousness is in contrast to modern apartments.

Previously, extended-family members occupied the lao-jia, and it was not uncommon for members of extended families, *fang* to reside there. Today, however, the family within a household is extended only to elderly parents, grown children and young grandchildren. It is becoming more common, however, for young couples to opt for a nuclear family arrangement, if they have the means, and there is an increasing (albeit still small) number of young married couples living on their own. When the family can afford it, or when their *qiao-qing* help them to acquire a modern shophouse apartment, young couples can afford to move out, an arrangement which is becoming fashionable and which reflects on the wealth and social status of the particular household. Most, however, cannot afford this luxury.

In recent years, modern apartment blocks of three- to four-storeys have been constructed by *qiao-qing* for their relatives. These buildings have modern piped water (pumped from wells), modern bathrooms (with a shower or sometimes with a long bath) and toilets. Many also have air-conditioning. This is a variation of the Singapore apartment type of living of the sixties and seventies. High-rise and high-density living has become the norm in Singapore, where the scarcity of land has made high-rise buildings a necessity, but the Anxi villages can afford lower-density housing. However, apartments are now seen as synonymous with modernity, and every villager wants to own and live in one. It is now common to find three- and four-storey buildings in the middle of agricultural fields, next to *lao-jia*. In most cases, one modern building usually houses one extended family. Within the extended families, each son and his family usually occupied one floor if there is sufficient space. Otherwise, two sons and their families may occupy one floor.

The third type is the two- to four-storey modern shophouse, with the ground floor occupied by retails shops and the upper levels used as residences. These are very popular in Peng Lai District and are found mainly in Peng Lai Zhen. A majority of these shops are small retail businesses selling clothing, shoes, small electronic goods, sundries, toiletries and dried foodstuffs. Usually, the upper levels are occupied by nuclear families.

The last type is the mud and wooden huts, where those with no overseas relatives and without financial means to rebuild continue to reside. These constituted the most common form of housing for a large number of the poor villagers. Today, a small number of villagers continue to live in them. Most are found in the hilly regions in the outskirts of Peng Lai district and are now a rare sight.

In the village environment, having a good house is more than just for comfortable living. It is a testimony of the social status, wealth and the material comforts that an individual household could offer. It also spells out to other villagers of the connection of the occupiers with the wealthy Singapore kin. It is also an important asset for marriage consideration. Having a good house is important for a good match. This is particularly so for those with grown sons who are seeking suitable brides.

The house is still considered as the single most important asset that an individual household possessed. In the villages where the paddy field and shops are communal properties, the house remains solely "individualistic". As such, the villagers look upon the house as the ultimate place where immediate family members could conduct their own individual and private affairs away from communal inspection.

A related aspect is the ownership of the house. For the first time since Communism, the villagers could record their names as legal owners of the house they occupied.

Reclaiming One's Ancestral Land

Another issue related to ownership of village land are those land that were taken from the Chinese overseas during the collective years. Under the present reform system, the Singapore Chinese are beginning to re-explore the possibility of reclaiming the land that originally belonged to them or their forebears. Although many would like to be able to reclaim their agricultural land, they were less concerned with this type of land than of their ancestral burial site, commonly known to the villagers as *feng-shui-di* (風水地).

The redistribution of farmland after the 1978 Reform has again become an issue of contention among the village households, mainly among those that were large landowners prior to collectivisation. Many of these have become wealthy through their connections with their Singapore kin. With decollectivisation, some of them had hoped that the land formerly owned by their ancestors would be reallocated to them. However, this was not to be the case, and there was much lamentation. There was little they could do beyond appealing for a reallocation. However, their chance of success is very slim. So, many simply resign and accept the outcome.

Among Anxi households, and especially among their Singapore kin, the issue of land ownership is an emotional affair. Land ownership, as Freedman said, was important for both the individual and the lineage, and today many households continue to express their desires to own a piece of land even though they are no longer engaged in farming. Some not only want to own a piece of land but also, more importantly, want to own their ancestral farmland.

Many villagers can recall the farmland of their ancestors and are able to point out their former family plots. This issue of land ownership is often tied to consideration of the old family house, *lao-jia* and the ancestral burial ground, *feng-shui-di*, and the remembrance of their past status, and to remind their descendants of local family history. During the collectivisation years, and especially in the aftermath of the Cultural Revolution, almost all burial grounds were exhumed and turned into agricultural land. With decollectivisation and the return of private plots, many villagers, together with their Singapore kin, have attempted to regain their former farmlands. Those with connections to local cadres have been able to arrange for the reallocation of former family plots to them, but others have been less successful.

For the Singapore Chinese, the desire is to rebuild the burial sites and the *lao-jia* in order to establish their family roots, *jia-gen* (家根). It was not easy for them to leave their ancestral home villages. For this first generation of migrants, the ties with Anxi remained unbroken, and they have been able to make use of kinship ties to establish *guanxi* ties with the village and town cadres to further their claims on their former farmlands through their village kin.

In Peng Lai District where links with emigrant kin remained strong, many original plots of land, with the *lao-jia* and *feng-shui-di*, were returned to the closest kin of the original owners. Larger stretches of farmland, however, were broken into small plots and allocated to other families during decollectivisation, and former landowners and their descendants could not claim more than their allotted share.

Although Singapore Chinese were considered as overseas comrades, qiao-bao (僑胞) by the official cadres, they were not allocated their original farmland. Few elderly emigrant men and women have been able to point out to me the larger stretches of land originally owned by their grandparents. They have come to accept that land ownership in village China is no longer the preserve of private individuals but is subjected to the discretion of the Chinese government. Even though they established strong social connections with the village-level and town-level cadres, their *guanxi* only permitted privileges within the boundary laid down by the central policy. Those allocated the lands surrounding their *lao-jia* and *feng-shui-di* regarded it as privilege treatment, a testimony to their *guanxi* networks with the right officials. However, not all were so fortunate. These people, at best, could only apply to the officials for the lease of land on which to relocate their ancestral graves and to build new homes, *xin-jia*.

To encourage Chinese overseas to visit, to contribute to the village economy and to assist with village reconstruction, the local government has adopted a flexibility in regarding requests by Singapore Chinese for *feng-shui-di*, and has granted them land to rebuild their ancestral graves on numerous occasions. This flexible approach has gained them much goodwill among the Singapore Chinese.

As suggested above, ancestral graves were located amidst agricultural fields. Lin (1947), in his work, *The Golden Wing*, has fully illustrated the significance of the ancestral burial site as a protector of the family. Freedman (1958, 1966) has also pointed to the importance of the ancestral burial ground as an important conduit for the flow of wealth into the family. It is therefore especially important to ensure that such site is not destroyed. However, Communist ideology dictated against this traditional belief and most of these sites were destroyed, especially during the Cultural Revolution, although a few tucked away in hilly terrain and hidden by thick bushes were neither desecrated or destroyed.

These *feng shui* lands were strategically located to oversee the village, the agricultural field and family home. Visiting and giving offerings to one's ancestors entailed climbing up into the hilly areas, which were often inaccessible by any kind of transport except sedan chairs. Most Singapore Chinese attempt to climb up the hills and trudge through the terraces to reach their ancestral tombs. Many elderly men and women have to be carried up on sedan chairs as, for most of them, the trip to Anxi would be incomplete without visiting and praying at their ancestral tombs.

(2) Development of Basic Infrastructure

A second area is the development of basic infrastructure. The most important is the construction of roads, bridges and power plants. Despite its poverty status, funding for basic infrastructure from the central and provincial governments remains miniscule. As mentioned earlier, from the 1950s to late 1970s, central funding per capita in Anxi remained at 20 Rmb. In the late 1970s, there was only 700 km of motor-roads with 2200 vehicles; no rail service and the two main rivers were navigationally insignificant (Lyons, 1994: 29). Many villages remained inaccessible by motor car. This was the case of Peng Lai until the late 1970s when Chinese overseas capital poured into the district to help with local road construction.

(a) Roads

Under the anti-poverty campaign, state funded basic capital construction was directed mainly towards transportation and communication systems and electric power stations and transmission lines (Lyons, 1994: 74). The most important is the construction of the Zhangping-Quanzhou rail line with 115 km running through Anxi with its western section completed in 1985. There was also the construction of the Xianghua-Longjuan highway and the Hutou-Jiandou Highway in the 1980s. By 1992, Anxi's road network increased to 1485 km serving the main towns. Since then, scheduled bus services plied between Xiamen City and other population centres (Lyons, 1994. 75). Even then, many of the outlying areas remained unserved by roads and the bus services. For example, buses do not go into Peng Lai town and villagers would need to take a localised version of motor rickshaw to reach the main road and take a bus if they wished to travel to the bigger cities.

The main arterial road leading from Xiamen to Anxi remained poor until two years ago. The result was that many visiting Chinese found it difficult to travel into Anxi. Movements of goods and people were retarded because of the poor road system. Although the county government has promised money to build roads, the progress of road building remained slow. The lack of governmental funding and corruption were seen as twin factors in the continued delay in road construction. This main road leading from Xiamen to Anxi has only been recently completed in 1997. Only the main roads were constructed with funds from the government.

There was also little funding for feeder and localised roads in the villages. Apart from the fact that there is insufficient fund for the construction, there was also a lack of political will to do so. Furthermore, in the emigrant districts, the policies of the central and provincial government have always been to encourage the Chinese overseas capital to fund these projects. It is therefore not surprising to see that little or no money is put into road construction despite pressures by the Chinese overseas.

In Peng Lai district, the Chinese overseas have been pressurising the local government to come up with funds for road construction without much success. One recent method used by the Chinese overseas is to split the cost of construction. The stretch of road leading directly into Peng Lai district was constructed under such a shared funding agreement. Apart from this, many of the localised roads were constructed wholly from funds from the Singapore and Malaysian Chinese. The result was that, from 1979 to 1991, a total of 91.1 kilometres of roads were constructed in Peng Lai district with overseas money (Anxi Xian Zhi, v.1: 361).

In 1995, the Long Men Tunnel was constructed and opened to traffic. The cost for building this tunnel amounted to 2 million RMB and was gain fully financed Singapore and Malaysian Chinese capital. This tunnel was burrowed through the mountain at Long Men Township which half the journey from Xiamen to Peng Lai from 5 hours to 2 1/2 hours instead of either travelling along the road following the river or through the hilly terrain.

(b) Bridges

The region is being cut into two by the Anxi River that flows through it. In the Peng Lai district, seven were built with qiao-hui. Altogether, these bridges totaled 267 metres and cost 2.5 million Rmb to build. The single longest bridge is 100 metres in length and cost 2.25 million Rmb to build (Anxi Xian Zhi, v.1: 379).

In our survey of Peng Lai District, we found that all the villagers mentioned that one of the greatest contributions made by Chinese overseas had been the construction of roads and bridges, and all were aware of the contributions made by Chinese overseas for them. Many of their Singapore relatives have contributed, in varying amounts, and villagers felt that without these contributions the roads and bridges would not have been built, or would have been of poor quality. They also informed me that without these contributions, the burden would have been heavy on the villagers, as all households would have been required by the local government to contribute to the construction costs. Even though the county government had promised financial assistance, money was not forthcoming, and it was only with the added contributions from the Singapore Chinese that the arterial road leading to Peng Lai was finally completed and opened at the end of 1996.

The older villagers were aware of large contributions by several Singapore Chinese. During the 1950s, 1960s and 1980s, three main donors from the Ke lineage in Singapore contributed to the building of three different bridges, allowing the villagers to cross the tributary of Xi River with ease. Other contributions also came from the Singaporeans, and one wealthy Singapore Chinese paid wholly for the construction of two bridges in Peng Lai district. Some of these bridges have the names of the donors inscribed on them.

In my interviews with the villagers, all mentioned that one of the most important contributions made by overseas Chinese is the construction of roads and bridges. All are aware of the contributions made by overseas Chinese in these areas. They feel that without the contributions of overseas Chinese, these roads and bridges would never have been built. They would not be able to access the regional towns and cities as readily as at present. They also told me that it would become a gross burden on all villagers if all households have to contribute to such infrastructure projects. Furthermore, the lack of funding from the county government has resulted in much delay to road building.

In general, there are three types of attitudes adopted by the villagers in regards to contributions by overseas Chinese. The first attitude states that the overseas Chinese have a responsibility to help them with such infrastructure projects. The majority of the villagers embrace this. The second attitude states that it is the responsibility of the county government to build the infrastructure in order that investments could be encouraged into the region. About half of the informants subscribe to this view. The third attitude is that the overseas Chinese should contribute if they have the ability to do so but should not be held responsible for such development. Only a handful adopts this attitude.

To the Singapore Chinese, they have come to see that helping to construct roads and bridges has become a way where they can become reunited with their ancestral village. To the men, it has become an important method of establishing social connections, *guanxi* with both the provincial, county and local cadres. Many of them are businessmen and establishing good connection is always useful for business purposes. Some of them have set up business in the larger cities and in Xiamen. A good guanxi is a good asset to have. For many others who have no business in Fujian province, giving donations and helping with infrastructure development means willing goodwill from all sectors - both the government officials and the villagers. In the eyes of the villagers, they would have achieved a higher social status and gain much social capital. With their status and the social capital they have gained, they are in a better position to negotiate with the government officials over the staging of the numerous socio-religious activities through the years. These activities often have the support of the village and county cadres. Another reason for their support in road construction is that a better road system simply makes their trip to their ancestral village a more pleasant and less dangerous one than before. Furthermore, it will encourage more of the Singapore kin to visit the ancestral village. This is especially important if they want to encourage the Singapore born younger Chinese of Anxi descent to visit the ancestral home. Thus to them, in calculating the financial cost of road development, they often weigh it against the social cost that they would gain. To them, the benefits that they derived often outweigh the monetary cost that they put in.

(3) Education and Schools

A third area is the building of schools and expansion of education. This area of development has high support from almost 90 per cent of the Singapore Chinese. Their main reasons are: (1) to raise the literacy level of the villagers as there is lack of education facilities and opportunities for the villages, (2) they see education as a way out of an agrarian village environment into an urban city, hence, out of poverty. This is especially so for village girls where many continue to receive a lower degree of education than the boys.

The provision of education for all the children of the villages has been an important priority. Peng Lai District is now officially regarded as a cultural district, *wenhua qu* (文化區) by the county government because of the number of educational facilities for village children and the relatively high literacy rate of its young population, in comparison with other mountainous districts, *shan-qu* (山區). The district and county cadres have expressed pride in this, and attribute the high literacy primarily to the work of the Chinese overseas who began to help with the provision of educational facilities as early as the forties. Today, contributions in the area of education have grown much faster than in other sectors.

From our survey, we found that few villagers go beyond the compulsory years of education. About 37 per cent of the villagers have some form of primary education; 27.5 per cent with secondary education; 16 per cent with post-secondary education; 5.5 per cent with teacher or technical education; 1.5 per cent with tertiary education and 18.5 per cent with no education. Of these, 95.7 per cent of male respondents have some form of education while only 48.3 per cent of female respondents have some form of education. In addition, of the 18.5 per cent with no education, 15.5 per cent of these are women. This is not surprising as the villagers continue to value sons higher than daughters. (See Table 5.1).

Table 5.1 Sex and Distribution of Education and Literacy

	No Education	Primary	Sec/Post Secondary	Technical	Tertiary	Total
Male	6	53	68	11	2	**140**
Female	31	19	9	0	1	**60**
Total	**37**	**72**	**77**	**11**	**3**	**200**
%=100	**18.5%**	**37%**	**43.5 %**	**55 %**	**1.5 %**	

Table 5.1 shows that the sex ratio distribution of education continues to reflect the bias towards the male children. Today, the general attitude is to provide at least ten years of education for all children, male and female alike. Among the wealthier households, the desire is to provide as much education as possible for the female children if their grades permit them to go on with their studies. In Peng Lai District in 1996 several young women had ventured beyond the village schools and attended teacher's training college in Quanzhou. Although among the villagers, they continue to have preference for boys, this attitude is gradually changing with some families treating their daughters with as much care and attention as they are given to boys.

Table 5.2 Age Groups and Education Attainment

Ages	No Education	Primary	Sec/Post Secondary	Technical	Tertiary	Total/%
20-29	2	3	16	0	0	**21 (10.5)**
30-39	3	10	25	1	0	**39 (18.5)**
40-49	11	19	15	3	1	**49 (24.5)**
50-59	15	17	15	4	2	**53 (26.5)**
> 60	6	23	6	3	0	**38 (18.0)**
	37	**72**	**77**	**11**	**3**	**N = 200**

Table 5.2 shows the level of education for each age category. It is clear that a high percentage 81.5 per cent have some form of education which led to Peng Lai District being considered as a "cultural district" where there is supposedly a higher level of literacy compared to other districts in the county. Forty-six per cent of those in the age groups 20-29 and 30-39 have attained secondary, post-secondary and technical education. Today, there has been a focus on encouraging the younger villagers to pursue higher education. The village schools are competing with one another to produce the best students to send to the best secondary schools and university. Children are encouraged to study and obtain good grades.

Educational reform has been a target of the village cadres. There are three main objectives: (i) to expand education in general; (ii) to encourage contributions to education from *qiao-qing*; and (iii) to upgrade teaching skills. Reform in education has also been one of the primary focuses of the Singapore Chinese, who have contributed substantially to numerous education projects. Since 1978, an expansion of educational facilities has included new buildings for the primary and secondary schools and new staff quarters for the teachers. The latter have attracted better teachers to the district, and this in turn has resulted in better grades for the children. Formerly, students had to travel to the county town for post-secondary education; today, primary, secondary and post-secondary education can all be acquired within the village setting. The local No. 8 Secondary School in Peng Lai District started offering post-secondary education in 1992 and has rapidly acquired a good reputation for producing good students. It has attained band 3 status and is aiming for band 2 status in the national examination system. In China, secondary schools are divided into 5 bands. Band 1 schools are the best academically and highly competitive. They are often found in big cities. To attain a band 3 status for a village school is an achievement. To attain a band 2 status is almost unheard of in rural China setting. So, it is an ambitious task that the No. 8 secondary school is trying to attain and they needed and relied a lot on assistance and resources from the Chinese overseas to help them realise their goal.

From 1979 to 1990, the number of primary schools in Anxi County increased from 355 to 424, and the number of students went from 84,557 to 97,387. The number of secondary schools increased from 4 to17 during this period, while that of post-secondary schools decreased from 15 to 10 with some schools offered combined secondary and post-secondary education. This same period witnessed an increase in the number of students in post-primary education from 21,750 to 28,518, of which 25,460 were in secondary education while 3,508 were in post-secondary education (Anxi Xian Zhi, v.2: 953).

Beginning in 1949 in Anxi County, 2 secondary and 17 primary schools were built with funds from Chinese overseas. After reform, Chinese overseas capital continued to finance educational projects, adding another 10 secondary and 12 primary schools (Anxi Xian Zhi, v.2: 974). It is estimated that in the last forty years Chinese overseas capital has contributed over 53 million Rmb to education in Anxi (Anxi Xian Zhi, v.2: 974). Such contributions are made, either by single donors or by groups of Chinese overseas, to a particular school, often one in their ancestral village. Thus *qiaoxiang* with a large number of wealthy visiting overseas kin have benefited greatly since the reform years, while those with few visiting overseas kin have fewer resources, and non-*qiaoxiang* have remained comparatively poor.

Indeed, an examination into the beginning of such schools revealed that many were, in fact, started because of overseas funding during the early years of Communism, and that subsequent funding came from members of the same lineage, so that these schools became associated with a particular lineage and surname group. Villagers of the lineage bearing the same surname were strongly encouraged to send their children to these schools, although children of other surnames were also admitted. It is not surprising that in these schools as high as eighty per cent of the students are of the same surname group. This situation is facilitated by the fact that although the villages are of mixed surnames, each village tends to be dominated by one surname group. It is often the visiting kin of the dominant surname groups that have contributed substantially to the schools and have a commanding voice in the school administration. Within Peng Lai District, three surname groups have schools affiliated with their lineages.

Case Example

In Peng Lai District, the Ke lineage dominates the Gui-Tou village. Within it, there is a primary and a secondary school. These two schools have assumed the name of a late donor, who was a Ke member, and are known as Chin Lai Primary and Chin Lai Secondary School, respectively.

Ke Chin Lai went to Singapore in the 1910s and had made his fortune by the thirties and forties. He returned to his home village and started the first village primary school in the thirties; in the fifties, he contributed another sum of money and built the secondary school. Since then, other donors from the same lineage have contributed substantially to improve educational facilities and the teaching environment in the district.

Contributions have also been made to the construction of teachers' quarters, in 1994 amounting to as estimated one million Rmb. This has been considered a very important project by the school authorities of No. 8 Secondary School, their main argument being that, since Anxi County is a remote county away from big cities, it has been difficult to attract good teachers and to retain those assigned to teach in the district. Because of Peng Lai town's relatively underdeveloped market economy, there have been no modern amenities, recreational or entertainment facilities. To compensate for this lack, teachers need to be provided with better accommodation. Until recently, existing accommodations were those built in the fifties by the teachers and villagers themselves, and were in extremely dilapidated conditions.

Thus, whenever the Singapore Chinese visited the villages, they would be taken on a tour to visit No. 8 Secondary School, during which various rundown buildings would be pointed out and the visitors would be asked to sponsor new projects. In 1994, sufficient funds were collected to enable the school to construct its staff quarter, and at the end of 1995 the first teacher household moved into the new building. Presently, the building is fully occupied by teachers, mostly from other districts, and the school is planning to construct a second building for teachers, to replace another old building. The school authorities hope that Singapore kin would again help with the financing. In 1996 when I was there, there were talks about asking the Singapore Chinese to help with equipping the schools with computer facilities.

According to the principal of No. 8 Secondary School, when the school was first built, donor Ke Chin Lai suggested that the school become an educational project of his Ke lineage. The school administration accepted this proposal and took contributions only from members of Ke lineage. The principal told me that by excluding members of other lineages from contributing to the school, the school administration hoped that Ke members would contribute more.

This has become the common strategy adopted by the various schools and a de facto policy in Peng Lai district. Today, in Peng Lai, different surname lineage adopts a school. Only members of that surname group could make contribution to the school. The school, on the other hand, would also only receive contribution from members of one lineage. Thus, the school becomes a de facto lineage school where students come from that lineage although admission is open to all surname groups.

According to a school principal, there are advantages to this practice. By making the school a de facto lineage school, the Singapore members would feel proud and contribute more to "their school". It also creates an environment where members of the various lineages would compete with one another to build better facilities for their "lineage school". Members would feel compel to give generous donations in order that their lineage school does not lack behind others. The school administration encourages such competition and indeed creates pressure to encourage more contribution from its members.

Because other schools adopted similar policy, this exclusion strategy worked well. Thus, each lineage informally adopts a school, and by associating the school with the lineage, lineage members become more generous in their contributions. At the time it was hoped that such arrangements would result in the various lineages competing with one another to contribute more to their respective "adopted schools". Here, "face" is at stake, and members of the dominant lineages want to win "face" for themselves. Understanding the psyche of the Singapore Chinese and promoting inter-lineage rivalry in educational projects have become ways by which local cadres attempt to solicit funds from their respective Singapore lineage kin.

The Singapore Chinese, on their own initiative and at times in response to suggestions from local cadres, have also established scholarships, awards and bursary for students of their "lineage schools". Students with the best results in a given year have been given awards, usually sums of money and memorabilia, for their scholastic excellence. Those who have been accepted into universities or other tertiary institutions have been given scholarships. Those students from poorer households were also given financial assistance and grants-in-aid to enable them to complete their studies.

In Peng Lai, the Singapore Chinese have contributed over several million dollars to the various educational projects including new buildings for schools, teachers' residences, bursary for needy students and scholarships for those with good results. At present, they are in the process of raising another million Rmb for scholarships and bursaries. It is estimated that the Chinese overseas have contributed over 53 million Rmb to education in Anxi during the last forty years. (Anxi Xian Zhi, v.2: 974).

The Singapore Chinese also establishes scholarships, rewards and bursary for students of their "lineage school". Students with best results for the year are given rewards, usually a sum of money and a memorabilia for their scholastic excellence. Those who make it to the university are awarded full scholarship for their studies.

To encourage teachers to perform and remain in the village, it is now a common practice to give additional salary and bonuses, better housing and living conditions to the teachers. This money also comes from the funds given by the overseas Chinese.

(3) Public Health and Hospitals

The third area of redevelopment is public health and provision of medical facilities. Being the poorest county, Anxi was and is still today somewhat neglected by the central and provincial government in the provision of health services. From the 1950s to late 1970s, the miniscule provision of fund did not stretch to include medical provision. The villagers were dependent on the barefoot physicians for assistance. In the Peng Lai district, there was only one government-run clinic that could provide elementary treatment. Serious ailments could only be treated in the county city hospital. However, it was beyond the reach of the villagers. In the 1980s, even though there was the anti-poverty campaign, the health sector continued to be neglected. Much energies then were channelled to infrastructure and enterprise development.

In Peng Lai district, the situation was no worse than other villages. However, since the early 1950s, it has benefited from financial support from Chinese overseas. Today, Peng Lai Hospital is the only medical institution in the district. It was established in 1953, with two expansions in 1972 and 1990. From the beginning, this hospital has been funded wholly from overseas Chinese capital. In 1953, the overseas Chinese donated 124,000 Rmb to the hospital. From 1985 to 1992, one million Rmb was donated to the hospital for equipment and medicine. Several million Rmb was contributed for the building of a new wing. Today, there is no charge for medical treatment and a nominal fee is charged for the medicine.

Apart from it, there are several medical outposts providing some form of basic treatment to the sick and the injured. Medical facilities in the district has been generally poor and of very low standard. In addition, some villagers have found it difficult to pay for treatment and medicine - this is especially the case for those living in the mountainous interior and those without the support of overseas kin. For these reasons most villagers have preferred self-medication. Today, however, the hospital has upgraded its services and is one of the most modern hospitals in the region. Because of its reputation, villagers from nearby districts travel to have their medical treatment there.

The hospital was established in 1953 as a medical clinic. In 1956, five Singapore Chinese joined together to raised a fund to help establish the Peng Lai Chinese and Western Medical Clinic, *Peng Lai Zhongxi Zhenliaosou* (蓬萊中西診療所), donating 124,000 Rmb; the facility was renamed Peng Lai Huaqiao Hospital in July 1956. In 1972, it was again renamed, as Peng Lai Public Health Institute, *Peng Lai Wei-Shen Yuan* (蓬萊衛生院). From 1984 till 1990 the hospital underwent various phases of modernisation and extension, financed wholly by Singapore Chinese capital. Then, in 1990, a new four-storey wing was added to the hospital. Three of the floors were for inpatients, the uppermost floor for meetings and to entertain guests. The contribution for this came from two sons and the daughter of a Singapore family and the wing was named after their late father, a big contributor to village reconstruction. About this same time, the hospital upgraded its medical equipment with funds contributed by other Singapore Chinese who, at the request of the hospital administration, also donated medical equipment, blankets, beds, refrigerators, a car, and other items of daily medical necessity to the hospital. Altogether, from 1985 to 1992, contributions totalled over a million RMB.

Like other public projects, the hospital continues to suffer from insufficient funding from the county and local government. Staff have been poorly paid and the increasing number of patients has made for a heavy workload for doctors and other medical staff - most of whom were trained in the Chinese medical system, although top administrators-cum-doctors have claimed knowledge of western medicine. While the hospital levies a small charge to cover medical expenses, this has been insuficient to defray increasing costs. Doctors have informed me that they often have to be out of pocket to treat the patients. The deputy director of the hospital related the following incident to me:

> Last year there was a peasant, a woman, aged twenty-two years. She was pregnant with twins but had no knowledge of it. Because the family was not well off, she did not even once visit our hospital or other clinics. Like many peasant women, on the day of her delivery, she went into labour at home alone. For over ten hours, she was trying to give birth, but the babies were in a breech position and she could not deliver. She was bleeding a lot and by the time her husband and other family returned home, she had already lost a lot of blood. She was already in a semi-conscious state. Her husband brought her to our hospital. It was a shocking sight. We had to try to save her life as well as the babies. We operated on her immediately. But it was too late: the babies, two sons, were delivered stillborn. Because of this, the husband was disgusted and refused further medical treatment for her. But we could not just discharge her like this. We hospitalised her and treated her. After she recovered and was discharged, her husband did not and could not afford to pay the bill of over 200 Rmb. He did not consider it worth it, as he had already lost two sons. As to her welfare, he did not show any concern at all. I had to pay the bill out of my own pocket, as the hospital does not have emergency funds to cover non-payment.

> Fortunately, after I mentioned this incident to one of the Singapore *qiao-bao*, he reimbursed me the amount and suggested that the hospital needed to set aside an emergency fund for such cases. Now, the hospital has decided to ask for contributions from the *qiao-bao* to help with this emergency fund. I hope everyone will contribute some to this.

Given their situation, the hospital authority has found it easier to turn to the Chinese overseas for donations than to ask for an increased budget from the government agencies and, since the 1980s, have engaged in intense lobbying for funds from Singapore and Malaysian Chinese. Funds are needed in all areas. The hospital has just completed the new wing, effectively tripling its capacity for hospitalisation and a staff quarter, and is now soliciting funds to purchase medicine so that local villagers can continue to enjoy relatively cheap medical care. Presently, a villager needs to pay only several Rmb for medicine; however, with the trend towards privatisation and with physicians allowed to engage in some sorts of private practice, health costs for villagers are expected to rise. In Peng Lai physicians employed by the hospital are now permitted to charge more in their private practices and still use hospital space. These are the *getihu* physicians, some of whom charge ten Rmb or more for consultation and medicine, making it extremely difficult for poorer villagers to receive medical treatment. The administration hopes that with contributions from *qiao-bao*, they will be able to continue providing low cost medical care for needy villagers while charging higher fees for wealthier villagers. Thus, to them, overseas contributions play a very vital role.

Funds continue to be needed to upgrade the medical equipment in the hospital, which is sparse. Only in recent years has the hospital been able to afford certain essential equipment such as X-ray machines, ultra-sound machines and ECG machines which, while they are basic essentials in hospitals throughout the world, continue to be seen as luxuries in village China. Without contributions from the Chinese overseas, this equipment would continue to be the privilege of the wealthy hospitals in the big cities, and of the privileged classes. In Peng Lai District, such facilities not only enhance the quality of medical treatment for the local population but also attract patients from other nearby regions. Thus the contributions of Chinese overseas have allowed the hospital to modernise and to expand into a relatively modern hospital with some advanced equipment.

The relatively high status attained by the hospital has made the Peng Lai villagers very proud of both it and their overseas connections. The hospital is seen as relatively well equipped, with modern equipment and a well-trained and well-disciplined medical staff. Before its expansion, it could only treat simple ailments, but today it has facilities for some forms of surgery; its modern X-ray machine helps to diagnose various diseases, its ECG machines helped to detect various heart malfunctions. It has good after-care facilities. In past years, many diagnoses and semi-complicated treatments could only be treated in the county hospital, two to three hours away, but today reasonably good health care can be found within the village.

Many villagers refer to the hospital as the Huaqiao Hospital, and feel the name truly reflects the concern of their *qiao-bao* for them. These were their responses:

> ... if the *qiao-bao* did not provide financial assistance, up till today, we would still be without a hospital. The hospital is clean by village standards and the doctors are good. We can now be treated for various illness and even have surgery done locally. We do not need to travel to the county hospital for surgery anymore. Besides, the charges are very

reasonable. Everyone needs to pay only a few Rmb to see a doctor and more for hospitalisation and surgery."

> I think it is good that the *huaqiao*, especially the Singapore Chinese, make big contributions to basic infrastructures in the village. It is especially good of them to make donations to the hospital. I think they should donate more so that we all can benefit from it.

By permitting rapid medical treatment, the presence of the hospital gives villagers a better chance of surviving life-threatening medical conditions - without it, the only alternative is dependence on their life-force, *mingyun* (命運), mitigated by the numerous deities. While this dependence continues for the adherents of the belief system, medical treatment now brings another dimension of hope. The hospital has thus changed the concepts of medical treatment and health and illness within the village milieu. Health and illness have been very much a part of living, and poor health and minor illnesses are considered part of routine living. Formerly, the old were expected to be infirm and awaited death. So were the young with illness. At least today, the hospital has given them some hope of survival. However, the changing of attitude remains a gradual process and many villagers continued to rely on supernatural elements to improve their health although some did it alongside modern medical practices.

Among the villagers, all are aware that the Chinese overseas funds the Huaqiao Hospital. They feel that this is an important facility and they feel that it is a good thing to have in Peng Lai. Among them, there is a gradual acceptance to use the hospital facility. This is especially so among the younger villagers who went there to consult over a minor ailment. Among the elderly, they continued with their home remedy for ailments such as cold and flu. To some villagers, the cost of the medicine, at 2 to 3 Rmb continues to be an expense that they do not wish to incur unnecessarily. Among them all, they all agreed that if there were a serious illness, they would go and consult the doctors at the hospital. However as the hospital is not as well equipped and the doctors not sufficiently well trained, those with serious illness will have to travel to the county hospital in Guanqiao or even Chuanzhou for treatment. There have been several serious cases where the villagers had to travel to Chuanzhou for medical treatment.

To the Singapore Chinese who are so used to western medicine and western medical treatment, the establishment of the Huaqiao Hospital seems the logical step to improve village infrastructure development. Many expressed disbelief that the central and provincial government did not provide funds for such an important service. They told me that they began to understand the meaning of "life is cheap in the villages" and began to realize that the various levels of government have no interest in the village life and village affairs. Given the reality of the situation, they are willing to contribute to establish some form of medical facilities for the villagers. This is even more so as their forebears were from the district and it was their ancestral village.

(4) Financing Small Businesses

The fourth area is to help transform the district from an agrarian to a petty commodity and trading economy. Until today, this strategy is met with little success in Peng Lai district.

The interior location, the mountainous terrain and the poor transportation are the main deterrent factors for industrialisation and commercialisation in Anxi. After the 1978 Reform and with the anti-poverty campaign on its way, Anxi continued to have very few industries or commercial enterprises. Most of these were cottage industries that made use of local resources and were geared toward local consumption. These included the production of paper, sugar, local alcohol, tea, handicrafts, rattan goods and furniture, and wood products.

As a result of the 1978 Reform, there has been an increase in industrial production for export. There has also been an increase in other forms of secondary and tertiary economic activities. In 1982, there were only 854 enterprises; by 1990, the figure had increased to 7,069. Main industries include farm machinery production, a power station, tea processing plants and construction; together the various enterprises employ a total of 37,304 workers (Anxi Xian Zhi, v.1: 353). Of the 7,069 enterprises, 194 were operated by towns, 810 by villages, 370 by the overseas Chinese bureau, and 5,695 by individual households (Anxi Xian Zhi, v.1: 354); 1,072 were involved in industrial production, 422 in agricultural production, 24 with construction works, 617 with transportation and roads, 4,285 with commercial and retailing activities, 642 in service industry, and 7 with other activities (Anzi Xian Zhi, v.1: 354).

In the Peng Lai District, in 1990, there were 114 enterprises employing a total of 2,479 workers. After reform, Peng Lai District witnessed the emergence of 3 cottage industries. These produce pottery, rattan goods and furniture, and tea processing and they are geared towards export. The industries make use of resources produced locally and employ local expertise. In 1990, the pottery and rattan factories each employed over twenty women workers in their late teens and early twenties. The clay pots and vases are made using local clay and are fired in local kilns, which were made by village men. After being produced, the products are brought to the factory where the girls weave rattan baskets, enclosing these vases and pots. These pots and vases in baskets are exported to the big cities of Southeast Asia, including Singapore. There have been talks about expanding exports to Europe. (Anxi Xian Zhi, v.l: 353).

From the 1978 Open Door reform onwards, the various levels of government officials have intensified their efforts to encourage Chinese overseas to visit and invest in the big cities and in their ancestral villages. The Chinese overseas, especially those with close qiaoxiang connections, were especially encouraged to invest in the emigrant villages in order that capital flow into these villages would bring about development in the rural sector. The Overseas Chinese Bureau in the emigrant counties worked intensely towards encouraging capital investments for infrastructure and enterprise development. County and district cadres made regular trips to Singapore to rekindle ties with their Singapore kin and to re-establish *guanxi* networks, hoping that through these social networks the Singapore Chinese could be encouraged to visit their ancestral home and to invest in Anxi in general and Peng Lai in particular.

This period coincided with a high growth rate in the Singapore economy and in the state's policy towards globalisation. The relatively wealthy status of the Singapore Anxi Chinese made them more prepared to deal with their ancestral home village in a generous manner, and when the village and county cadres came to Singapore to ask for financial assistance for infrastructure development, they, under several local leaders, contributed substantially. It is possible to argue that such generosity was also a reflection of their search for cultural identity, which lead them to re-evaluate their ties with their ancestral home. They looked towards their ancestral source of origin, not so much for moral sustenance, but as a locale for discharging socio-moral duties. Participating actively in village reconstruction and making the emigrant villages prosperous was thus one way of reflecting their own well being.

In addition to the Open Door policy, the lifting of restrictions on travel to China by the Singapore government meant that Singapore Chinese could travel to China without the need to apply for exit permits. In addition, the potential of the China market and the low labour costs there led many Singapore Chinese to invest in China by setting up factories and various types of businesses in the port cities and special economic zones of Xiamen, Hainan, Shenzhen and Suzhou; but the Singapore Anxi Chinese have also focused on development in their ancestral villages. Although village and county governments were eager to encourage capital investment in industry and manufacturing, these Singapore Chinese were less interested in this - to them, economic rationalism dictated that they set up factories in port cities and the special economic zones rather than in the villages, where there was little economic infrastructure to support these types of investments. Yet they were still interested in assisting their immediate kin to develop some kinds of small businesses and enable them to move out of their agrarian background.

Solving Unemployment with Enterprise Development

By encouraging Overseas Chinese to invest in local industry rather than to support cultural and religious activities in the villages, local government hopes to solve the unemployment problems of the Anxi region.

A rapidly growing population as a result of the partial failure of family planning and the shrinking of cultivable land area has made for a large pool of surplus labour. Traditionally, agricultural involution in paddy growing had been insufficient for absorbing surplus labour; emigration was one result. Today, the district hopes the new market economy can solve the unemployment problem. At present, the county town is in a transitional stage while the Peng Lai district market town is attempting to transform its economy without much success.

Interviews with the official cadres have elicited following expressions of hope that Singapore Chinese or other groups of Chinese will return and set up factories in Anxi and Peng Lai:

> It will be good if the Singapore Chinese come and invest here. They should come and set up factories here. We are very short of electricity and they should come and set up a power plant here.

> The county government and the Singapore Chinese have co-operated and set up a power plant. They should now concentrate on industries, such as the garment industry, to help solve our unemployment problems.

> These Singapore Chinese have their priority wrong. They are only interested in the cultural and religious functions and are willing to spend large sums of money on these. When it comes to setting up factories, they are not so willing to do so. Some even reject this suggestion outright.

While industrialisation and the market economy are the goal of the official district and county cadres, many have very sketchy ideas of how to go about the transformation, as they themselves have very little exposure to, or knowledge of, the operation of a market economy or of industrial development. This lack of exposure has meant that the majority find it hard to articulate what they expect of industrialisation, or the types of factories that are appropriate for the economic needs of Anxi. Many simply expressed that, as long as there are factories, the villagers would be able to work and earn an income, and this will solve the unemployment problems. These were their responses:

> I do not know what types of factories would be good. But any type of factory would do. As long as there are factories, these would be good for our economy and our people.

> I would like to see manufacturing factories. But I have very little idea over what types of manufacturing would be appropriate for Anxi. I guess I would leave the decision to the Singapore investors. They would have better ideas than we would here. After all, they are businessmen.

> I would like to see factories that will absorb many workers. Maybe light industries such as garments, bags, etc. are good for us.

However, there are several cadres who have some knowledge of the operation of a market economy. While they too hope that the Singapore Chinese will come and invest in the county, they have reservations about their success in encouraging these investments. They feel that the central, county and district governments do not play a sufficient role, pointing to their lack of commitment to develop basic infrastructure. To them, governments at various levels have failed in their promise to build more roads and other transportation facilities, as well as power plants that would provide the necessary energy to run factories. The arterial road from Xiamen City to the county town and Peng Lai was delayed for several years due to lack of sufficient funding on the one hand and corruption on the other.

Corruption is a widespread phenomenon in China, especially in the rural areas. Bribes and kickbacks line the pockets of officials at different levels, leaving only a small amount for the construction of basic infrastructure. In the case of the arterial road, the level of corruption, according to the villagers, increases according to the length and quality of road completed. Since the arterial road was to pass through several counties, each county government was required to contribute to the construction of the stretch of road that would run through the county. The county government, on the other hand, distributed financial responsibilities to its district governments. Thus, going through the various counties, various stretches were completed while others were not; in the various districts, some stretches were better constructed than others. According to the villagers, in districts with less corruption, roads are in better condition and new roads are built faster than in others. Under pressure from the Chinese overseas and with additional contributions from them, this road was finally completed in 1996, to the relief of all, especially the Chinese overseas.

In an economy in transition from agriculture to petty commodity trading and cottage industrialisation, the issue of employment has taken on new meanings. Previously, farm workers had surplus time during off-seasons. With the shrinking of farmland, there are now many non-farm workers who are unemployed. Furthermore, the villages now produce many young men and women with ten years of education who have no desire to work on the farm but want paid employment. As the transitional economy has been unable to generate sufficient jobs, such young people sit around smoking and engaging in idle conversation. It is such scenes that lead Singapore Chinese to label them "lazy".

Convincing the Singapore Chinese to set up factories in Anxi County has been an uphill battle for the county cadres, especially as concerns Peng Lai District. Until today, the Singapore Chinese have remained lukewarm in their attitude towards large-scale capital investment here. However, a few members whose ancestral home is within Peng Lai District have financed small-scale garment factories and other enterprises set up by their village kin in addition to the considerable financial contributions that they have made for infrastructure development.

Enterprise Profile in Peng Lai District

The Singapore Chinese have given small amounts of capital to their immediate relatives to start small manufacturing and retailing businesses within the district. Like in many rural counties, the villagers are opting to become self-employed and own small businesses. In my survey, there are 2 factory-owners, 17 shop-owners, 5 self-employed drivers, 1 photographer, 1 ironsmith, 1 carpenter and 1 artist. They form an increasing pool of self-employed individuals who operate within the limits of the reformed socialist market system.

Most are small retailing businesses geared towards local needs and consumption. Attempts at export-oriented small industry failed because of its interior location and poor work skill.

Today, over one hundred shops are found in the Peng Lai district. These shops sell a variety of goods including clothes, personal toiletries, small electrical goods, transistor radios and cameras. A booming tyre business is found to cater to the rapidly emerging car population in the district. Service shops have become very popular. There are now several ladies' hairdressing salons and two photographic studios. Some shops have pinball machines that cater to children and for twenty cents the children can have some form of modern entertainment.

An important business is called "the religious and dead industry" that caters to the emerging religious practices found in the villages. Shops emerge to produce religious paraphernalia such as joss sticks, streamers, candles, joss papers, house for the dead, *ling-wu* and fire crackers. The revival of religious activities and ancestor worship has, to a large extent, fuelled the vibrancy of this type of business. They have also helped to reinstate traditional skills and handicrafts that are essential in the making of these religious items. They are extremely profitable and those who could produce them are able to make substantial profit. A religious celebration or a gong-de could amount to 5,000 Rmb or more and an equivalent amount could be spent on purchasing the paraphernalia. The challenge is to attract more overseas Chinese to visit and stage communal religious fairs in the village. Because of the contribution to the village economy, religious activities have been encouraged by the villagers and tacitly approved by the village and county cadres.

For the first time since Communism, there is an emergence of "the flesh industry", i.e. prostitution in Peng Lai. I was told by several villagers that a small number of "immoral and indecent women", *bu-zhen-jin nu-ren* (不正經女人), from other parts of China now lived in the district and catered to out of town men who came to Peng Lai for business and stayed overnight. A few of these women are "mistresses" of these businessmen. The villagers, especially the women, do not welcome this kind of work. They felt that these prostitutes and mistresses have contaminated the village.

Creating a Moral Economy

By contributing substantially to the above areas of activities, the Singapore Chinese have assisted substantially in village redevelopment, thereby transforming the very poor villages into economically prosperous emigrant villages that are also culturally vibrant. I would now turn to answer the question that I posed earlier on, that is, "why do the Singapore Chinese feel obligated to assist and contribute to village reconstruction?"

The main consideration that compels the Singapore Chinese to regard the redevelopment of the ancestral village as their moral responsibility lies with two main sets of forces that form a moral economy which binds these Singapore Chinese to their ancestral village. The first set of reasons lies with the attitudes of the Singapore Chinese. Here it is their understanding of, identification and affinity to their ancestral village. This is very much shaped by three factors, namely the collective memory, their sense of moral duty and their moral consciousness. The second set of reasons lie with how the village leaders and cadres and villagers, through cultural concessions and moral persuasion, further bind them to the moral economy.

Moral Duty and Sentiments of Singapore Chinese

The attitude of the Singapore Chinese plays a very important role in their continued interest in their ancestral villages and their role in village reconstruction. Many of them continue to have strong sentiments. Their understanding of, identification and affinity to their ancestral village is shaped very much by the collective memory of their ancestral village as discussed in chapter 3. Many of the first generation Singapore Chinese continue to have fond memories of their ancestral village as they recall their childhood and young adult life in the village. They also recall the extreme poverty of their ancestral village. It is this sentiment of what the village was like and the memory of poverty that is instrumental in pushing them to assist in village reconstruction whenever they are called upon to help.

A second reason that they gave is a sense of moral duty. Among this group of Singapore Chinese, they continue to be governed by a Confucian sense of moral duty to their ancestral village. Confucian notion of remembering the source when one is drinking water, yin-shui-si-yuan is a phrase frequently invoked by my informants. They told me that they should not forget their ancestral home. They do not have to like it or embrace it. But they should not forget it. To many of them, this is where their parents and grandparents were from. And they have some knowledge of the place. To remember the ancestral home is also taken to mean that when they have been called upon to help with rebuilding the village, they should not turn it down. They also found it difficult and embarrassing to turn down offers to help. One common comment made is that "when the elders come to us for contributions for village projects, it is hard for us to turn it down. Somehow, it just did not seem right to say no. We usually gave whatever they asked from us. Generally, we would be asked to contribute S$500 or $1000. After all, it is our ancestral village".

A third reason given is that when they returned to their home village, they are confronted with real poverty and an underdeveloped social and economic structure. For the first time, some began to understand what village life is all about and village structure which is vastly different from an urban city. This is especially true for the Singapore born Chinese. One said, "before visiting Anxi, I imagined that the villagers were lazy and did not want to work. After visiting Anxi, I begin to understand that it is not because they do not want to work, but rather that there is no work for them to do. Apart from farming, there is little they could do. We also understand that the government has very little interest in helping the region to develop. So, among some of us, we decided to help with setting up a hydroelectric power plant. We also helped our relatives to start up some small businesses to cater for local needs. But we are more reluctant to build factories here because it is impractical to do so. It will be profit-losing".

A fourth reason that the Singapore Chinese give is that of relative wealth and guilt feeling. They told me that "presently, we are relatively well off and comfortable. We also do not wish that our village kin would starve and live meagrely. They don't have to live the way we do in Singapore. But at least, we could help them to live comfortably by village standard. After paying visits to the place, we realise that many of them live in very poor conditions and have few material goods. So, we should help a little".

Finally, a fifth reason lies with the desire to maintain continuity between the two groups of Chinese. To some, the relationship between the Singapore and Anxi Chinese is likened to a thin thread. Once broken, it will be very difficult to maintain. One informant commented that "our relationship is like a thin thread, it should be maintained at all cost, so that our future generations have reference to their ancestors and their source of origin. If it is broken, then the future generations will not be able to search for their ancestral roots and they would become headless."

Cultural Concession as Cultural Capital

A second set of reasons is the actions and attitudes of the Anxi village leaders, cadres and villagers. By permitting and assisting the Singapore Chinese in the areas of religion and ancestor worship, these village leaders and villagers have created a set of cultural capital where they can use them effectively as bargaining chips in exchange for village redevelopment. Here, two forces, cultural concession and the extraction of social capital, worked in favour of the villagers.

On the part of the village leaders and cadres, they are able to identify the psychological needs and provide cultural concessions to the Singapore Chinese. These village leaders told me that many of the older Singapore Chinese are interested in religious activities when they visited their ancestral village. So, within their power, they facilitated the reproduction of such cultural and communal practices. At the same time, they provided full support and assistance for the rebuilding of the ancestral house and temples.

By giving cultural concession in the form of permitting and helping the Singapore Chinese to stage large communal ancestor worship and religious celebrations and allowing the rebuilding of the ancestral house and temples, these become tangible forms of social capital. In so doing, they created a source of social capital and established good guanxi for themselves. This social capital and the network of guanxi and reciprocity serve to bind the Singapore Chinese further into the moral economy where they would be called upon to contribute and assist with various aspects of village rebuilding. Once in it, they found it difficult to extricate themselves out of it.

At the more immediate level, the Anxi villagers have also actively promoted a series of moral sanctions to publicise their Singapore kin who fail to discharge their moral duty. James Scott (1985), in his study, explores the passive resistance of the peasantry towards the landowners. In my case, the moral economy involves active forms of sanctioning. In both cases, the relationship is one of patron-client.

i) Labelling - The villagers openly describe those Singapore kin who failed to help with their immediate needs or village reconstruction as having become "*huang*" [H], "*fan*" [M], i.e. "uncivilised", "babaised" or "detribalised" - like the natives of Nanyang and have no sense of propriety and *qing-qin* (kin sentiments). It is also used against those who persuade others not to contribute to their ancestral home. The villagers also commonly labeled the Singapore born Chinese, as "*huang*" because they are generally less interested and sympathetic to the rebuilding of the ancestral village and often tends to distance themselves from the villages. They also behave very differently from the older Singapore Chinese in manners and attitudes. Many of them also speak the English language and some could not speak the Fujian dialect well. In the eyes of these villagers, these Singapore-born Chinese, usually the younger generations, have betrayed their ancestral origin.

ii) Moral Persuasion - The villagers also invoke their close kinship relations as part of the moral suasion to entice the Singapore Chinese to help with the reconstruction. They often invoke phrases like "we part of one family"; "blood relatives"; "*luo-yeh-gui-gan*" - that the leaves will have to search for their roots"; "that they should remember the ancestors"; "*yin-shui-she-yuan* - that when they drink water, they should remember the source"; "irrespective of wealth, one should not be divorce from the ancestor; and "they are offshoots from this family and this lineage".

Social and Economic Changes

By engaging in the building of the old houses, roads, bridges, schools and hospital, the Singapore Chinese have helped to redevelop and alleviate the poverty-stricken Peng Lai village and transformed it into a prosperous township. Such rebuilding has put into motion the wheel of economic development. It has brought about a boom in the construction industry and other related businesses. The filtering-down effect has far-reaching consequences for the village/township economy.

During the construction boom, almost 70 per cent of the able-bodied men are engaged in some form of construction work. Others are involved in retailing and service industry. Likewise, the large communal religious fairs and ancestor worship have also led to an increase in the number of people engaged in this trade. These are important economic activities that the villagers are beginning to pursue in earnest.

As the village moves away from a pure agrarian economy into a mixed economy, the farms become neglected. Today, many men are involved in some kind of capitalist pursuit or have moved to the neighbouring towns and cities to work. They have left the women to work in the fields. Increasingly, it is the village women who are active farmers. Other wealthier households that have financial support from their Singapore kin also no longer worked on the farms. They either rent their farms to the poorer villagers or engage workers to work on their farms.

The rebuilding of the old houses, new houses and shophouses have also impacted on the land use pattern. Substantial farmlands have been encroached upon for the building of these new buildings. As a result, there has been a shrinking of arable land. Despite this, the villagers have adopted an optimistic outlook. Many have expressed that they no longer want to work on the farm and find that such work is both difficult and without prospect.

Under the influence of their Singapore kin, many desire to move out of the village setting and into the towns and cities. Those with wealthy Singapore kin have been able to move to the towns and cities and start small businesses. Some have also managed to go overseas, especially to Singapore for employment. In Singapore, many work in electronic factories and printing houses.

Conclusion

The rebuilding of the ancestral village and the economic prosperity that these ancestral villages experience is the result of the working of the moral economy, one that is based on collective memory and a sense of moral duty on the one hand and the extraction of social capital through cultural concession given by the village leaders and members on the other hand.

The relationship between the Singapore Chinese and their Anxi ancestral village can be seen in the following manner. Among the Singapore Chinese, the family, *jia,* continues to be seen as the most important primordial social group which needs to be held together despite of all adversities. The lineage, zhong-zu, is thus an extension of the jia where its primordial-ness hinges on the inter-connectedness of its people through both the collective consciousness and social conscience. Here, the moral conscience is embedded in their perception of their self-identity, their identity vis-a-vis their village kin and their identity within the Singapore nation-state. Moral conscience is also crouched in Confucian morality where loyalty and compassion led them to return to their home village and help with village reconstruction.

The success or failure of ancestral village reconstruction and its transformation is also dependent on how the Anxi Chinese transform social relations into social capital and impose it onto the Singapore kin, making it extremely uncomfortable for them not to provide any form of assistance.

In the final analysis, it is the intersection between these two sets of forces that are responsible for the creation of a moral economy that the Singapore Chinese found it hard to ignore.

Notes

1 For a discussion on early remittances by overseas Chinese to China, see Hicks, G.L. (ed.), 1993, *Overseas Chinese Remittances from Southeast Asia 1910-1940*, Singapore: Select Books.

2 For a discussion of this, see Chen, Kezhen, 1994, *Anxi Huaqiao Zhi*, Xiamen: Xiamen University Press.

3 Other uses included the starting of small businesses, the purchase of equipment and electronic goods and the financing of marriages.

Photo 1 Constructing a Bridge across River Xi

Photo 2 The No. 8 Secondary School

Photo 3 New and Old Houses

6 The Bond of Ancestor Worship

Introduction

With the coming of the Singapore Chinese after the reform years, the social and cultural life of the villagers became more colourful and exciting. The last decade has witnessed a revival in both traditional socio-cultural and religious activities. Much cultural life now centres around three types of worship: (i) that of the ancestors, which involves the ancestral house, *zu-zai* [M] (祖宅) or *zhor-chu* [H] (祖厝) and the performance of meritorious deeds for dead ancestors, *gong-de*, (公德); (ii) that of the living, which involves rites for the flow of descendants, *juan-ding*, (涓丁); (iii) that of other deities, which involve the celebration of the Buddha's birthday (佛誕), communal village celebrations, the procession of the county deity, Q*ing-Shui Zu-Shi-Gong,* (迎清水祖師公) and the rebuilding of Q*ing-Shui Zu-Shi-Gong* Temple and its environs, known locally as Qing-Shui-Yan, (清水岩), and the reconstruction of small village temples, devoted to various local deities, such as Zhou-Yue-Miao (州月廟) and Peng Lai Shi (蓬來寺). These religious activities can be broadly divided into communal and individual.

This chapter and the next will explore religious revivalism in the *qiaoxiang*. In this chapter I will explore the significance of ancestors within the Chinese cosmology and the revival of ancestor worship of the Ke Lineage in Peng Lai District, and the extent to which ancestor worship and related practices are gradually being reproduced to cater for the increasing, overt needs of the Singapore Chinese as well as for those of their village kin. Practices associated with ancestor worship, in fact, now permeate village life, and bring together Singapore Chinese and their village kin ritually to acknowledge their common ancestors, thereby forcing them to acknowledge the kinship ties that exist between them, however illusive they may be.

I will also examine the extent to which religious rituals and culture are reproduced in the village environment, and the extent to which the revival of ancestor worship is relevant to the contemporary Chinese family, lineage and village. To what extent is this revival the result of a request for cultural continuity, and to what extent is it purely an instrumental act aimed at luring the Chinese overseas to the village to help with financial contributions?

Another issue to consider here is the question of cultural authenticity. Is this revival a reflection of the understanding of ancestor worship by the Singapore Chinese alone? To what extent has the practice of ancestor worship changed with the interaction, in contemporary time and space, of different sets of social players and social environments?

Bridging the Social Gap: Ancestors and Ancestor Worship

Who are the ancestors? Throughout Chinese history, ancestors, both living and dead, are an important part of the Chinese family, lineage and community. They are collectively seen as both source of origin and transmitter of Chinese culture. Records of ancestors, their roles and their significance, are found in numerous writings. One of the earliest works to revere ancestors is the Confucian *Book of Filial Duty, Xiao-Jin* (孝經), in which Confucius outlined proper treatment towards elders. Descendants were extolled to treat their living parents with filial-ness, *xiao,* (孝), and their dead ancestors with ritual propriety, *li,* (禮). It is thus important to treat both living and dead ancestors with respect and human-ness, *ren,* (仁).

Ancestors also occupy a central position in Chinese cosmology. Death is not seen as the ultimate cessation of life (De Groot, 1964, vol. 1: 4), but as the separation of *yin* (陰) and *yang* (陽) energies. After death, the spirit, *hun* (魂) moves from one realm of existence, the human world, *ren-jian,* (人間), where the physical form is visible to the naked eye, to the netherworld, *yin-jian,* (陰間), where the dead assume a spirit status in a form undetectable to human eyes. Ultimately, the dead aspire to attain a godly status and to reside in the heavenly realm, *yang-jian,* (陽間) (Yang, 1961: 150-151). In the after-life, either in the netherworld or the heavenly kingdom, the dead continue to interact and interface with the living in the human world.

The disposal of the newly-dead with proper rituals, *sang-li,* (喪禮), and the treatment of dead ancestors by proper conduct of ancestor worship, *ji-zu,* (祭祖) are seen as essential[1], and all descendants, from the emperor downwards, were required to carry out ritual duties to their ancestors. Among Confucianists, such acts express "gratitude towards the originators and recalls the beginning" (Yang, 1961: 44). The construction of ancestral halls, *zong-tang,* (宗堂) and memorial halls, *ci-tang* (祠堂), allowing descendants to perform sacrificial offerings and ancestor worship, were found both within palaces and in villages (Freedman, 1958: 81-91).

Ancestor worship thus provides continuity between the living and the dead. Dead ancestors, like other sentient beings, interact with the human world in various ways. They are especially concerned about their immediate kin members and are known to assume a protective role over the welfare of their family. It has been argued that when the burial site of the ancestors is propitiously located, its *feng-shui* harnesses the *yang* energies, *yang-qi* (陽氣) of the ancestors to protect and to accrue benefits for the descendants

(Freedman, 1966: 118-154). Performing regular ancestor worship and conducting correct rituals are important acts of respect and propitiation to ancestors, both being offerings and sacrifices that guarantee that ancestors protect rather than harm them. Spiritual attacks by ancestors were, in fact, considered justifiable if descendants neglected them, especially if ancestors had turned into lonely ghosts, *ku-hun* (孤魂) or wandering ghosts, *you-hun,* (游魂).[2]

Ancestors and ancestor worship are important in bridging the social gap between the Singapore Chinese and Anxi villagers, as they are important among the Chinese in overseas communities. In Singapore, Chinese households continue to uphold ancestor worship, often within individual households, although there is also communal ancestor worship in the memorial halls and in temples. The present trend is towards placing ancestral tablets in such temples, where individuals can now lease space in the memorial halls of the temples for the purpose and then visit and worship individually, while communal worship and offering can also be conducted by the temples' monks or nuns (Tong, 1982).

In China, the 1978 reform made it possible for ancestor worship to be conducted openly in the villages. Before this date, overt communal ancestor worship was prohibited in the villages, even though some individual households worshipped in private (Parish and Whyte, 1978: 283); since then, the villages, especially the emigrant villages, have witnessed a great revival of communal ancestor worship and related rituals. Along with ancestor worship, performing meritorious deeds, *gong-de* (公德), performing the rite of gratification for the flow of descendants, *xie-zu-juan-ding*, and resiting the burial grounds, *feng-shui-di* have become important ritual activities relating to the dead. Among the emigrant villages, building of lineage ancestral houses has become important. All these activities reflect joint effort by Singapore Chinese, who provide financial and emotional support, and Anxi Chinese, who provide labour and active participation. These activities have become the hallmark functions of a prosperous emigrant village, *qiaoxiang*.

Reinventing Lineage Ancestral House, *Zu-Zai* [M] (祖宅), *Zhor-chu* [H] (祖屋)

One of the most important aspects of ancestor worship is the construction of the lineage ancestral house, *zu-zai*. A search through the Ming and Qing Historical Records reveals records of ancestral temple, *zu-miao* (祖廟); lineage temple, *zong-miao* (宗廟); and lineage ancestral temple, *zong-ci* (宗祠), but there is a visible absence of *zu-zai*. Could it have existed as a localised version of the above? Or is it a different social institution altogether?

From its functions, it is more akin to *zu-miao* or *zong-miao*, but it also has functions similar to those performed by *zong-ci* or *ci-tang*, found commonly in Chinese communities overseas where such halls allow groups of Chinese to commemorate and worship their ancestors. Yet *zu-zai* is more than the above. It provides the members with a physical space that helped them physically to locate their ancestors, allows individuals to engage in dialogue and come to terms with the social reality of the past, and allows them to understand and "feel" the social experiences of the ancestors.

Among the Singapore Chinese, the recreation of *ci-tang* is a common feature among the clan associations. These are memorial halls where clan or lineage members gather periodically, on specific occasions, to worship their ancestors - a practice, which continues today. Memorial halls were erected during the early years by Chinese migrants living in various parts of the world in order to fulfil the duties of ancestor worship. These socio-religious institutions helped migrants settle into new environments.[3] *Zu-zai*, however, were not reproduced, as there can only be *zu-zai* at the original physical space where ancestors originally planted themselves in a locality. This locality, for the Ke members is Anxi. To the elderly Ke members, they continue to see Anxi as their ancestral home. As such, they see themselves as the Singapore branch of the wider Ke lineage. In any case, there is no attempt on their part to create a separate lineage from that of the Anxi one.

Following reforms in China, the Ke branch and its lineage members in Singapore and Anxi were able to obtain approval for the reconstruction of the lineage ancestral house, the [M] *kui-tou-zu-Zai* or *kway-tau zhor chu* [H] (魁頭祖宅). There was much sentiment for doing this and for reinstating ancestor worship, as it would enable the separate branches of the Ke lineage to come together after five decades of separation. This includes branches in Singapore, Malaysia, Indonesia and Taiwan. For Ke lineage members, the zu-zai serves "not only as a memorial to remember their ancestors" but also as "a reminder of (their) origin" and would be "an important visible monument for the future generations if they want to trace their cultural roots", acting as a reminder of the existence of their lineage from its beginning through the present and into the future.

In Anxi, ancestors are worshipped in several places. Communally, ancestors are worshipped in the *zu-zai*, which is communal property where every member can lay claim to his or her ancestors and where he/she can go to honour his/her ancestors on special occasions marked by communal celebrations. All households belonging to the lineage participate in these activities. At the individual level, each member can erect an ancestral altar for his or her immediate ancestors. For some well-to-do families, an ancestral shrine room might be created, where the ancestral tablets are placed and the immediate ancestors worshipped, simply on a daily basis and more elaborately on special occasions. For wealthy families, the *lao-jia* may be converted into a private ancestral house, to be used solely for the worship of family ancestors.

In the survey, both Singapore and Anxi informants responded positively to the idea of the reconstruction of the *zhor-chu*. The Singaporean Ke members overwhelmingly supported the reconstruction, with a few wealthy members contributed large sums while the majority contributed what they could afford - sums ranged from several hundreds to tens of thousands dollars (Singapore). Several active elders in Singapore acted as leaders in this fundraising exercise, their high social status within their community allowing them to raise the money with relative ease. Many contributed because their immediate forebears had migrated from Anxi.

The supervision and the actual work of reconstruction were left in the hands of the Anxi lineage members. On several occasions during the reconstruction, the Singaporeans visited the site. The Anxi team took great care to ensure that the project stayed within the budget and was completed in time, and that the house was well constructed. They told me that the Singaporeans expected them to be efficient and corruption-free. The Singapore members feared that corruption would hinder the completion and quality of the project. Both sides felt that they need to maintain a level of mutual trust.

As a memorial building, the present *zu-zai*, now completed, is built in traditional Chinese architectural style, with a curved tile roof. The building comprises a large shrine hall and an uncovered front courtyard. The shrine hall is divided into three main sections: in the middle, there are built-in shelves reserved for the ancestral tablets; to the left, an altar is reserved for *kui-xing-gong* (M) or *kway-sin-gong* (H) (魁星公); and to the right, there is an altar for the earth god, *tu-di-gong* (土地公). Both the shrine hall and the adjoining courtyard are sufficiently spacious to allow for the attendance of a large congregation of lineage members at religious events.

The *zu-zai* is regarded as the residence of the ancestors and the location of their original home and, as such, is considered the physical source of the lineage, and there can be only one ancestral house for each lineage. Hence, a *zu-zai* would not be recreated by a lineage branch, unless it wished to establish itself as separate and sever ties with the existing one.

The *zu-zai* can be conceptualised as both a physical and a socio-religious space[4], a visible reminder of the origin of one's lineage. It is the place where the values of the first ancestors were laid down for descendants to follow. It is thus a marker allowing a group of Chinese to lay claim to common ancestry and to proclaim them as related kin, irrespective of present geographical location. It has become an extremely significant marker for the two groups of Ke lineage members: since the eighties, the intensity of social interaction between the Singapore and Anxi Ke has markedly increased, as evidenced by the numerous communal celebrations held in the *zu-zai*.

Since its construction the *zu-zai* has facilitated the process of grieving for the dead. It has also allowed both the Singapore and village women to become primary reproducers of religious rituals within the once male-dominated village social structure: women have been both active proponents of, and participants in, the elaborate religious rituals that have accompanied the revivalism.

The *zu-zai* is a nexus of power. Emanating outward from this centre of power flow the traditional values of wisdom, compassion and morality. Those within the core area (i.e., the Singapore and village elders) are expected to perform the ancestral duties befitting the senior status that is bestowed upon them. The values ripple through the various layers of social relationship, moving from the centre to the outermost periphery, so that all kin may benefit from their association with the *zu-zai*. The wealth and social prestige of individuals is only recognised when they are converted into virtuous deeds that benefit the community as a whole: philanthropy and charitable works are essential to ensure that social status is recognised within the lineage, to be recorded in the lineage ancestral house, especially after the death of individual contributors. To the Singapore Chinese, wealth, on its own, has little value. Only when it is converted into social deeds do those in possession of it gain an everlasting "fragrant" name. The *zu-zai* thus represents the source, the ritual contents, and the core traditional values of the lineage.

The Rite of Gratification for the Flow of Descendants, *Xie-Zu-Juan-Ding* (謝祖涓丁儀式)

Religious rites and communal celebrations are significant events in the lives of Anxi villagers. The daily monotony of working, tending the house and going to school is now broken by these periodic communal activities. One villager said, "It is good to have these activities. They light up the atmosphere". Another said, "Our children have more exposure to Chinese cultural activities." Some said that, compared to the previous decades, "with the increased number of Singapore kin visiting our village and their concern about religious activities, our village has become less dull". They have also affirmed, "We will support these activities. We will buy some joss incense and papers and go and pray to our ancestors or the village gods". A teacher mentioned that "It is also good for our village economy. These religious functions will need manpower to help with the various activities. Indirectly, they create some kinds of part-time jobs for some of us here". A trader also said that "They are good for our "incense and oil", *xiang-you* (香油) business and for our village economy. That is why even though some of us might not believe in these religious practices, we will continue to support them".

The term *xie-zu* means "thanking the ancestors" while *juan* means "continuous flow" and d*ing* means "descendants". Taken together, *xie-zu-juan-ding* is thus the expression of gratification to ancestors for a continuous flow of descendants - i.e., for the continuity of the lineage. On the occasion of this consecration ritual, over twenty Singapore members arrived to participate, most having arrived several days before the ceremony. The ceremony was important to open the door of the ancestral house and to install the ancestors in their rightful position. It was held in 1988 after the completion of the *zu-zai* to "express gratitude towards the ancestors and to open the doors of the *zu-zai*". Since then, the doors of the *zu-zai* have been opened for communal worship and celebrations, events which occur several times a year and which include the Spring Festival or Chinese Lunar New Year, the *Qing-Ming* (清明節) and the *Zhong-Yuan* Festival (中元節) or *Pu-Du* (普渡). On these occasions, the doors of the *zu-zai* open and members are expected to participate in both communal and individual worship of the ancestors. Individual households prepare several dishes, bring them to the *zu-zai* and offer them to their communal ancestors. In this the role of women is expressed by their participation, as these activities bring the women out from their private domestic spheres into the public sphere and establish them as *bone fide* members of the lineage.

Within the Ke lineage, there are twelve founding ancestors. These founding members were honoured during the ceremony, and ancestral tablets one foot high and four inches wide, each with intricately carved gold-inlaid edges and each inscribed in the middle with the name of an ancestor in painted gold characters, were prepared and installed in their rightful position.

On the day before or on the morning of the celebration, individual households, and particularly the women, busied themselves with preparing traditional rice cakes, slaughter poultry and cooking. About mid-morning, women and men took tables and the prepared food to the *zu-zai*, arranging the tables in neat rows in front of the *zu-zai* and placing the food as offerings to the ancestors. Because of their number, the households were divided into two groups, one of which made offerings in the morning and the other in the late afternoon. A variety of Chinese cakes, poultry, meat and fruits were offered to the ancestors; incense was also offered to the ancestors, but on an individual basis. At a stipulated time, priests or monks performed the liturgy and rituals. The sessions lasted about an hour each. After the religious performance, each household burned paper money as offerings to the ancestors. After the session the lineage members collected their food, placed it in a basket, picked up their tables and returned home. The food was then eaten as lunch and dinner.

On the day of the celebration itself the appointed tablet-carriers, all elderly men, arrived dressed in a variety of styles - some in traditional high-collared gowns, *qi-pao* (旗袍), others in western-style suits. The rest of the participants dressed casually. The ancestral house was packed with lineage members, but other villagers were also present. The master of ceremonies, a local village cadre known for his speaking ability, read aloud the *zhang-cheng* (章程). This informs the community of the history of the Ke lineage, of the achievements of its descendants, of the glorious past, of the achievements of the founding ancestors and of the desire to "fragrance" the lineage through the restoration of the ancestral house. After the introduction, the tablet carriers stepped forward and honour their ancestors. As the master of ceremonies read out the name of each founding ancestor the tablet carrier with that ancestor's tablet carried it with both hands to the front of the altar, while the master of ceremonies introduced the ancestor and read out his achievements. The tablet-carrier, with a lineage-member on hand to assist him, then climbed onto a chair, knelt forward and placed the tablet in position behind the deified Anxi guardian ancestor, Qing-shui zu-shi-gong. Tablet-carriers were instructed to place the tablet carefully in position, as, once the tablets were placed on the altar, no adjustments would be made. I was told by the tablet-carriers that it was not easy for the elderly tablet-carriers to carry out their task, as they had to climb on to the chair and to lean forward to place the tablet with both hands.

The ceremony took about two hours to complete. Afterwards, firecrackers were lit to mark the joyous occasion, and incense papers were burned for the ancestors and gods.

After this formal ceremony, individual lineage members including men, women and children strolled into the ancestral house and offered their own prayers to the ancestors. The ceremony had also attracted many villagers, who displayed a great curiosity, and some of them went in to investigate while others watched from outside. Those who visited the ancestral house were invited to a bowl of noodles, while the lineage members were invited to a luncheon feast. The feast concluded the consecration ceremony, but the ancestral house remained open for the whole day, allowing members and non-members alike to visit and witness the restored ancestral house. It was a proud day for the lineage members.

In recent years, many Singapore Ke lineage-members have planned their visits to Anxi to coincide with communal ancestor worship. Such occasions provide them with a legitimate excuse to visit the ancestral village. On such occasions, younger members accompanied their elderly parents for a visit. In traditional China communal ancestor worship was the responsibility of male elders, but this is not so today, and women have become important participants - in fact, female members of the Ke lineage are often the main participants in communal ancestor worship.

It is the case that Singapore lineage members are given priority treatment when it comes to ancestor worship. One local lineage member said,

"We are host and they [Singapore kin] are guests, so they should be invited to worship the ancestors communally". Another commented that the Singapore kin have priority because "we must know our behaviour, they have come all the way from Singapore, so it is only right that they are given priority to worship our ancestors as they only come, at most, once or twice a year. We can always worship them on other occasions, as they only come, at the most, once or twice a year. There is no need to fight with them over this". A third villager suggested that "the Singapore Chinese are very enthusiastic about cultural and religious activities. They are firm believers and participants. That is why they are prepared to travel all the way back to Anxi for such activities. And they are willing to contribute substantially to these kinds of religious activities. If they pay so much for the celebration, then, would it not be right for us to stop them from communally worshipping our ancestors".

Women, including married and unmarried daughters, and younger members are seen as an integral part of the lineage. One reason given for the incorporation of women and younger members from Singapore in communal ancestor worship is that Singapore women are seen to be more interested in religious activities than their male counterparts. They undertake food preparation, give offerings and instruct the preparation for the religious occasions. They also give instructions for ritual performance. The breakdown of traditional social structure under Communist rule and the changing social environment in Singapore have made it easier to incorporate women as important players in communal ancestor worship. They are also seen by some as representing their husbands, if and when the latter have not returned for the occasion. Likewise, young Singapore men and women are invited to communal worship - by incorporating them, it is hoped that they will feel part of the lineage and become interested in Anxi.

Opening the Doors of Ancestral House, *Kai Zu-zai Men,* (開祖宅門)

Individual members can also "open the doors of the ancestral house" (*kai zu-zai men*) if they want to honour and give thanks to their ancestors for their achievement and success. Several Singapore Ke have done this, one example being a man who honoured the ancestors in appreciation for the achievement of his son in attaining the highest academic qualification - in this case, a doctorate. To him and his village kin, this was an honour that would "give fragrance to the name of the ancestor and his family". "Opening the doors of the *zu-zai*" is considered an important act for sharing the achievement and joy with the lineage. This privilege is now extended to female members of the lineage after much negotiation between the Singapore and the Anxi elders. Women who have attained great achievement can now open the doors of the ancestral house. So far, there is one case and it is considered an achievement in the rural setting.

Before one is allowed to "open the doors of the *zu-zai*", both Singapore and village elders must agree on the appropriateness of the occasion. In the above-mentioned instance, having decided that the occasion warranted the opening of the doors of the *zu-zai*, the family and the son were invited to return for the ceremony. The date was set by the family concerned. With the date set, the family and the prodigal son made arrangements for opening the *zu-zai-men*. Prior to their return, village kin made preparations, bought the necessary religious paraphernalia, had a plaque with the name of the son and his academic achievement prepared and arranged for a feast. Invitations to all lineage members were issued.

By staging various religious functions, whether *xie-zu-juan-ding* or *kai-zu-zai-men*, the lineage is expressing its presence and social dominance vis-à-vis other lineages in Anxi. Through these religious activities the sense of lineage identity, which was hidden and buried prior to the reform years, is recreated and articulated openly. One lineage member said, "It is good to have a *zu-zai* and that we can identify with it". Another felt that "It is good that the Singapore Chinese and we, the Anxi people, are able to identify our ancestors again. It makes us feel like one people".

When wealth and success have become part of the social fabric of emigrant villages, then other criteria are needed to measure the social status of these emigrant villages and to differentiate them from one another. The old fashion criterion of knowledge, the production of scholar-literati in the Confucian sense, has now become equal to, if not more important than, material wealth. Similarly, becoming an official now has more appeal than before.[5] Such recognition can only elevate the status of one's lineage in competition with others. In the words of one, "not every emigrant village could produce a doctor, *bo-shi* (博士)".

Meritorious Deeds, *Gong-De* for Ancestors: The Rite of Inclusion

Among Chinese, disposing of the dead in a ritually correct manner is imperative for the dead to become transformed into ancestors. The passage from death to ancestor status involves various stages: cleansing the body of the dead, mourning, funerary, performing meritorious deeds, *gong-de* (公德), burial and ancestor worship. The performance of these ritual stages allows the dead to move from being a dead person, to being a spirit and finally to becoming an ancestor. The transition from one stage to another can be regarded as a rite of passage. Van Gennep defines rites of passage as "rites which accompany every change of place, state, social position and age" (Van

Gennep cited in Turner, 1969:94). These are transitional stages which are "marked by three phases: separation, margin and aggregation" (ibid: 94). In the case of the dead, the dead person is separated from the living. Its soul is split into two parts, *hun* (魂) and *po* (魄). The *hun* part which is imbued with *yang qi* (陽氣), or *yang* energies, moves into the heavenly realm, while the *po,* which is imbued with *yin qi* (陰氣), or *yin* energies, moves downwards to the netherworld, *yin-jian*. Here it undergoes various stages of punishment, according to its karma, as it gradually moves through the ten gates of the netherworld. This is the stage of separation. At this stage, the soul is in a liminal stage, "between and betwixt" (Turner, 1969: 95) - it is a wandering spirit in a state of limbo which has yet to find a permanent home either in the netherworld or in the heavenly world. Only after passing through the ten gates of Hades does the soul finally come to rest. This is the phase of aggregation, when the spirit is reintegrated within the cosmological world, re-emerging as an ancestor to the living and as a spirit with a permanent abode in the other realm. It is no longer a wandering ghost nor is it in a state of transience. Its permanent ancestral status is recognised through the acts of ancestor worship, conducted by its descendants.

In Anxi, the Communist policy of simple burial rites led to burial without the death rituals that Chinese have traditionally seen as essential for the dead to be transformed into ancestors. Death rituals were secularised and simplified, and cremation became common, as ground burials were considered to take up valuable space and resources (Whyte, 1988: 289-316). After the 1978 reform and the liberalisation of religious practices, visiting *qiao-qing* and village kin reinstated several after-burial rituals to provide for the material and spiritual needs of their ancestors. The *qiao-qing* consciously reinstated the rites of *gong-de* and select a geomantically aligned burial ground, *feng-shui-di* to complete the mourning process, and performing rituals for the dead has now become important in village life, as many of the dead had not been given proper burial during the previous period, or had had their graves exhumed. Since the 1980s, *gong-de* and *xie-zu* (謝祖) have become the main preoccupations of many Singapore Chinese and their village kin, and a booming cottage industry has grown up specialising in catering for the material needs of the dead.

In my survey, I found that a majority of the households, and particularly those with Singapore connections, have conducted *gong-de* for their dead ancestors during the eighties and nineties. In 1994 and 1995 there was a rush to perform *gong-de* among members of the Ke lineage, who all wanted their ancestors to be included in the lineage genealogy. In 1995, the lineage started to "mend the genealogy", *xiu-pu* (修譜). It was anticipated that the new entry of names into the lineage genealogy, *zu-pu* would be completed by mid-1996, and the *xie-zu-juan-ding* ceremony was scheduled for the tenth lunar month of 1996. I was told that only those ancestors that have been given a *gong-de* could be included as *bone fide* ancestors in the genealogy. Hence, members whose ancestors have not been given *gong-de* felt obligated to perform the rite or be shut out of the lineage forever. Exclusion from the genealogy would leave a gap in the individual family tree, thereby sabotaging their descendants' attempts to rediscover their own social identity.

What is *gong-de*? Literally speaking, it is "public virtues and morality", "meritorious deeds". The origin of such a ritual can perhaps be traced to a combination of Buddhist and folk religious beliefs. There are various interpretations of its origins and its ritual content. However, among the Singapore Chinese, the Buddhist interpretation of karma and merit-making has influenced the understanding of this ritual,[6] although both the villagers and their Singapore *qiao-qing* find it hard to provide me with a satisfactory explanation. Orthopraxy here seems to be more important than the ideological intrigue of orthodoxy.[7]

At any rate, for villagers and *qiao-qing* alike, *gong-de* is essential for their ancestors for various reasons. First, it is the ritual, which provides merit to the dead. This is the Buddhist notion that the transfer of merit to the dead can make up for the deceased's bad karma and provide the dead with the energy to move up from the underworld to other planes of existence.[8] Some Singapore Ke are able to explain this to me. Unlike the Buddhist transfer of merit, however, *gong-de* is also performed to inform the relevant gods of the virtues of the dead. By telling the gods of their achievement, the dead can be elevated to various statuses within the religious hierarchy, at the apex of which the dead, because of their virtues, become deified as godly beings. At the base of the hierarchy, the evil of the dead is rightly punished. *Gong-de* is thus also a rite of redemption, whereby the wrongdoing of the dead can be redeemed through the efforts of the living, so that the deads eventually become ancestors.

Secondly, *gong-de* is a rite of transition, which allows the dead to advance from the status of "dead person" to that of ancestor. The majority of the informants are aware of this function. They told me that the dead, like the living, have wants and needs in the netherworld, and therefore need various resources - including material goods such as a spirit/soul house, *ling-wu,* or *ling-chu* [H] (靈屋) - are necessary to keep the ancestors from becoming "hungry ghosts" and to help them live through the required period in the netherworld. Further rites are then required to install them permanently as ancestors. In this sense, the dead is treated according to what Ahern (1981) said about the similarities between the worlds of the dead and of the living. To this group of Chinese, *gong-de* is the last major rite that needs to be performed for the dead, without which the cycle of death and rebirth would be incomplete.

Third, *gong-de* is a rite of inclusion whereby the dead ancestors are incorporated into the wider lineage community, allowing the dead and the living to co-exist. In this especially important rite the dead are formally invited to become part of the lineage and are honoured in a communal manner with a position in the ancestral house and individually within the family's domestic altar.

The rite of *gong-de* is thus an essential rite of passage, which serves to bring ancestors in the lineage structure, and failure to perform it will exclude them from the lineage. It allows the dead as "wandering spirits" to be transformed into ancestors. These ancestors would be recorded in the genealogy.

In Anxi villages, *gong-de* is performed by both the Singapore Chinese and their village kin for their closest relatives, such as grandparents, parents, siblings and at times, parents' siblings. It might also be performed for those who died in Singapore but who in life continued to regard themselves as part of the home village. Many of the *gong-de* performed in recent years has been for those who had died over the previous decade or two as, for political reasons, the rite was not conducted for some forty years. By reviving *gong-de*, lineage members rethink their relationships with the dead, and this has revived an interest in Chinese cosmology.

The rite consists of a series of rituals performed over a period of three to five days, depending on the family. The first ritual is usually the *yin-hun* ceremony, and the last is the situating and positioning of the ancestors, *an-we* (安位) through which he or she is given a permanent home. In most households, the ancestral tablet and ancestral altar is prepared beforehand within the household; at the end of the *gong-de* rite the soul of the ancestor, captured within the ancestral tablet, is placed on the ancestral altar, his/her final and permanent resting-place. Each day, two to seven services are performed for the ancestors. The ritual performances on the first and last days involve the participation of all kin, while those in between are performed by the monks or priests and the immediate family members for the dead. Most family would request three to five services for their dead ancestors, which are considered as adequate and sufficiently ostentatious for the occasion.

During the rites, mourners are required to perform as directed by the monks or priests. This involves moving around in the confined space, directing the soul back to the village and to the home where it will reside as an ancestor.

The rite of passage over the bridge of no return and through the ten hell gates rescues the "soul" of the dead from the netherworld by directing it to the ancestral spirit world, the *yin-hun* (引魂). During this rite, either Buddhist monks or Daoist priests (the Singapore Chinese prefer Buddhist monks) direct the eldest male descendent (who carries the incense urn, or *xiang-lu* (香爐)) to carry the *yin-hun* streamer, which shows the soul of the ancestor where to go. The eldest male is followed by the rest of the family.

For this ceremony a family usually employs three, five or seven Buddhist monks, usually from the Qing Shui Yuan Temple; the number depends on the amount the family is willing to spend. The charge for Buddhist monks is higher than for Daoist priests. The main reason given for the Singaporean preference for Buddhist monks is that they are better-trained and are full time religious personnel with some knowledge of Buddhist liturgy, able to recite the variety of sutras required on the occasion. Daoist priests, on the other hand, are perceived to have a different type of training and to be suited for religious functions other than the care of the dead ancestors.

The *ling-wu* prepared for the deceased in this ceremony is a two- to three-storey paper house that is beautifully decorated with the intricate details which might be used in the house of a living person. Although the *ling-wu* is shaped in the traditional style, it is accompanied by numerous items required for modern living, such as a motor car, a television, a video cassette recorder, etc.; as well as maids, paper money, chests of gold and silver ingots, incense sticks and other religious paraphernalia. All these items are made of paper.

During the ceremonial period, an opera or puppet troupe may be invited to perform for the dead and the living.

Mourners were traditionally required to dress in proper mourning attire, which includes mourning clothing made of coarse hemp material and a headdress made of similar material. Presently, however, both Singaporeans and villagers simplify the attire. Mourners now wear their own clothing, with a thin hemp overdress over it. Grandchildren are required to dress in blue: they now dress in blue tee shirts and navy blue pants.

At the end of the *gong-de* a feast is given for all lineage members; by attending the feast, the members accept the dead as part of the lineage structure, completing the process of inclusion and allowing for emotional closure to take place.

The cost of performing a *gong-de* ranges from several thousand to over twenty thousand RMB. This cost includes all the religious paraphernalia, the spirit/soul house, *ling-wu*, also known as the grand house, *da-wu* (大屋), the services of the monks or priests, service money to participating kin, food, drinks and all meals for the monks and Singapore and village kin. If the *gong-de* is an elaborate one, with five to seven services a day, the cost for the monks goes up considerably, often by several thousand Rmb. Higher-quality *ling-wu* and religious paraphernalia may also add to the cost, and an opera or puppet performance, if held, will add another several thousand Rmb. The final feast is a must and costs several thousand Rmb. A budget of ten to fifteen thousand Rmb is a thus a moderate budget for a *gong-de* ceremony. For most Singapore Chinese, they would spend at least ten to twenty thousand RMB for a sufficiently grand gong-de to impress the village kin.

A Case Example of *Gong-de* Performance

In 1995, the Chiu family in Singapore decided to hold *gong-de* ritual for four of Mr. Chiu's ancestors - his father, mother, grandfather and grandmother. Discussions were then held between Singaporeans and villagers, and the tenth lunar month of that year was set aside for the ritual. Several family members from the Singapore side, including Mr. Chiu's mother, second son, eldest daughter and eldest daughter-in-law, would be the representatives from the Singapore family. From the village, the next of kin included Mr. Chiu's eldest sister and her family, the family of his deceased sister and an assortment of distant relatives. Chiu himself was in ill health and did not attend the ritual.

There are two main stages in this ritual performance namely the preparatory and religious stages.

Preparation

After deciding on the date, the Singapore and village kin discussed the scale and elaborateness of the occasion. They decided to have a three-day service and requested Buddhist monks to perform seven ritual sessions each day. They wanted the *gong-de* performance to be sufficiently grand to impress the villagers with their proper treatment of their ancestors.

Having decided on this, the villagers prepared all the necessary items for the occasion; the Singapore Chinese would send money. The initial amount sent was 20,000 Rmb.

The usual site for *gong-de* is the family residence. In most cases, this means the *lao-jia*, but for the Chiu family it was a modern three-storey building. They thus erected a covered canopy for the spirit/soul house on a vacant piece of land adjoining their building. The building provided shelter for the mourners during the ritual performance.

A village kinsman arranged for the purchase of the required religious items by placing orders for the *ling-wu* and quantities of incense, joss papers, candles and other items. Instructions were given for the size and elaborateness of the *ling-wu*: a three-storey building constructed in the traditional Chinese architectural design. The *ling-wu* came with a number of houseboys and maids, and modern apparatus such as a television, a car, a videocassette recorder, a bicycles etc. All the items were made of colourful foil and paper. The *ling-wu* cost 3000 Rmb. Two big treasure chests, large candles, large quantities of a variety of joss papers (for the dead, the gods and the spirits) and incense sticks were also ordered, to be brought to the site a day or two in advance. This religious paraphernalia had to be ordered well in advance because of the large quantities required. Four ancestral tablets inscribed with the names of the ancestors were also prepared.

The family, being Buddhist, requested Buddhist monks instead of Daoist priests for the occasion, and these were arranged for through the chief monk at Qing Shui Yuan Temple. Five monks were hired, to ensure that the place would be filled with "heat and noise", re-nuan (熱鬧). The cost for the monks for three days (seven sessions per day) was 2,800 Rmb. This was considered a bargain by the Singaporeans, as, in Singapore, the same service would cost a minimum of 40,000 Rmb. Monks need to be booked in advance, as the revival of religious activities in village China has brought about an increase in the demand for religious personnel, and there is now a general shortage of monks for various religious functions.

A restaurant was asked to cater lunch and dinner for the three days. About seven tables were set for the participants at 250 Rmb each, with another, vegetarian one for the monks at 270 Rmb. On the final day, more elaborate food was provided, and each table cost 310 Rmb. The food was cooked in the restaurant and brought to the ceremonial site. The restaurant also provided tables and chairs.

All village kin related to the family (including distant ones) were informed of the event and were invited to participate. Every participant was given a sum of money to be part of the mourning team. This is the so-called affinity money, jie-yuan-qian (結緣錢) for the purpose of establishing relationship with the dead. Anthropologically speaking, this is one way to ensure a good turn-out of mourners, the family being concerned to ensure that there would be a large crowd, thereby adding prestige to the occasion, as a big group of mourners performing ritual weeping is a testimony to the wealth and status of the family. This reflected on the social status of the Singapore Chinese, in that not only their kin but also other villagers were able to participate in the performance of the ritual.

Several days before the actual ceremony, a temporary canvas canopy was erected. Two days before the performance, the ling-wu arrived and was placed in position, with a large table set up in front on which were placed the four ancestral tablets that were made for the occasion. In front of the tablets were placed a set of each of the following daily items: wash basins, facial towels, tooth brushes and mugs, and clothing. Fruits, rice cakes, one pig's head, poultry and dried food were also placed on the table as general offerings. An incense urn holding lit incense sticks and two large lit candles were placed for the ancestors. In the family's house, the altar to the Buddhist deities and the ancestral tablets were cleaned. Fruits and dried vegetarian food were offered to the deities and ancestors.

The Singaporeans arrived in the village two days before the ceremony. On arrival, they were shown the preparations and were informed of the ritual itinerary. Singapore women would then supervise the preparation of ritual food for the ancestors.

Gong-de Rites

On the first day of the *gong-de*, at about four o'clock in the morning, the household awakened and prepared for the occasion. After a quick breakfast, family members within the household dressed in the appropriate coloured attire. Village kin arrived in the house and also readied themselves for the ritual acts. Close kin dressed with a hemp overdress; other, more distant kin and friends dressed in their daily attire with a piece of coloured cloth, the size of a 2-inch square pinned to the sleeve. This signified the social distance of these kin to the dead ancestors according to the five-grain, *wu-ke* (五殻) categorisation. The monks arrived at the appointed time and were offered a simple vegetarian meal.

All participating members assembled in the shrine hall inside the house. The beating of a gong by a monk signalled the start of the *gong-de*. The monks then began to recite a Buddhist sutra. The principal mourners from Singapore were instructed to recite the Buddhist prayers, after which the chief principal mourner recited a *cho-yuan* (湊文), or petition seeking permission from the Buddhist deities to conduct the rite of *gong-de*.

After preliminary prayers, the entourage then made its way to the head of the Anxi River, about half an hour's walk away, and began the rite of directing the ancestral souls *yin-hun* to the *ling-wu* site, which would be their temporary home for three days. The monks led the way, followed by the chief male mourner carrying the *yin-hun* streamer. He was followed by other kin.

By the riverside, the monks recited prayers inviting the souls of the dead ancestors to rise and follow them home to their rightful place. After the third invitation by prayers, a close kin threw a pair of wooden cups, *mu-bei* to see if the ancestors agreed to be led home by the mourners. Before the start of this journey home, however, the ancestral spirits had to be ritually cleansed and to present themselves in a purified form, for as wandering souls they were polluting and dangerous. They were thus told to "take a bath", and a straw mat rolled into a cylinder was placed upright on the ground to serve as a temporary bathroom for the purpose. The monks then recited prayers, which purified and cleansed the ancestral spirits. After this spiritual cleansing, the ancestral spirits and the entourage journeyed to the *ling-wu*.

On arrival at the *ling-wu*, a charm (*fu*) was burned on the gong to signal the start of the rite of ushering the ancestral spirits and transforming them into ancestors. The monks then recited several types of prayers, after which the tablets of the ancestors were dotted with red ink, symbolising the taking of position by the ancestral spirits in the tablets. This dotting was witnessed by all thirteen local deities where they were specifically invited by the monks to witness this occasion. Their names had been written on paper tablets placed at the site of the *ling-wu* during the preparatory stage. These thirteen were to act as guardians and witnesses. They were given offerings and invoked at each session by the monks. Apart from these occasions, these deities resided in their own temples scattered throughout the district.

During each of the seven daily ritual sessions, a different Buddhist text was recited, including the Diamond Sutra, *Jin-Kang-Jing* (金鋼經); Kistagarbha Sutra, *Di-Chang-Wang-Jing,* (地藏王經), Amitabha Sutra, *O-mi-to-jing,* (阿彌陀經), Heart Sutra, *Xin-Jing,* (心經), Lotus Sutra, *Lien-Hua-Jing,* (蓮華經) and Water Sutra, *Shui-Chan-Fa-Jing,* (水懺法經). During each ritual session, the monks led the mourners from the Buddhist shrine hall at the home to the *ling-wu*, the principal male mourner carrying incense and four bamboo sticks bundled together, to represent the four ancestral souls. This symbolised the carrying of the Buddhist light to the dead where the flame is used to light up the *ling-wu*. The Buddhist deities were also called upon to witness this ritual service for the dead. Through recitation of the Buddhist sutras, the living imparted good merits to the dead ancestors in an attempt to help the dead to reduce their store of bad karma and increase their good karma. The motive text, *biao-wen,* (表文) was read, making the objectives of the *gong-de* known to the Buddhist deities and local gods. This text was carried by a second mourner from the Buddhist shrine to the *ling-wu* and placed on the table in the shrine, to be burned at the end of the ceremony.

During the first session of the first day, the mourners were told to offer personal effects to the dead. Watches and jewellery worn by the Singapore descendants were taken and placed on a tray as offerings; these were returned to the mourners at the end of the session, they are symbolic expressions of one's feelings towards the dead.

During each daily ritual session, the monks led the mourners from the shrine hall to the *ling-wu*, continuing the sutra recitation throughout the journey. When they reached the *ling-wu* they assembled in front of it, with the principal mourners and other kin behind them. The rite of *zhou-jin*, aimed at increasing good merits for the ancestral spirits, then began. A Buddhist sutra was recited, during which the monks led the mourners, circling around the *ling-wu*. A second ritual act, *nian-shou*, followed, during which the names of the four ancestors were recited, and they were informed of the merits imparted to them. At the end of the ceremony this list of merits would be read out aloud and would be burned to inform all deities of the dead's achievement. During the recitation, mourners were required to kneel and pay obeisance to the ancestors. Towards the end of the ritual, offerings of wine as libation was made to the ancestors. The wine was poured into a basin where a young pine sapling was planted, signifying the rebirth of the ancestral spirits as ancestors. Each kin offered libations to the ancestors. This is the rite *dian-xie*. After the libations, the mourners were instructed to kneel three times, after which the monks led them back to the shrine hall, concluding the ritual session.

The ritual was repeated seven times daily, with an hour of rest in between, so that a total of twenty-one ritual sessions were conducted over the 3-day period. On the final session of the third day, the principal male mourner presented a pair of lanterns to the attending married daughters and married granddaughters, who offered their merits to the ancestors. These were "longevity lanterns", *chang-shou-deng*, (長壽燈), the recipients of which are blessed with eternal life and prosperity. The final act was to seek permission, through *mu-bei*, from the Buddhist deities to offer all material goods and treasures to the ancestors.

The final session had begun after dinner and had ended at about 10 PM. Afterwards, the *ling-wu*, chests of gold and silver ingots, large quantities of paper money, and all the ritual paraphernalia made of paper and the bamboo sticks, streamers, and clothing that were for the ancestors, were all burned in a bonfire. The ancestral tablets were taken and placed on the ancestral altar in the shrine hall, the permanent resting-place for the ancestors.

From now on, the ancestral spirits would be proper family ancestors, to be worshipped as such. Before the *gong-de* they had been wandering spirits, dissatisfied and full of anger, polluted and unclean, barred from entering the household by the guardian gods because of their status. Now cleansed, ritually transformed and given a permanent home, they had become proper family ancestors to be worshipped, whose task was to protect and bless the family with good fortune and wealth.

For three days, the mourners, village kin and friends participating in the *gong-de* had been provided with lunch and dinner. The gong-de ceremony is considered as a family affair and only members of the Ke lineage and some close friends were invited. Other surname groups usually stood as bystanders and watched the ritual performance. The gong-de was not considered a "red" occasion, as death is a polluting event, and those associated with it can become polluted too. Those who participated were given good luck charms - usually, red thread would be given to participants. In addition, the participants were given money. Those who had accompanied the principal mourners to and from the river during the *yin-hun* rite were given 20 Rmb, while those who had participated in the various sessions and offered incense to the ancestors were given 30 Rmb each day. The closer village kin were given 60 Rmb each per day. These were given at the end of the final session each night. Often, the last session ended at around 10 or 11 each night.

Throughout the day, during and in between the ritual sessions, visitors came and paid their respect to the ancestors, engaged in conversation with the mourners and showed their support, and received cakes, biscuits, fruits, nuts and candy. Men (but not women) were also served beer and offered cigarettes, the total cost of which amounted to over 5,000 Rmb. The total cost for the three-day *gong-de* ritual came to 50,000 Rmb.

Resiting Burial Grounds, *Feng-Shui-Di*

Other concerns of the Singapore Chinese have been to search for their ancestral graves and to rebuild the burial sites of their ancestors. The locals call this "making *feng-shui*" (做風水). The Cultural Revolution had destroyed many graves and had converted burial sites into agricultural lands; the few sites, which had not been destroyed, were those on the hillsides. For most Chinese, maintaining their ancestral graves, *feng-shui-di* (風水地), is important, and it would have been an extreme act of unfilial-ness not to reconstruct an ancestral grave. It is also important to Singapore Chinese to have an ancestral grave sited in a good *feng-shui* location to bring good fortune to all descendants.[9]

Since reform, Singapore Chinese have returned to Anxi to restore their ancestral graves. Those left in ruins for the past forty years have now been repaired and restored, and regular maintenance has made them clean and tidy. It is now possible to spot these ancestral graves that dot the paddy fields from a distance, as there is no need now to hide them in tall grass, and many villagers are now proud to display their ancestral graves publicly.

What about ancestral graves that were destroyed, and the land given to different families for cultivation? This is a situation that has created much dissatisfaction among overseas Chinese. While some families have been able to buy back original gravesites and to restore ancestral graves, others have not been so fortunate. These latter may apply for new sites from the local government. Some Singapore Chinese have applied for burial sites from the *zhen* government and have been able to rebuild their ancestral grounds.

Competition for Feng-Shui-Di

Competition for good *feng-shui* burial sites is keen. Most persons are willing to search for a good *feng-shui* site and pay a relatively high price for it. Usually this involves buying certain hilly sites from their owners, whether these are villagers or district government. In most cases this is a relatively straightforward transaction.

Although lineage members have been known to fight for the same *feng-shui* site, this was often seen as unacceptable and was discouraged. It was very rare for a member of a lineage to buy another member's *feng-shui* site, especially when an ancestral grave was already in place. There was such a case in Peng Lai District, however, which created much rivalry, tension and ill feeling between the two families involved. The case involved two

Singapore families with village kin. The son of Family A had purchased the ancestral burial site of a member of Family B without his knowledge, the transaction having taken place between the son of Family A and the married daughter of Family B, who had agreed to the sale. Having purchased the land, the son of Family A constructed their house there, and only later did the son of Family B know of it. Within the traditional Chinese lineage, all land had been inherited by sons, and married daughters had had no rights to land inheritance, nor did they have say in the disposal of any land, including ritual and burial sites. Even today, married daughters are considered to belong to their husbands' families and therefore do not have rights to make decisions regarding the disposal of the land of their natal families. In this case, the married daughter was seen as having overstepped her authority when she sold the ancestral burial site to Family A without informing the living brother in Singapore, while the son of Family A was regarded by fellow lineage members as having behaved in an ungentleman fashion, failing to observe lineage rules and obtaining the burial site by devious methods.

There is thus a conflict between the social expectation of kin relations on the one hand and the modern rule of competition on the other. *Feng-shui* land is a scarce commodity and, according to the modern individualistic ethic, those with the means might compete in purchasing it, for personal gain. However, among local lineage members in Peng Lai, such modern rules of competition continue to be inapplicable to the acquisition of ancestral burial sites. The above case thus has aroused much ill feeling and discontentment among lineage members, who viewed it with grave concern, and it was seen as unethical and devoid of social gallantry for lineage members to commit such acts. The operation of lineage rules can only be effective if all members subscribe to them - otherwise, they fall apart.

The case also involved "face". By taking away the ancestral site, Family A was not giving face to Family B - behaviour detrimental to lineage solidarity. However, the village elders did not dare to intervene, as the case involved a Singapore person, aggressive and wealthy. Although the Singapore elders "had a word" with him, they could do nothing about it. The honourable thing would be for Family A to return the land to Family B, but this was not done. For the present, there continues to be a latent tension between the two families, although they continue to be polite to each other.

It has become a duty for the Singapore descendants to repair and restore the *feng-shui* gravesite to its former glory. Like the ancestral house where the ancestor's yang spirit resides, the ancestral grave is where the yin-spirit of the ancestor comes to rest and is a visible reminder of one's immediate ancestors and of the benefits derived from them. For the villagers, taking care of the gravesite is also testimony of filial piety and of that of the overseas Chinese, whom they feel to have prospered as a result of the good *feng-shui* of the ancestors. In this connection the phrase: *fu-gui-bu-li-zu* (富貴不離祖), "wealth is not divorced from ancestors", was quoted to me - an argument indicating that the overseas Chinese should not neglect their home villages and their lineage members within it.

Ancestor Worship by Singapore Chinese

Ancestor worship is commonly conducted in Singapore by the majority of the Chinese. Within most Chinese households, there is an altar for the ancestral tablets of the immediate ancestors, and the offerings of incense to the ancestors are a daily routine. On festival and religious occasions as well as on the death anniversary of the immediate ancestors, offerings of food, incense and paper money are made to these ancestors. In recent years, family members have placed some ancestral tablets in temples, where family members go to make their offerings. Ancestors and ancestor worship continue to occupy a prominent central position in the Chinese community in Singapore.

Our survey shows that the Singapore Chinese concern for their ancestors and their practice of ancestor worship stretch back to their ancestral villages, and that the majority of the Singapore Chinese are aware of the existence of ancestral houses and the practice of communal ancestor worship in their home villages in Anxi. The ancestral house in Anxi is a reminder of their origins and allows their ancestors to be remembered and worshipped in a collective manner. The house is also a place where their future descendants can go in search of their roots. One Singapore-born second generation Chinese expressed this in the following way:

> It is important to have an ancestral home so that we are reminded of our ancestors, of the sacrifice they have made in order that we have our present position. Without them taking the risks, developing the place, the lineage, and eventually allowing some to emigrate overseas, we might still be stuck in Anxi and not in Singapore. It is this unyielding ancestral spirit that we should not forget.

These Chinese can be divided into three categories: the first consisting of those who emigrated as adults to Singapore; the second, of those who emigrated as children; and the third, of Singapore-born with Anxi-born grandparents and parents. The responses of these three groups concerning their ancestors and ancestor worship allow us to understand their sentiments, as well as the tensions that arise as a result of inter-generation attitudinal differences.

Among the first and second groups of Chinese, worship of the immediate ancestors is the most important duty, which they perform conscientiously. Without fail, there is an altar to the ancestors within their domestic households, where daily offerings of incense are carried out by the women. On festive occasions and the death anniversaries of immediate ancestors, offerings of incense, joss paper and food are made. On the Qing Ming and Chung Yang Festivals, the sweeping of ancestral graves and the offering of food and religious items are standard practice. Most of this category does not fail to visit the gravesites, where offerings are usually given at the gravesite, as well as within the household.

Religious practices in Singapore have taken new forms and the new trend is to place ancestral tablets in temples, where ritual offerings continued to be offered on festival and death-anniversary occasions. So that worship is not forgotten, the acts of worship are now often entrusted to the monks and nuns in the temple.

These first-generation migrants fully support the reconstruction of *zu-zai* in Anxi, and either they or their spouses have contributed to it. The reconstruction, carried out and completed in the late 1980s, were considered the most important activity that they had done for their ancestral village. One informant commented: "How can we let the *zu-zai* become broken down and not care about it? Even if we have to save on our eating, we should contribute to help with the reconstruction. It is the house of our ancestors. So, it is our ancestral home".

Apart from the lineage ancestral house, several wealthy Singapore Chinese have also converted their *lao-jia* into family ancestral houses. As the *qiaoxiang* become wealthier and as the villagers move to live in new modern buildings, the *lao-jia* becomes vacant, and many are now uninhabited and decaying. Given the fact that these are now surplus housing, some of the wealthier Singaporeans have decided to turn them into sacred spaces solely for the use of their immediate families - an action which symbolises the relatively high status of these families. This has not been criticised by the official cadres, partly because they do not want to offend the Singapore Chinese and partly because their status as surplus housing makes such use more justifiable. By turning them into family ancestral houses, the buildings will be maintained in good condition. Many of the younger villagers prefer not to live in them if they can avoid it as the *lao-jia* is considered old style even though some are new and equipped with modern amenities. Some of the *lao-jia* are rented out to poorer villagers and outsiders who lived in Peng Lai district. But many are left vacant. There is a case where a *lao-jia* with all the various extensions amounted to a 73-room building but is only inhabited by the elderly parents of the family. The children have all moved out either to cities and towns. Those living in the district has also moved to live in the modern three-storey building.

To worship their ancestors in Anxi has become an important rite of passage for first-generation migrants, as it reincorporates them into the lineage structure and reintroduces them into their home villages. It is thus of great importance, and, since reform, the large majority of them have made visits to their ancestral villages to perform communal ancestor worship in the lineage ancestral house. They time their visits to coincide with these activities, and it is these activities that encourage them to return for visits, without which many feel less inclined to visit, stating that they would become very bored if there were nothing to do while they were in the village. The communal religious activities allow them to be meaningfully occupied.

As has been discussed, the Singapore Chinese, together with the village elders, decide on the scope of ceremonies and pay most of the costs, although, at present, some of the wealthier village kin also contribute financially.

Because of the heavy involvement of the Singaporeans and the wealthy villagers with ancestor worship and all types of village religious activities, the villagers regard the practitioners as "primarily interested in religious activities", and some label them as "being superstitious", mi-xin-de (迷信的). This label is especially given to the Singapore women who occupy their time in the village with all sorts of religious activities.

Among the third group, the second and third generation Singapore Chinese, a fairly large number feel the need to know something of their ancestors - at least of their great-grandparents, grandparents and parents. They seek to fill in their family genealogies. For some of them, it is to answer their children's questions that they begin to search for knowledge of the ancestral home and their grandparents. Some are interested in reconstructing the social history of their immediate families - migration experiences, early life in Singapore, difficulties and sufferings, and success. Others are less ambitious, wanting only to know a little history about their ancestors. Yet many have visited their ancestral villages, and some have gone back several times.

All in this group are aware that their parents have contributed some money to the reconstruction of the lineage ancestral house, and they have supported this. Although they have not contributed themselves, they all express their willingness to do so if asked.

For this group, too, the ancestral house serves as a visible reminder. For some, it is a reminder of their good fortune. These are some of the responses:

> Anxi people used to be very poor and because of this, we had very low status in comparison with other lineages in Singapore. Some members used to hide their origin. But today, thanks to our ancestors, the Singapore Anxi people have become rather prosperous and the lineage has elevated its status to

become one of the top eight lineages in Singapore. Not only do we no longer hide our origin, we are now proud of it. In fact, some non-Anxi people try to become one of us.

Even though we are Singapore born and consider ourselves Singaporean ... especially now that we are relatively well off, we should not completely ignore our ancestral root. The Chinese saying "wealth should not be divorced from ancestors" (*fu-gui-bu-li-zu*) is very true. Without our ancestors, there will be no us and thus, no wealth. Thus, wealth comes from the blessings of our ancestors. If this is so, we should not forget our ancestors, for by forgetting them we would undermine future wealth.

There is also a small group of this third category and they are indifferent to the construction of the ancestral house. They express no sentiments for it or the ancestral village, which they have never visited. To them, Singapore is their home and the ancestral village and ancestral house hold no meaning. Neither do they wish to participate in communal ancestor worship, nor do they see the need to return for visits. However, they do not prevent their parents or siblings from visiting and participating in village activities, as they recognise that their parents and others continue to harbour sentiments towards the ancestral home.

Ancestor Worship by Village Kin

Ancestor worship was banned in China until very recently. During the early days of Communism, some families continued to perform ancestor worship secretly behind close doors, while others modified ancestor worship and changed it into a ritual-less reverence, as recommended by the Communist regime. It was only in the eighties that the *qiaoxiang* began to stage communal ancestor worship and individual families to worship to their immediate ancestors.

Among the villagers, there was overwhelming support for the reconstruction of the ancestral houses, and they were very pleased that the Singapore Chinese contributed to the total cost of construction as, given their financial situation, they could never afford it - each lineage household would have had to contribute two to three hundred Rmb, and this was (and still is) a hefty sum for the villagers. As we have seen, however, the villagers were primarily responsible for the actual work.

In our survey, support for the reconstruction of the ancestral home was found in the following responses:

There is a need to reconstruct *zu-zai* because it is important for us to remember our ancestors, *zhor* [H] (祖) and having a lineage ancestral house (*zu-zai*) will help us to remember them. It is a place for us to memorialise, *ji-nian* [M], *ki-liem* [H], (記念) our *zhor*. It is important to understand our history and what our ancestors have done for us. Ancestor worship is important because it helps us to understand our ancestors. So, it is a good idea to reconstruct our ancestral house. Our Singapore relatives, whose roots are also from here, would be able to come here in search of their origin and history.

The continuity of a group of people is dependent on the continuity of this house. Praying to ancestors will help the younger generation to remember, *liu-lien* [H], (留念) their ancestors. It is especially important for the *hua-qiao* because this is their root and without it, it will be hard for them or their future descendants to search for their own roots and identity. Ancestor worship is important because it is a tradition and a cultural practice of our people. The ancestral house is also a symbol of our respect for our ancestors. They [*hua-qiao*] should come back and pray to them especially now that they are well off because wealth should not be divorced from our ancestors. The ancestral house would also allow us and the *hua-qiao* to recognise the significance of our common ancestors and their duty to help us.

It has now become an important focal point where Anxi people from overseas come back and pray to our ancestors. This is very important for the unity of the lineage and allows for interaction and the rekindling of kinship and social ties between them and us. Ancestor worship is an important ritual and by participating in it, they would have stronger feelings for their home.

Why should the Singapore Chinese pay for the reconstruction? What part do the ancestors play in bringing the two groups of Chinese together? The following are the attitudes of the villagers towards these two questions.

They are wealthy and we are poor. They can afford it but it would be very hard on us if we had to contribute.

They are also part of the lineage; an offshoot from us, and hence they have the obligation to do so.

They did it because they want face. Even if we want to pay, they would not have let us. They would feel insulted if we offered. They have such big egos.

This reconstruction has been good for the local economy. It provided jobs for some of us. Also, the ritual activities and their need for religious items have also helped some of us to get extra income when we supply them with the religious items. These are important [activities] to pull back some overseas money. For the sake of this money, we will participate in these activities.

The reconstruction of the ancestral houses is important to attract more Chinese overseas to visit our village, and this will prevent a break in kinship ties. It has encouraged more Chinese from Nanyang to come back. It is especially important to attract the younger Chinese back to our village. Otherwise, they would forget us completely.

It is also very good for the dead. Now, our dead ancestors can enjoy a little and have a nice house to live. This is to compensate for the lost years after the Cultural Revolution.

Others feel that by contributing to the ancestral house and performing ancestor worship, the overseas Chinese

...must have thought of the home village and our ancestors. The *zu-zai* is a way of bringing together and galvanising different sections of the lineage together. It is because of our ancestors that our people are spread to different parts of the world. Having an ancestral home will allow us to preserve our historical memory of our ancestors and to remember the different branches of our descendants overseas.

It also provides the Chinese overseas with an opportunity to search for their ancestors, thereby developing their love for their home village and family. It can also help maintain relationships and sentiments between village and Singapore kin and help us to get to know one another better.

It is important for the promotion of our lineage [vis-a-vis other lineages] and helps to unify future generations through "blood relationship". It is also good for the future of lineage and for a smooth life for all of us.

Attitudes of Official Cadres towards Ancestor Worship

In Peng Lai District, the construction of lineage ancestral houses and the performance of communal ancestor worship ceremonies have been made possible because of co-operation and support from the district and county official cadres. Since the reform years, the Singapore Chinese and the official cadres have maintained a close relationship which has facilitated the carrying out of many projects, both social and economic, without much obstruction. Most cadres see ancestral activities as significant cultural practices, especially for the district cadres, some of whom have participated in them. At an instrumental level, the concern is to encourage the flow of Chinese overseas capital into the *qiaoxiang* and other parts of Fujian. Encouraging and supporting these cultural activities are seen as important for strengthening the relationship between the Chinese overseas and the region.

Prior to reform, ancestor worship practices were considered superstitious - they were prohibited, and those who took part in them were persecuted. Today, they are construed as cultural traditions. To understand this transformation of attitude, we need to understand the roles of village cadres within the village politics.

Our survey showed village cadres to be very much part of the Singapore-*qiaoxiang* connection. Through the years, village cadres have maintained strong ties with their Singapore kin, and since the reforms they played an important role in encouraging the Singapore kin to contribute and help with village reconstruction. For the most part, they have encouraged and supported religious fairs and ancestor worship in these *qiaoxiang*. By supporting the Singapore Chinese, they hope to revive the traditional cultural practices and at the same time, create a network of *guanxi* and reciprocity. Because of the goodwill that support for ancestor worship and religious functions creates, the flow of Chinese overseas capital into these villages has helped transform the economic status of the region. The village cadres have also become important figures at both district and county levels, as the fact that they have connections and are able to encourage their Singapore kin has made them important in the eyes of the county government, who now increasingly tap into these *qiaoxiang* connections to help with county level development. In this way some village cadres have become influential in both village and county politics.

Although township (*zhen*), county (*xian*) and provincial (*shang*) cadres are openly more restrained in their support for ancestor worship and religious fairs, most will attend the activities and feast when invited by Singapore Chinese hosts, as ancestor worship and its related activities are seen as important parts of Chinese culture and thus are given official support. In relating to ancestor worship and the construction of ancestral houses, a formal response by one of these cadres was:

> It depends on how you look at this. If it is purely religious practice, then it is superstition and we would not support it. But this is the ancestral house and they are engaged in ancestor worship. This is our ancestral place and it is very important for the future generations. It is a place to remind us of our ancestors and to remember them. Through it, we will be able to foster closer relationships among our blood relatives, within the villages and with the Chinese overseas. This will also allow them to develop stronger bonds with their home village. The ancestral house is a place where we, the Chinese, search for our ancestors and roots. It is also beneficial to the lineage and provides an opportunity for the Chinese overseas to express their love for their motherland and home village. Because this is a cultural practice and not a superstition, we would support it.

At *xian* level, responses of the cadres can be divided into three types:

1. *Sentimental*, emphasising the existence of the ancestral house as a help for the Chinese overseas in searching for their cultural roots and ancestors. These responses categorise the early emigrants as a group of kinsmen who were forced to emigrate because of poverty in the villages, who should not be discriminated against by not acknowledging their present status and needs to search their roots, *luo-yeh-gui-gan*. These respondents hoped that such acts would strengthen their sentiments towards the home village.
2. *Moral*, emphasising ancestor worship activities as a concession to remind the successful and wealthy Chinese overseas not to forget their ancestral home, *fu-gui-bu-li-zu*. These respondents considered Chinese overseas as *qiao-bao*.
3. *Instrumental*, emphasising this concession that is needed to establish further contacts and *guanxi*. Such cadres hoped that the Chinese overseas would contribute money to schools and hospitals and help with infrastructure development, not only in their own ancestral village but in the county as a whole.

Table 6.1 Attitudes of Cadres Towards Ancestral House and Ancestor Worship

CADRES	AGREE	DISAGREE	DON'T KNOW	TOTAL = N
Village	29 (97%)	0	1 (3%)	30
District	17 (94%)	1 (6%)	0	18
County	41 (82%)	5 (10%)	4 (8%)	50
TOTAL	87 (89%)	6 (6%)	5 (5%)	98

Table 6.2 Reasons for Supporting Ancestor Worship by Cadres at Different Levels

CADRES	SENTIMENTAL	MORAL	INSTRUMENTAL	TOTAL=N
Village	45%	20%	35%	100% = 30
District	42%	5%	53%	100% = 18
County	15%	0%	85%	100% = 50

There is a small group of district and county cadres who feel that the Singapore Chinese have their priorities wrong. They did not agree to the reconstruction of ancestral houses and ancestor worship, but wanted the money to be used for schools and to fund educational needs so that future generations of Anxi villagers would be literate. They see ancestor worship and its related activities as a waste of money, resources and labour.

Moral Sentiments and Moral Duty

The Chinese understanding of Confucian teaching explains their attention to the moral code of behaviour. The concern here is with their place of origin, hence their emphasis on roots, *gen* (根) and ancestors, *zong* (宗). In the *Xiao-Jing*, the family, *jia* (家) constitutes the most important social institution within which an individual functions on a daily basis, and the interaction with its members is a routine part of existence. The living elders need to be respected and the dead ancestors to be revered in a ritually correct manner, *li* (禮). In our case, this means ancestor worship.

Among the Singapore Chinese, Confucian teachings of moral responsibility continues to influence the way this group of Chinese perceive their ancestors, family and lineage. To be a gentleman, *junzi* (君子), one needs not only to understand but also to articulate the value of propriety and to perform the necessary rituals. Understanding one's roots, family and lineage, and worshipping one's ancestors, are thus important means of expressing one's moral cultivation. These moral sentiments, in turn, influence the Singapore Chinese to revive the economic and socio-cultural structures of their emigrant villages.

"When drinking water, remember the source" (飲水思源). Despite the physical and social distance between the Singapore and Anxi Chinese, it is possible to argue that the Singapore Chinese continue to have strong sentiments towards their ancestral home, which is deeply embedded within their individual and collective memory. Some Singapore Chinese told me that they do not have to like or to embrace their ancestral home, but that they should not forget it. In remembering the ancestral home, many feel obligated to assist when the need arises. This is also a matter of face, as they find it embarrassing to turn down appeals for help. One typical comment is that "when the elders come to us for contributions for village projects, it is hard for us to turn it down. Somehow, it just did not seem right to say no. We usually gave whatever they asked from us. After all, it is our ancestral village".

When visiting the ancestral village and performing ancestor worship, Singapore Chinese come face to face with the social reality of village life and village poverty. Some begin to understand the restrictions and lack of opportunities within the village structure. One said, "Before visiting Anxi, we all thought that the villagers were lazy and did not want to work. After visiting

Anxi, I begin to understand that it is not because they did not want to work, but rather that there is no work for them to do. Apart from farming, there was little they could do. They also have very few leisure activities. So, among some of us, we thought that by staging religious and cultural activities, village life would be enriched".

In the present liberalised socio-political environment, many feel that they now have the opportunity to conduct ancestor worship, and complete what they previously could not do. They see the failure to conduct ancestor worship and *gong-de* "...as if something is still incomplete. We have to do it. Otherwise we would feel remorseful, *nei-jiu* (内疚)". Given their commitment, enthusiasm and willingness to pay the expenses, they have been able to encourage and revive the interests of their village kin in such activities. In so doing, the Singapore Chinese have helped to revive not only ancestor worship but also other socio-cultural and religious activities in the emigrant villages.

Sentiment has also pushed Singapore Chinese to maintain continuity with their kin in Anxi. One expresses the relationship as follows: "Our relationship is like a thin thread, it should be maintained at all cost. So that our future generation have reference to their ancestors and their source of origin. Otherwise, they would become headless". Headless here means that they could not trace their ancestral origin.

Support and Rivalry

Supporters and opponents can be differentiated by generation and educational background. Generally, it is the younger and the better educated who are less supportive, arguing that the Chinese overseas misuse their resources, which should be used for village infrastructure development and to revitalise the village economy. These opponents are in their twenties and thirties. A few school teachers in their fifties, too, do not approve of such practices but did not oppose them, feeling that the revival of ancestor worship has indirectly contributed to the social life and economy of the village and stressing the need to adopt a more flexible attitude towards their Singapore kin as, by contributing to socio-cultural and religious activities, the Singapore Chinese have also been made aware of the needs of the villages, and many have now contributed to village economic development. To these opponents, it is a matter of trading one thing for another.

The staging of communal ancestor worship and related activities has resulted in competition and rivalry for leadership roles. Those with good relations with their Singapore kin and with the appropriate skills - usually village elders, but also some younger villagers - become leaders. The *guanxi* network among lineage members is important in selecting village kin who have character and are reliable, trustworthy and able to organise the activities, as they are entrusted with money and responsibility for preparation for the communal activities and religious fairs.

In Anxi, elderly men and women with intimate knowledge of the rituals of ancestor worship are the main players in them. In this sense, the authority structure is one based on seniority and knowledge. Here, we find that village elders are able to reassert their authority in the area of ancestral rites, thereby recreating a niche for themselves. Several of the village elders have become "core members" in planning and organising communal ancestor worship and are assisted by a group of younger villagers. They worked closely together with their Singapore kin. A majority of them are in their sixties and seventies.

Understanding ancestral rites is often an important criterion to becoming an active lineage member. Those with the knowledge and skills are the ones approached by the Singaporeans to assist in such activities, and so there is competition and rivalry among the villagers to portray themselves as skilful in matters relating to ancestral rituals. By becoming actively involved in these activities, villagers can gain much social prestige and recognition, and also material and financial benefits. In an environment where the elderly are increasingly considered a burden to society, the roles played by these village elders have helped restore their self-esteem and reincorporate them as productive members of the lineage.

The relationship between Singapore and their village kin is not tension-free. When it comes to worshipping the ancestors on a communal basis, the Singapore Chinese are given priority. Invariably all the Singapore kin attending communal ancestor worship in Anxi are given priority. They all participate in communal ancestor worship irrespective of age, sex and seniority - in the front rows, carrying incense sticks and participating in the ritual acts. Among the villagers, only the elders are invited for these rituals, the younger kin being excluded. This has created dissatisfaction among some villagers, who accuse the Singapore Chinese of buying their way to the central position. One commented that, "because they contributed to this function, they are given such prominent placing in the worship. We should also be entitled to it. After all, we also have a share in the ancestor. Why should they be the prominent ones?"

Ancestor Worship as a Ritual Form and a Life Philosophy

Ancestor worship is seen important as "it allows us to express our sentiments to our parents and ancestors in a ritually correct manner". The restoration of the ancestral house has allowed lineage members to perform the ritual acts of (thanking the ancestors) *xie-zu* and (worshipping the ancestors) *bai-zu*, two important forms of ancestor worship which are done communally.

We have seen how the revival of ancestor worship in the village has materially transformed the *qiaoxiang* by enriching the calendrical cycle of activities with ritual performances and social activities and with the accompanying feasts, which have become a symbol of the relative abundance of food and the higher standard of living than that of non-emigrant villages. We have also seen that the important functions of ancestor worship include the socio-moral one of integrating the members of the family and the lineage, in a manner which dictates the roles and reinstates the positions of members within the community and which helps to bind two groups (Singaporeans and villagers) of the lineage together, re-establishes social and structural continuity among them, and   provides a historical past within which the present generation of lineage members can find ancestral and cultural roots. By engaging in correct ritual forms, *li*, each member has become a "moral person", an "honourable person", who fulfils his/her responsibilities to family and lineage and in so doing re-establishes a niche for him/herself in a society that is fast losing its traditional moral values. Participants in ancestor worship rituals have thus become champions of traditional moral and cultural values amidst the influence of modern education, modern mass media and technology.

Are we witnessing a cultural renaissance among the Chinese in this part of the world? Can we see ancestor worship as a part of a wider social process at play in East Asian societies - one in which Confucianism, in its various forms, is emerging as an important ideological and social force driving all aspects of society, from economics to politics and down to individuals and families? Ancestor worship, as a transcendental ritual form of Confucianism, could thus be seen as an important socio-religious force galvanising members of a lineage together and resulting in an interlocking social network where moral and social capitals have to be handed out periodically to establish one's honour and morality. Such a conception would indicate the emergence of a moral economy and would explain the philanthropic activities of the Singapore Chinese in their ancestral villages.

In witnessing the emergence of a kind of cultural renaissance, one central issue of concern is that of cultural authenticity. To what extent are the rituals subjected to varying forces that influence and change their contents and meanings? Our findings show that the ancestral rituals practised today in the village are an interactive product of villagers and Singaporeans, with the level of authenticity therefore subject to mutual negotiation. Old rituals are reproduced, simplified or elaborated and new ones invented to suit the occasions and the needs of those concerned. It is therefore more appropriate to say that ancestor worship is an evolving ritual form aimed at satisfying the cultural needs and the problem of theodicy of the two groups.

In conclusion, ancestor worship remains a potent force among the Chinese, both within village China and in the overseas environment, as is shown among the Singapore Chinese. It recounts the story of family and lineage, draws on the moral economy of its members and forbids them to forget their ancestors, lineage, home village and village kinship structure. It is this force encapsulated in various formulae such as "not forgetting the source", "wealth not being divorced from its ancestors" that constantly pricks the individual's moral conscience and leads him back to his place of origin. It is this that is instrumental in re-establishing continuity between the Singapore and Anxi Chinese.

Notes

1   For a discussion on death rites and ancestor worship, see DeGroot, J.J.M., 1964, vol.1.

2   Among the Singapore Chinese, this is one main reason for staging large scale communal sacrificial offerings to the wandering ghosts during the Hungry Ghost Festival *(Zhong-Yuan-Jie)* during the seventh lunar month.

3   For a discussion, see Yen, C.H., 1986.

4   For a discussion on the relationship between space and social structure, including identity, see Castells, M., 1976: 60-84; also, Harvey, D., 1985.

5   In recent years, those overseas Chinese with high official titles in their adopted countries have been given due acknowledgement by the provincial government. One example here is the restoration of the ancestral grave of the former President of the Philippines, Corazon Aquino, when she visited her home village in Hong-jian Village, Long-hai County, Fujian.

6   For a discussion of karma and merit-making, see Obeyesekere, G., 1968: 7-40.

7   The debate on whether the practice of Chinese religion is a matter of orthodoxy or orthopraxy is discussed extensively by J.L. Watson, who favours orthopraxy; while Whyte argues for the importance of orthodoxy. See Watson, 1988: 3-19; also Whyte, 1988: 289-316.

8   The six Buddhist planes of existence are Heaven, Human, Azuras, Animal, Preta and Hell. See Daye,D.D., 1978: 123-126.

9   A discussion on *feng-shui* can be found in Feutchwang, S., 1974.

7 Religious Revivalism

Introduction

Chinese religious orthodoxy is an important part of Singapore-Chinese socio-religious life. One of the earliest social institutions established by the Chinese in Singapore was the temple, which catered to the religious needs of the early migrants. Since then Singapore Chinese have continued to hold Chinese religious practices both at individual and communal levels. Today, Chinese religious orthodoxy continues to have a communal function, which is served by the ritual ceremonies and religious fairs that continue to be part of the religious landscape, enabling participation in communal expression that fosters a sense of group identity and solidarity.

Among the Singapore Anxi Chinese, the orthodox practices of Chinese religion continue to play a significant role. Today, they reproduce the communal religious rituals they have come to understand as important for their lineages. They have also built a temple, Peng Lai Si (蓬萊寺), named after their home district. They are able to get the temple named after their ancestral home because the majority of them came from the same district. Within this temple, their guardian god, *Qing-shui-zu-shi-gong*, is housed. On various occasions, communal fairs are organised for lineage members.

The 1978 Reform in China brought a revival of religious activities in Peng Lai district, and visiting Singapore Chinese have been instrumental in reinventing ritual practices in the villages. The small scale, individualised religious practices during the early years of reforms have gradually given way to large annual religious fairs, now a common sight. Ninety per cent of village households belonging to the same lineage participate in them. In recent years, more Singapore Chinese visit their home villages to take part in these religious fairs. This chapter examines religious reproduction in the *qiaoxiang*, focusing on the centrality of *Qing-shui-zu-shi-gong*; the revival of religious fairs and the implications for the lineage identity of Singapore and village Chinese.

Chinese Religious Orthodoxy: Its Contemporary Roles

Chinese religious orthodoxy can be seen as consisting of two structures, the ritual and the ideological. Each can exist independently of the other. Irrespective of whether it is the rituals or the ideologies that are being considered, Chinese religious orthodoxy remains an important aspect of Chinese culture. In one study, Watson sees the standardisation of ritual as central to the creation and maintenance of a unified Chinese culture (Watson, 1988: 3). To Watson, it is the ritual performance rather than the meanings behind it that are crucial. Thus, he argues that "what is clear and explicit about ritual is how to do it - rather than its meaning" (Watson, 1988: 5). On the other hand, scholars like Rawski explore the meanings behind these ritual practices. She argues that, although the practitioners themselves might not be aware of the meanings behind each ritual practice, a complex structure of meanings does exist for all ritual practices and it is important to acknowledge the existence of such a system of meanings (Rawski, 1988: 22). In my own work, I argue that Chinese religious orthodoxy consists of the surface, manifest structure which is grounded in rituals and actions, as Watson does, but at the same time recognise a deep latent structure which provides the Chinese with an identifiable, common cosmological worldview. Taken together, these two structures allowed Chinese communities throughout the world to practice an identifiable form of Chinese religious orthodoxy, the latent structure often changing less than the surface, manifest structure, which is subjected to addition, subtraction and modification due to changing socio-cultural, economic and political environments.

Chinese religious orthodoxy is an eclectic mix of three main ideologies - Daoism, Buddhism and Confucianism - interwoven with folk beliefs and animism. This syncretic mix did, and still does, determine the practice of a majority of the Chinese. Various scholars categorise Chinese religious orthodoxy in various ways. Attempts at ideologically 'pure' religious practice were confined to a small elite minority - in former times, the state and the literati, who favoured institutional forms of religion, either Confucianism, Buddhism or both (ibid). A more diffused form of religious practice was that of the masses (Yang, 1961) - formerly this meant, for the most part, the peasantry (Granet, 1975).

As a system of rituals, Chinese religious orthodoxy can be seen as a system of social action, the performance of which required the co-operation of individuals who followed the direction of leaders (La Fontaine, 1985: 11). In such ritual practices rules govern each action and each participant, and there are also prescribed sets of actions to be followed in a set of rituals (La Fontaine, 1985: 11). Other rules concern those to be excluded.

In contemporary Chinese society, it is the better-educated and professional classes that favour scriptural purity. Among Singapore Chinese, only in recent years has there been a rise in scriptural Buddhism and an emerging trend towards Reformist Buddhism, while Chinese religious orthodoxy has continued to be represented by communal religion; yet there is a new division between individual spiritualism and communal religiosity. The latter is now interpreted as part of Chinese cultural tradition and thus is supported by various Chinese groups - and, very recently, by the Singapore state. (Kuah, 1994; Kuah 1998a). Chinese religious orthodoxy is practised by many groups of Chinese: lineage groups, surname associations, temples and occupational groupings all participate in the various communal religious celebrations.

The reproduction of Chinese religious orthodoxy among the Singapore Chinese is not a systematic process. The early migrants first engaged in this process of religious reproduction. Ritual elements changed according to the perceptions and understanding of practices by the migrants through the years. What they remembered as traditions, they reproduced and practised - in many cases, with very little idea of the meaning behind them. These practices were important as they provided the early migrants with cultural familiarity and continuity in a foreign environment. Today, these rituals constitute an important part of Chinese culture, providing the Chinese with a distinct cultural identity in the face of new challenges. The challenge facing Chinese religious orthodoxy today is that of restructuring it and turning it into a rational, modern religion that fulfils the spiritual and social needs of individuals and the collective whole.

Among the Singapore Anxi Chinese, religious orthodoxy fulfils another important function: it provides a bond between them and their village counterparts in Peng Lai District. Through ritual practices, they are able to express their sentiments towards their ancestral villages and their village kin. By staging religious fairs and participating in ritual practices, these two groups of Chinese are brought together. These ritual practices serve as cushions against the initial shock of reuniting with village kin, and as an important dialogue platform for the two groups, who have been separated for several decades, providing a ready topic for conversation and thus reduced embarrassment due to lack of conversation topics. This is particularly important for the men, as many of them find it difficult to make small talk, so that involvement in some sort of work becomes a desirable aim when they visit the villages. Thus the staging of communal religious fairs becomes a way out, as conversations are directed towards preparation and the actual ceremony. It also provides an important cultural bond for the women. Most Singapore and village women are involved in the preparation of food and religious paraphernalia for the ancestor worship as well as being very active in individual and communal ancestor worship. Through cooperation in these chores, the women are brought closer together. To a large extent, Chinese religious orthodoxy provides the *qiaoxiang* with communal fairs that enable all villagers to participate and rediscover a religious culture that had been suppressed from the Cultural Revolution until recently and to express overtly individual religiosity and spirituality that had been covered by secularism.

Centrality of *Qing Shui Yan* and *Qing-shui-zu-shi-gong*

When the Singapore Chinese visit Anxi, one of their primary aims is to visit Qing-Shi-Yan and make offerings to their religious ancestor, *Qing-shui-zu-shi-gong* [M] or *Ching-Shui Zhor-She* [H]. Ninety per cent of them do this. Why is *Qing-shui-zu-shi-gong* so important to the Singapore Chinese? Why is it also important to the villagers? In fact, this deity provides the two groups with a shared religious ideology and allows them to engage in communal religious activities as members of the same ancestral village/district. Being member of the same lineage helps to further lessen the social distance between them.

The temple complex, Qing-Shui-Yan (清水岩), is located at the southeastern outskirts of Peng-Lai District. It is 760 metres above sea level and nestled in a hilly area with beautiful greenery. From Peng-Lai market town, it takes about twenty to thirty minutes by car to reach the foot of the temple, and then another fifteen to twenty minutes to climb the steps on foot to reach the temple itself. It is an imposing temple complex built in traditional Chinese architectural style, with arched roofs. The main building is made of red bricks and granite slabs, giving it distinction in the rustic rural landscape. Its position at the top of a peak commands a panoramic view of the villages below it. To the villagers and Chinese overseas, the position of the temple - located in the hills with a river flowing by and overlooking the villages, *bei-shan wan-shui,* (背山望水) - is considered to have exceptionally good geomancy, *hou feng-shui.*

This temple is dedicated to a Buddhist monk who is popularly known as *Qing-shui-zu-shi-gong* (literally, Clear-water Deified Ancestor), the name given to a historical figure who lived during the Sung Dynasty and who was renowned for mystical powers that saved the lives of many villagers. There are several versions of both his origin and his mystical power. One version has it that his original name was Chen Pu-zu, and that he was born into a family whose poverty forced them to send him to a monastery at a very young age. Because of the harsh conditions, however, he left the monastery, travelled, and eventually reached Anxi. He liked the place, settled there, and lived the life of a recluse, practising Chan meditation. He was rumoured to have attained a high level of spiritual power. He was seen as a compassionate monk, who often gave rice to the poor villagers. After his death, the villagers build a temple in his honour.

Another version has it that he was a monk from nearby Yongching County known as Chen-Yin, who had become a monk at a very young age. His knowledge of dharma, mystical powers and compassion were widely known to the villagers in the region. During the 6th year of Northern Sung rule, Ching-Xi (present-day Anxi) suffered from a bad drought. The local inhabitants begged Chen Yin to perform the rite for rain. After the drought, he remained behind and lived in the temple at An-Yi-Zhang-Yuan-Shan. In addition to his life as a monk, he was a practising physician, who treated the villagers' diseases with herbal medicine, about which he was very knowledgeable. He also helped build bridges and roads. In his spare time and over a period of 18 years he rebuilt the temple he was living in, afterwards renaming it Qing-Shui Yuan. His efforts, diligence and compassion won the hearts of the villagers. He reportedly arrived at Qing Shui She in 1101 and died at the age of fifty-five years (Anxi Xian Zhi, 1994 v.2: 1127-1128).

Qing-shui-zu-shi-gong is commonly known as *wu-mian-zu-shi-gong* (烏面祖師公) because of his black face. One version has it that during his nineteen years as a recluse practising meditation in the cave he was constantly disturbed by the spirits who, on one occasion, attempted to kill him by blowing on the lamp for seven days and seven nights. He survived the ordeal, but his face was badly burned and was black.

He is also known as the "dropping nose ancestor", *luo-pi-zu-shi-gong* (落牌祖師公) among the Taiwanese today. One story has it that the nose of the statue of Zu-She Gong was torn off when part of the roof of the cave where it was housed collapsed. It was later fixed back in position, but since then, whenever he senses natural calamities, his nose drops off, to be found in front of his chest or buried in his sleeve - a sign for the villagers to prepare for the coming disaster. Another story claims that he disapproved of unclean worshippers making offerings to him, and that his nose drops off whenever this occured (Lou, 1977, Zhenxiang zazhi bianjibu, 1987).

After the monk's death, and in commemoration of his contribution to the place, the villagers continued to build various pagodas and to expand Qing-Shui-Yuan into an impressive temple. Gradually, the monk assumed a transcendental status and became a deified person and was worshipped as a deified ancestor by the villagers. From 1164 to 1210, Qing-Shui-Zu-Shi-Gong was posthumously honoured by the Southern Sung imperial palace four times, each time with two characters having the following respective meanings: "ever-ready", "great wisdom", "ultimate compassion" and "extremely charitable". He was much loved and worshipped by the general population of Anxi County. Today, even though Qing-Shui-Yuan is known as a Buddhist temple, the main shrine houses this wu-mian zu-shi-gong.

Qing-Shiu-Yuan has undergone two main phases of development, the first being that of the Northern Sung and Southern Sung eras, after which it was honoured as a Buddhist temple by imperial decree during the Southern Sung. Since then, during the various dynastic epochs, additional honours led to new additions to the main temple, expanding it and transforming it into a renowned sacred place.

The second phase of development has been the modern period,

starting towards the end of the nineteenth century. In 1899, the main shrine of the temple complex underwent an extensive renovation, and two new buildings were added to it. In 1933, the complex was destroyed by a heavy rainstorm, which caused the walls of the main shrine, and those of other buildings, to collapse. It was then left in a state of ruin until 1953, when Chinese overseas started to rebuild it. From 1953 to 1976, a group of Chinese overseas collectively renovated and extended the temple complex. It now stands as a complex of three buildings. The main shrine is called the *Zu-Shi-Dian* (祖師殿) and is devoted to *Qing-Shui Zu-Shi*. In 1978, a temple management committee was formed to manage the complex, and the following year the complex was modernised with a telephone, street lamps and a sealed-surface road winding up the slopes to the temple.

Qing-shui-zu-shi-gong has, through the centuries, become the guardian deity of the people of Anxi County, and the villagers of Peng Lai have regarded it as their ancestral deity. His black face is now considered a symbol of good virtue and righteousness. He is widely known for his deeds in helping those in need of assistance, and is a protector of the villagers from natural and human calamities. Because he was supposedly a historical figure and not a mythological one, he is called a deified ancestor, *zu-shi-gong*.

An Emigrant's Deity

In rural China, there was formerly very little flow of information, including that concerning the existence of other gods and deities than those already known. Villagers thus clung to their known gods and deities for all socio-psychological needs. On the eve of emigration, many those were to travel would pray to *Qing-shui-zu-shi-gong* for guidance and for a safe journey. Other deities, such as the Goddess of the Sea, *Ma-Zu* (媽祖) (also known as Heavenly Empress, *Tien-Hou* (天后) only became popular with the emigrants after they came into contact with her in the coastal ports of Fujian.

To the Anxi Chinese emigrants of the nineteenth and twentieth centuries, *Qing-shui-zu-shi-gong* was a source of encouragement and moral support, a protector against banditry and the uncertainties of the journey, and the only deity known to many of them prior to emigration. He was also a source of compassion and the villagers relied on him for blessings and to solve their communal and personal problems, big and small. He was known to answer most requests because of his mystical powers and was thus spiritually powerful, *ling* to these Chinese.

The emigrants from Anxi made their way through the hills to the coastal cities and to Singapore. In the foreign environment, Chinese social institutions existed to help these newly arrived migrants with their social and economic needs, providing temporary shelter and employment; but their fears and innermost needs were assuaged by their faith in *Qing-shui-zu-shi-gong*. In this environment, every migrant was in great need of emotional support, and while they provided each other with whatever mutual support they could, they were often left to manage their own emotional needs. They turned to *Qing-shui-zu-shi-gong* for support and derived comfort from knowing that he was there to help them. The fact that *Qing-shui-zu-shi-gong* was their ancestral deity made the sense of security greater, as he was there exclusively for them. During the early years, there were religious fairs held in temples that provided a reprieve from the mundane routine of coolie life, where ritual activities and gods were communally shared. These activities were important in serving as a base for socialisation and social networking; but *Qing-shui-zu-shi-gong* continued to provide an inner sanctuary for the Anxi migrants to turn to, be it for spiritual needs or social consultation.

Today, *Qing-shui-zu-shi-gong* reflects the proud achievement of the Anxi Chinese in Singapore and continues to be a constant source of support to them. He is also a visible reminder of who they are and where they come from - a testimony of their origin and cultural roots; of their hardships and blessings that they came to accept as they built their social base and sank their roots into Singapore society. *Qing-shui-zu-shi-gong* is there to prick their conscience, to remind them not to forget their ancestral home as the process of planting their roots in foreign soil is completed.

Qing-shui-zu-shi-gong is a historical person, a deified hero and a Buddha; but he also represents the coherent socio-religious system that these Anxi Chinese have come to embrace in their changed social environment, reminding them of their cosmological worldview and allowing them to reproduce aspects of their religion that were and are fulfilling their needs in Singapore.

Temples devoted to *Qing-shui-zu-shi-gong* can be found in various Chinese overseas communities as in Singapore, Taiwan, and Malaysia where he is also known popularly as the "dropping nose *Zu-Shi*".

Situating *Qing-shui-zu-shi-gong* in Singapore

By the early 1950s, the number of recent migrants from Anxi to Singapore had grown substantially. There were about 60,000 people from Anxi in Singapore. Some of these emigrants were from Peng Lai District. Two social institutions emerged to cater to this increasing number of Anxi people in Singapore. The first was Anxi Association, *Ann Kway Hui Guan* [H] (安溪會館), formed in 1921 to provide a social roof for the migrants. It has recruited members from Anxi County and organised several communal religious and cultural fairs on an annual basis and continues to provide a space for social interaction on a daily and weekly basis. Today, it has its own premises and is open to all members.

The second institution established was the Peng Lai Temple, built in 1951 to provide for the religious needs of the Anxi people and to house their guardian ancestral deity, *Qing-shui-zu-shi-gong*. The original temple - small in size, with one main shrine and a small area for the temple caretaker - was built from contributions given by twelve persons. In 1985, it was subjected to urban renewal and urban redevelopment, and the land was returned to the Urban Renewal Authority (URA) for compensation. A choice of several locations for rebuilding was given, which would be leased to the temple authority at a rate several times below the market rate. The committee for Peng Lai Temple bid successfully for a site that has an area of about 20,000 square feet and a leasehold period of 35 years. The site was leased at a cost of S$270,000.

In the 1980s, many small temples were also subjected to urban renewal and were given summons by the Urban Renewal Authority to relocate[1]. At the same time, the URA has released several parcels of sizeable plot of land earmarked for religious purposes. Those affected temples could bid for the land to build their new temple. In 1985, several temples were also served with relocation notices. The committee of two temples, Zhong-Ting-Miao and Ming-Shan-Gong, first approached Peng Lai Temple with the intention of joining it. Members of these two temples were also from Anxi and also worshipped *Qing-shui-zu-shi-gong*. Given the fact that there are not so many parcels of land to be distributed to all temples affected by urban renewal, the government has encouraged temple premise sharing among temples. Since each temple had its own deities and worshipped a common *Qing-shui-zu-shi-gong*, they saw the feasibility of sharing a temple premise. By combining resources, they are more likely to succeed in bidding for the government designated religious plot of land. By claiming that several temples share a plot of land, they are also in a stronger position to bid for a plot of land in competition with other Chinese and Christian organisations. Furthermore, by pooling resources together, they could also build a bigger temple. The parties all agreed to the use of the name "Peng Lai Si".

During this period of planning and construction, four other temples heard of their combined efforts and decided to join in the project, and so met with the organising committee of Peng-Lai Si to discuss the possibilities of joining the temple as co-partners. These four are Che-Chi-Tang, Pu-An-Tang, Shui-Kou-Tang and Xiang-Fu-Ting. Organising members of these four temple organisations were also from Anxi County and also recognised *Qing-shui-zu-shi-gong* as their guardian deity. At the meeting the groups got on well and were accepted into the Peng-Lai-Si Project. Thus, Peng-Lai-Si became a combined project of seven temple organisations and was jointly co-owned by all of them.

In 1986, the Peng-Lai-Si Fundraising Committee was established, with members from the seven temples, representing the nine surname groups found in Anxi. These are Lin (林), Ke (柯), Li (李), Zhang (張), Liao (廖), Liu (劉), Wen (温), Xie (謝) and Chen (陳). With renewed effort and an increase in funds, construction work began on Peng-Lai-Shi in 1989 and was completed in 1991. The total cost of construction amounted to S$1.7 million.

The temple is constructed in traditional Chinese architectural style, with elaborate carved tiled roofs, with dragons and phoenixes on top of it. It has one main shrine hall, with a high ceiling. At both sides are offices on the first and second floor. At the front podium, the building is supported by four cylindrical pillars, with carvings of dragons and phoenixes, transported from Suzhou. In front of the building is an open space where religious fairs are held.

The new Peng Lai Temple is co-owned and shared by the seven temple groups. Each group has a management team that looks after its own religious functions, while the Peng Lai Temple management team looks after the maintenance of the temple. Within the temple, *Qing-shui-zu-shi-gong* is the main god and is shared by all. He is positioned in the centre of the main shrine. On both sides are constructed seven pavilions, each housing a group of guardian deities from the seven previous temples, above which are written the original names of the temples. The temple is opened to all, but especially those who claim ancestry from Anxi.

The temple holds several communal religious functions a year, both for *Zu-Shi-Gong* and the guardian gods. To begin with, there is an annual celebration of the birthday of Zu-Shi-Gong on the 6th day of the first lunar month. This is the most important inter-lineage communal religious function, commonly referred to as *Zu-Shi-Gong-Dan* (祖師公誕). Other communal religious celebrations include Spring, Qing-Ming and Zhong-Yuan festivals, occasions where members from all the surname groups go and make their offerings to Zu-Shi-Gong. Communal celebrations of this nature, shared by all surname groups, are organised by a joint multi-surname committee.

A committee composed of members from different surname groups is selected on an annual basis according to the "will of Zu-Shi-Gong". The selection process is conducted at the end of each *Zu-Shi-Gong-Dan*. Members from all surname groups representing individual households, family business groups or individuals assemble in front of *Zu-Shi-Gong*. As each name is put forward, the person kneels and offers *mu-bei* to *Zu-Shi-Gong*. The person with the highest number of positive replies from *Zu-Shi-Gong* becomes the stove-master, followed by the deputy stove-master, secretary, financier and others. These persons then manage the organisation of *Zu-Shi-Gong-Dan* and other communal functions for a year. Individual names and those representing corporations are submitted for the selection process.

There are also birthday celebrations for each group of guardian deities from the seven temples, participated in by members of the particular temple group. The celebrations are organised by their respective management committees, chosen in the same way as the Peng Lai Si management, but with only the group concerned participating in the selection process.

Peng Lai Temple serves members at two levels. At the wider, communal level, it serves original Anxi members and their descendants, who come together to worship *Zu-Shi-Gong*. In this they all identify with the common deified ancestor, *Qing-shui-zu-shi-gong*, the territorial deity identified with Anxi County. This galvanises people from the county together and creates a sense of being insiders, from the same area, *tongxiang* (同鄉). Members from all the seven temples usually attend these functions.

In terms of status, the seven satellite temples are equal with one another but lower than Peng Lai Temple. They are of a parochial nature, represent a district within the wider Anxi County, and serve their own members, each temple group making offerings to their own guardian deities. Each temple has one day per month when rituals, *fa-shi* (法事) are performed for its members. On that day, only members of the relevant group come and make offerings.

For those who pray at Peng-Lai Si, the temple is a visual representation of their understanding of the relationship between their ancestral home village and their religious practices - a relationship of communalism and collective consciousness. It presents to them their own deity, and those who recognise it are insiders - members of the same village, district or county. But besides being a space where communal religious worship occurs, it is also a social space where interaction among members from different groups occurs - a place where friends are made outside immediate kinship circles. These intra- and inter-lineage interactions are most common when there is a communal function. Peng Lai Si, a temple based on both the territorial (Anxi County) and district or village (*tongxiang*) affiliations of its members, is unlike other temples in Singapore, where individuals go and seek assistance of specific gods and goddesses. Its members formed one big socio-religious community and, at the same time, spilt themselves into seven smaller socio-religious communities.

Celebration of Zu-Shi-Gong's birthday coincides with the Lunar New Year. On this occasion, the organising committee arranges food, flowers, and incense and joss papers, which are placed on the table and offered to *Zu-Shi-Gong*. A Chinese opera troupe is invited to perform for both gods and temple members, and Daoist priests are invited to perform religious rites. Offerings are made to the heaven and the deified ancestor.

On this day, members, especially women, turn up in great number. They arrive in the late morning with joss sticks, incense papers, fruits and sometimes food to present individual offerings to Zu-Shi-Gong. As on most religious occasions, worship is conducted on two levels: there is the communal offering to *Zu-Shi-Gong* and the individual offerings by individuals. The worship is a simple act involving the lighting of the incense sticks, the placing of the flowers in the vases provided by the temple, the laying of the fruits and food on the plates and offering them to *Zu-Shi-Gong*, and prayer. Incense papers are burned as an offering at the end of the ritual, which takes ten to fifteen minutes.

Although most members arrive in the morning, they may arrive at any time of the day. By mid-morning, however, the crowd gathered in the temple has grown to a hundred or more people. During the morning, women visit and perform their offerings. Many are elderly women, who generally spend several hours in the temple before returning home. Most stay for a luncheon prepared by the temple organisers. There are also a small number of women in their thirties and forties who often accompany their mothers or mothers-in-law to the temple. Some of these stay behind and join in the conversation while others, after offering incense to the gods, leave the elderly to socialise among themselves and go out.

On this occasion, the social and kinship networks of the members are clearly displayed to everyone. The majority is related to each other, either sharing surnames or coming from the same ancestral village. Each member is thus known to others, and there is a high level of sociability. At the lineage level, women are related to each other through husbands of the same lineage, and many have known each other for the past three to four decades - many, in fact, knew each other in their ancestral villages prior to emigration. Their relationships have been strengthened through their years of association in Singapore, where they have provided moral and other support in times of hardship, especially during the early years of migration, and where, at present, they provide mutual support for the elderly and those who are suffering from illness. These cross-lineage ties of support and friendship have developed into important networks within which the women can draw strength in times of hardship and happiness.

Celebrating the birthday of *Zu-Shi-Gong* is a joyous occasion for all members. After their obligatory worship the women greet one another, settle down in small groups and talk among themselves, catching up with one another on a range of issues ranging from the marriages of children and grandchildren, health, recreation, food, fashion and other mundane issues, mostly centring on their families. It is a time to exchange news and to renew kinship and friendship ties as, while most have their own circles of relational kin with whom they regularly interact, this occasion provides opportunities to rekindle relationships with those whom they meet less regularly. After lunch, many make their way home, leaving a handful behind to continue their conversation.

Other religious functions, such as those for the guardian gods of the seven temples, are celebrated in much the same way, but within smaller groups.

On these communal occasions, individual religiosity is consigned to a secondary position, to the individual acts of worship and offering. Men usually gather in groups during the night, after making offerings of joss incense to the various gods, to engage in conversation. Topics range from business to politics to events in their home villages in China. Although it is most common to see elderly men at the temples, younger men in their 30s and 40s are also present, as well as a handful in their twenties. They, too, join in the conversation. These younger men have either accompanied their parents to the temple or come as representatives of their parents to perform the worship and to pay monetary dues to the temple.

Membership in Peng Lai Si is exclusive, not open to the public, the criterion for entry being based on ancestral territorial affiliation. Members are most likely to be of Anxi origin, although outsiders do visit the temple. Membership is based on a household system rather than on individuals, unlike in modern evangelical Christian movements where individual membership is the norm. Participation and belief are two separate issues: those who participate in communal worship need not be believers. In most cases, it is the ritual participation that is significant.

Anthropologically, these religious activities fulfil several functions. First, they provide opportunities for the elderly to meet and rekindle their relationships. Second, they provide opportunities for younger members to get acquainted with one another. They also allow economic networking among the younger members: among the younger men who visit the temple, many have now taken over family businesses - thus, going to Peng-Lai-Si allows them to develop *guanxi* and form business partnerships. They enable younger women to be inducted into the wider kinship network and become recognised as daughters-in-law, thereby providing them with a patrilineal identity. By encouraging the participation of younger members, identity with the lineage and ancestral district can be ensured.

Reviving Religious Orthodoxy in Anxi

A common remark made by Anxi villagers is that when Chinese overseas return to their ancestral villages, they are predominantly preoccupied with religious activities and are willing to spend large sums of money on them.

Why are the Singapore Chinese preoccupied with conducting large communal religious fairs in their ancestral villages? What are these communal religious fairs? What is the impact of these affairs on their social and kinship life?

Before 1978, the conduct of religious activities was extremely low key. Individual worship took place, but was conducted quietly, with hardly any burning of incense or offering to the gods. The small number of Chinese overseas who visited Qing-Shui-Yuan gave incense, paper money and food offerings, but the majority of villagers continued to conduct their worship discreetly with incense and little joss paper. Even at the beginning of the reform years, discretion continued to be the rule regarding religious activities. By the mid-1980s, however, closer relationships between official cadres and Singapore Chinese brought about a greater degree of freedom for religious activities. Communal religious fairs, since then, have become public events for all villagers to participate in.

When the idea of reform was gaining popularity in the mid-seventies, village and county cadres were looking for means to boost the economy. The cadres of these *qiaoxiang* negotiated religion in exchange for capital investment and infrastructure support at the village level. They first agreed to the renovation of Qing-Shui-Yuan by the Chinese overseas, agreeing that it was an important historical temple worthy of preservation. The temple had long been an attraction to the Chinese overseas and over 80 per cent of Chinese overseas visiting ancestral villages in Fujian made pilgrimages to it. By renovating it and according it the status of a tourist space, it was hoped that it would become a major tourist attraction in interior Fujian and encourage more Chinese overseas to visit the area. Such rationalisation was in congruence with the national ideology of national heritage preservation, and was also in line with the national push to encourage Chinese overseas to visit China and ultimately to invest in China - hence the temple reconstruction of 1976 described above. Even afterwards, however, there was little religious activity by the villagers beyond the discreet domestic worship of deceased grandparents and local gods carried out mostly by elderly women, with only occasional visits to the temple to make offerings and ask for the blessings of Qing-Shui-Zu-Shi-Gong.

Beginning in the 1980s, however, religious fairs became common in the *qiaoxiang* villages. Among these were the welcoming procession of *Qing-shui-zu-shi-gong, ying-Qing-shui-zu-shi-gong* (迎清水祖師), the worship of Heaven, *bai-tian-gong* (拜天公), the "welcoming of god and lighting the fire", *ying-shen ying-huo* (迎神迎火), and the birthdays of the various buddhas, *fo-dan* (佛誕). Groups of Singapore Chinese returned to participate in these celebrations. Usually a local household would be selected as the main organiser and sponsor of each event, the chosen person being known as the buddha head, *fo-tou* [M] or *puo-tau* [H] (佛頭).

Most households in our survey participated in communal religious functions. Only three families of Christians did not participate in any village religious events, although they continued to perform ancestor worship, including communal ancestor worship. Generally, the villagers practice orthodox religious traditions and are interested in rituals, as are their Singapore counterparts, but most do not concern themselves with religious ideology, whatever concerns they have in this regard being expressed in ritual form. The revived ritual practices are significant to them because they are considered part of the wider Chinese tradition. More significantly, they answer their this-worldly needs - local deities, gods and buddhas are consulted about health and illness, material concerns, marital problems and social relationships.

As in Singapore, the elderly are more religious and participate wholeheartedly, while the younger members are less enthusiastic - although they, too, continue to support religious activities. Elderly villagers see religious practices as important in satisfying their this-worldly and otherworldly needs; whereas younger villagers feel ritual practices, and religion in general, as less relevant to their lives; and some view religion as superstition, not to be encouraged. However, given the highly emotional attachment of their elders to these rituals, many feel it best to go along with their elderly parents, grandparents and Singapore kin. Many of the young say that they do not believe in religion at all, and attribute their attitude to their secular education; yet a large majority continue to assist and participate in the ritual celebrations.

Some villagers' comments concerning this religious revivalism are the following:

> Before they came, the village was very quiet. Now that our relatives come regularly, the place is full of life. They usually come in a group and organise religious fairs. We have ceremonies like welcoming the deified ancestors, *ying-zu-shi*, rite for the flow of descendants, *juan-ding-yi-shi* and, most recently, rite for thanking the genealogy, *xie-pu-yi-shi*. I think it is very good to have these religious celebrations to enliven our life here. It is also good to see so many of them returning and visiting their ancestral village. Before this, there were very few outsiders to our village. Now, it is different. We feel that the village has come alive.

> "I personally do not really believe much in these rituals and their efficacy, but the old ones do. But, I think these ritual activities are not just religious in orientation. They are more important for creating a communal spirit among the villagers, but also between the villagers and their Singapore relatives. It is also important for us to show interest in these activities so that the Singapore Chinese will return more frequently. If there is nothing

for them to do when they visit the village, then they might not be inclined to return as often as they do now. These ritual activities occupy their time and minds and so when they return, they are always busy and doing something. In this sense, it is good that we have these religious celebrations. Furthermore, they create some kind of festive mood and villagers tend to be more gregarious. The general atmosphere tends to be one of happiness and excitement. This is good for the social and spiritual life of the villagers and the district".

The communal religious fairs attracted much attention because of their grandeur, and the atmosphere of excitement has encouraged individuals and households to participate in them. Like the ancestor-worship celebrations, the several yearly religious functions add life to an otherwise mundane social environment. As in Singapore, they can be divided into two types: individual or household worship, carried out on festive occasions or when the need arises; and communal participation in religious fairs.

Today, there are three types of communal religious fairs. The first is the district level fairs which involve all the lineages of the district, of which the most important is the annual welcoming of gods and fire, *ying-shen ying-huo* (迎神迎火) celebration. The second is the annual lineage level fairs, which, for the Ke lineage, is the welcoming procession of *Qing-shui-zu-shi-gong* on the sixth day of the first lunar month. The last are the small-scale fairs organised by individuals or groups of visiting Singapore Chinese.

It is possible to argue that the this-worldly needs of the villagers are similar, in general, to those of the Singapore Chinese, and that it is this shared religious ideology, with its focus on ritual practices which both groups embrace and understand, that allows the two groups to come together to engage in religious reproduction, recreating those aspects which are relevant to their needs. This shared ritual understanding also provides them with a common platform to discuss other concerns, which may be irrelevant, or only obliquely relevant, to the ritual system. The revival of these communal religious fairs has been made possible as a result of the efforts of the Singapore Chinese, with the active support of the villagers.

Fo-Tou and Religious Fairs

The district-wide *ying-shen ying-huo* religious fair was revived only in 1990. The important selection of the buddha head, *fo-tou* [M], *puo-tau* [H] or chief organiser of the fair was traditionally based on an annual rotation cycle among the nine surname groups in the district, and this procedure was instituted when the fair was revived. Thus, each lineage gets to have a member appointed *puo-tau* once every nine years, and when this occurs it becomes imperative that both the lineage's Anxi and Singapore members become involved in the fair, both as helpers and as participants. By involving themselves, the lineage gains much "face" and creates a good name for itself and its members, which is important for maintaining its overall social standing vis-à-vis other lineages.

Although the position of the buddha head is based on rotation, the year that a lineage is asked to serve is done through a selection process. When Peng Lai district revived its first religious fair, all surname groups would be required to submit their name for selection. On the second year, the surname group that was the buddha head for the previous year was required to refrain from submitting its name. This leaves only eight surname groups bidding for the position of the buddha head. This process will go on until the last surname group becomes the buddha head and a new cycle begins. For the selection of the surname group to become the buddha head for a particular year, the members relied on the following method. In a simplified religious rite, a representative from the each qualified lineage is required to throw *mu-bei* in front of Qing-shui-zu-shi-gong, who stands as witness to the selection process. The lineage with the most number of positive throws becomes the *puo-tau* for the coming year. Usually a lineage learns that it will become a *puo-tau* one-year ahead of the schedule as, at the end of each celebration, those lineages that have not had a *puo-tau* are required to compete for the position. After the selection, the lineage concerned is required to select a team to head the preparation for the following year's celebration.

Being a *puo-tau* is prestigious for the lineage concerned, but it is also involves a huge burden of responsibility - for the expenses, preparation and staging of the fair, as well as for its scale. When a lineage is selected to name a *puo-tau*, an ad hoc committee of members from among both Singaporeans and Anxi villagers is formed, the majority of whom are lineage elders. The actual preparatory work - booking the monks and the opera troupe, arranging the feast and the religious paraphernalia, etc. - is carried out largely by the villagers, the Chinese overseas arriving in the district only shortly before the fair.

Within the lineage, members vie for the position of *puo-tau*. The selection procedure is similar to that at the inter-lineage level. Interested individuals or households are invited to participate in the selection process, which is again witnessed by *Qing-shui-zu-shi-gong*. It too involves the throwing of *mu-bei* in front of the deity, the person with the highest number of positive throws becoming *puo-tau*. Because he is expected to arrange for labour and to provide financial contributions for the fair, it has now become a norm that the position of *puo-tau* falls on the shoulders of a lineage member who is relatively wealthy - generally a wealthy villager or an overseas member. In the last few years some village households, with the support of their overseas kin, have successfully vied for the position. The related village kin are required to carry out the preparatory work in the absence of the *puo-tau* if he resides overseas.

For the Ke lineage, the main religious fair at the lineage level is the welcoming procession of *Qing-shui-zu-shi-gong*. The committee members are given one year to prepare for the celebration. Giving oneself sufficient time to prepare for the celebration is important, as this is the first time that most of the *puo-tau* are organising a large-scale communal religious fair and it allows them to seek help and advice from other members who have been *puo-tau* and who have the experience of organising such an event.

Within a lineage, there is usually a core group comprising both Singapore and Anxi members who are most active and interested in its affairs. These are mostly men, ranging in age from fifties through eighties. They are the ones who really organise the function. In most cases, it is the local members who are involved in deciding the details recruiting manpower for the jobs that need to be done prior to the actual days of celebration. Usually, younger men from within the lineage are recruited for a variety of tasks, including cleaning and decorating the shrine, erecting the opera stage and purchasing the religious items. These young men are normally available on short notice and are counted on to do odd jobs and run errands for the celebration. The Singapore elders, on the other hand, having agreed to the general outline of the celebration, do not concern themselves with the details. Although they remain intensely interested in the preparation, about which they are kept informed by their Anxi counterparts, they are more involved with the pragmatics of funding, which they easily attract from Singapore lineage members. They also encourage and co-ordinate the attendance of the Singapore lineage members who intend to participate in the celebration. A third concern is the invitation of village and county cadres to attend the function and the feast.

During this preparatory period, the two groups of kinsmen remain in close telephone contact with one another, and the Singapore members might also make several trips to the village, although, as discussed, most of the actual work is left to the Anxi counterparts to carry out. The cost of the celebration is calculated, and funds are collected from lineage members in Singapore and then handed to the core members of the Anxi group to be spent on the necessary items for the celebration. Each cost is carefully recorded by the treasurer; contributions from the members are posted outside the ancestral house during the celebration. The cost of a communal religious fair ranges from forty or fifty thousand Rmb to over one hundred thousand Rmb, or even more if it is on an extraordinarily lavish scale.

Anxi members attest to the need to develop trust between the parties when it comes to large-scale joint celebrations where one party contributes capital and the other has labour power. The parties must ensure that the preparation is conducted smoothly, that the fair is of a sufficiently large scale, and that the large sum of money is spent wisely. On this last point, I was told that during the earlier years, there was much corruption, with individuals pocketing expenses. Now, strict accounting is carried out.

Sometimes, individuals or groups of Singapore Chinese decide to stage a religious fair in appreciation of the assistance given by the local deity or by *Qing-shui-zu-shi-gong*. They and their villager kin then arrange and prepare for a celebration on a much smaller scale. For these small-scale religious fairs, the cost includes the following:

(i)   An opera troupe for about 5,000 Rmb, or a puppet show for about 3,000 Rmb, for several nights of performance. Often both are staged. These performers must also be provided with accommodations and food. This entertainment is one of the two most important and costly items for the celebration.

(ii)   The hiring of Daoist priests or Buddhist monks to lead the religious procession and to perform religious rites. This could amount to another 4,000 to 5,000 Rmb, depending on the number of monks or priests and the duration and intensity of the performance.

(iii)   Religious paraphernalia often cost as much as 3,000 to 4,000 Rmb.

(iv)   The feast, for at least 10,000 Rmb.

Thus, the total cost would be from twenty to thirty thousand Rmb, at the minimum. For lineage-level religious fairs the cost often amounts to 100,000 - 200,000 Rmb; the cost of district level fairs is sometimes double that of lineage celebrations. In Peng Lai District, district-wide fairs have amounted to 400,000 Rmb.

For district and lineage level celebrations, the grandeur of the celebrations is ensured through the co-operation of various authorities. In most cases, the occasion is declared a public holiday, with schools closed. The primary and secondary school principals respond to requests by getting pupils and students to perform dances and musicals, adding to the already joyous atmosphere. On such occasion, each student participant was provided with dress, drinks and 20 Rmb - the sums, however, vary with the lineage. Many students look forward to these occasions, when they can enjoy themselves and have new clothes and money, and when they do not need to attend classes.

Trust and Rivalry

To organise a big communal religious fair requires trust and co-operation among the organisers, a fact attested to by both Singapore and Anxi Chinese. The Singaporeans often worry about the failure of the villagers to make the preparations successfully, while the villagers worry about too much interference from the Singapore Chinese who do not know much of the cultural traditions. Since the reform years the two groups have developed mutual understanding of their respective needs and have worked amicably to stage religious fairs. However, the Anxi members continue to feel that they have to be vigilant in their efforts. In the words of one village member,

> When they entrust us to do something, we should be reliable and do it well, otherwise they would lose trust in us. We cannot blame them for being cautious, as there have been cases in the village where some [Anxi] people have been entrusted with a large sum of money for some projects. Instead of working on the projects and spending the money on them, they spent it on themselves. The result was that things were done halfway and incompletely. The Singapore people had to put in more money and get other people to do the job. When these kinds of incidents happened, the Singapore members were very unhappy and lost trust in us. We were also very upset by these incidents as it reflected very badly on us. Not all of us are like that. We like to see ourselves as reliable and trustworthy and able to be counted on to do the job well. Thus, we will do our best to ensure that there are not even little incidents that would disrupt this religious celebration.

Sometimes, when individual members failed to trust the other party, mutual co-operation could not be carried out. The result was the creation of tension between the two groups of members. In one incident, a village kin was entrusted with the full amount of expenditure for a large religious celebration. He was expected to communicate with the relevant people for the purchase of the religious paraphernalia, organise Daoist priests and Buddhist monks and arrange for a puppet show and a village feast. He took the money but the celebration was not organised on a grand scale as expected. Furthermore, the quality of the religious items was considered as inferior grade. Likewise, the village feast was not considered up to standard. There was dissatisfaction among the lineage members - both the Singapore and the village members. At the last minute, some members provided additional funding to rectify the situation by ordering better grade religious items and asking the restaurant owners to improve the menu for the feast to save face for the lineage. In many cases, there was close co-operation among the Singapore and the village kin and when they realised that the entrusted member could not carry out the expected duty, others would be assigned to take over.

Although there could be dissatisfaction, it was never allowed to surface and become outward antagonism. Sometimes, the guilty party would be pulled aside by the lineage elders and given a warning. In most cases, they would be black marked and no future work would be entrusted to the person. The Singapore kin have also exercised restraint in their comments on them when they were in the village. However, upon returning to Singapore, they did not hesitate to speak their mind to other members.

Usually, there is a careful selection and those who are known to be honest and capable are entrusted with the task. In most cases, there is a high level of trust, and the relationship between them is generally good. The task is usually performed to the satisfaction of all.

Participating in the Religious Fairs

As mentioned, when an individual becomes a *puo-tau* for a communal religious fair, the participation of his lineage members, and especially of the overseas members, becomes extremely important. This symbolises a visual display of the social solidarity and strength among them and of the overseas members' recognition of their ancestral roots. The participation of village members poses no problems: whenever there is a religious fair, most village households participate in it. However, encouraging the Singapore members to visit Anxi and participate is not easy, as they need to be convinced of the value of these socio-religious visits. This is especially true for the younger members, who have very little understanding of Chinese tradition and Chinese religious orthodoxy. In recent years, however, largely due to the efforts of the older members to persuade their children and grandchildren to accompany them and to better organisation on their part, many Singaporeans have come. Group travel arrangements are now the norm, and individuals need only inform the leaders for arrangements to be made on their behalf. Such events now regularly draw a group of thirty or more Singapore members, and the *xie-pu-yi-shi* celebration at the end of 1996 drew over seventy Singapore Chinese.

When visiting Anxi for religious events such as these, it is customary for the Singaporeans to stay with their closest blood kin. Those without relatives, or with relatives without a house to put them up in, usually book into the Overseas Chinese Guest House, *Qiao-Lian-Suo* (僑聯所).

Since the reform years, many Singaporeans have begun to visit their ancestral village on a regular basis, some as annual pilgrims. They are thus no longer considered "newcomers" or "uncivilised guests", *fan-ke* [M], *huang-ke* [H] (番客) by the villagers: the constant flow of Singapore Chinese into Anxi is now a routine part of the social landscape, and their arrival no longer raises eyebrows or causes the excitement, enthusiasm, and expectation of the earlier years, but is now expected. Upon arrival, they rest and are briefed on preparations for the event. The men gather and discuss final preparations, while the women busy themselves instructing their female village counterparts to purchase incense, candles, joss papers and fruits and making individual offerings to the ancestors in the ancestral house. Over the next few days, the women visit the Qing-Shui Temple and make offerings to Qing-shui-zu-shi-gong.

The few days leading to the celebration are busy with last-minute preparations, with men looking after the external events while women involve themselves with food preparation and ritual items needed for the various rites. The various roles for the men are spelled out. Although the *puo-tau* and other active members are to play the roles of religious elders and to lead the procession throughout the various ritual performances, on most occasions younger members substitute for the elders after one or two rounds, because of the tediousness of the performance.

The village atmosphere transforms dramatically with the coming of the Singapore Chinese and the impending celebration. There is intense communication between households, and reciprocal visits between Singapore Chinese and their kin. At night, the men might gather at a particular household, sipping tea, drinking liquor and discussing the coming events. Likewise, women gather together and talk. The social atmosphere is one of festivity and the mood increases as the celebration draws nearer. Children too are keenly aware of the upcoming celebration and become wildly excited about the event, as the schools announce the holiday. Village routine gives way to festivity and celebration, and most villagers become involved in the celebration one way or another.

Emergence of Household Temple and Wayside Shrine

Apart from communal religious fairs linked to Qing-Shui Temple, local temples have also been reconstructed, the most famous being the Zhou-Yue-Miao. Local temples often have a shrine hall where worshippers go in and made their worshipping to the gods. Small wayside shrines housing local deities are stashed in street alcoves, and they too have been revived. Most of these are relatively simple in appearance but are distinguishable by their traditional arched roofs and the constant smoke streaming from the joss incense placed there by worshippers and passers-by. They occupy small areas and have three enclosed sides, with the front facing the street left open. Within, the local god is placed on a concrete platform, together with a medium-sized incense urn, two candle stands and an oil burner with a wick that burns continuously. These wayside shrines are maintained by nearby households who add oil to the burner, replaced the candles and offer incense. Passers-by too make such offerings. However, not all wayside shrines are maintained in good condition, and some have been left to await rehabilitation by the villagers or (more often) the Singaporeans.

Small local temples and wayside shrines do not, in fact, attract much attention from the Singaporeans, as the gods are not known for supernatural abilities. Some villagers and Singapore Chinese give offerings of incense and candles if they are in the vicinity, but most do not seek out these temples to worship. The local temples are mostly patronised by local villagers, mostly by elderly women, although occasionally, a younger woman might pass by and offer an incense stick. These village gods are nearby, and so it is easier to go to them than to Qing-Shui Temple.

Religiosity or Superstition

In the village world, where religion and overt religious practices have been suppressed for several decades, the sudden revival of communal religious fairs and large scale worshipping have brought about mixed feelings and confusion for some. Chinese overseas who visited the home village to perform large-scale communal worship expect their village kin to have the same level of religiosity as themselves, but this has not generally been the case. I have argued that ritual practices have provided the two groups with a shared activity that allows for social bonding to occur. Yet there continue to be differences at the micro-level. Differences in religious experience, religiosity and interest have led to a boundary between the two groups, between "insiders" and "outsiders", which they must confront.

In our survey, we found that the villagers have varying attitudes towards religious practices. Almost every villager felt that religious functions were very closely linked to the Chinese overseas and their needs, which were responsible for the religious revivalism and for the expenditure on religious activities. These are some responses:

> It all depends on what they want to do (the types of rituals) and we do not agree or object to these. We just do as what they suggest. Because they believe in these practices, we should try to accommodate and support their practices. By supporting them, we hope that they will visit us more often.

> It is now fashionable to stage religious activities and we have to participate in these activities. If we do not participate, we will not be giving them face and this will not be good for our family and the lineage as a whole. Our village would also lose much face. On an individual basis, sometimes, I participated in them more actively than other times.

We feel obliged to support these practices as they [Singapore Chinese] wanted these rituals. These rituals are important to them and fulfilled their needs. If we do not give them this support, they might not befriend us. Also, many Chinese overseas believed that their success is due to the blessings of Zu-Shi-Gong. So they returned to give thanks to Zu-Shi-Gong and organise big religious fairs in his honour. We should be understanding regarding this.

The majority of villagers were supportive and participated in the communal religious functions. They also visited Qing-Shui Temple occasionally and prayed to Zu-Shi-Gong, although mostly in company with their Singapore kin. In addition, some prayed to the local village gods. They feel the large-scale religious events provide "noise" and "heat" to the village. In contrast to the years after the Cultural Revolution, when everything was quiet and socially lifeless, the religious events breathe some life into the once sedate village atmosphere.

In contrast, the younger villagers found the religious practices to be wasteful, arguing that the large funds for ritual events could be put to better use, to help with village reconstruction. They feel there should be a limit on the celebrations. Some, however, look upon the religious revival as a way of exercising religious freedom, which had not been possible since the sixties, so that being able to carry out these activities freely was refreshing. However, they also expressed the fear that if the *qiaoxiang* do not exercise discretion over the conduct of religious celebrations, the government authorities might impose restrictions, which would be detrimental to religious freedom. Another reason for disapproving of large-scale celebrations is that they are seen as a leisure pursuit of rich Chinese overseas that highlights the differences in social status between themselves and the villagers. Still others consider the rituals as superstition and regard the Chinese overseas as superstitious *(mi-xin-de)* in their preoccupation with them on their visits.

There are three Christian families in Peng Lai District. Among those Christians who do not participate in these non-Christian religious rituals include a 21- year-old woman from a Christian family and a 51-year-old housewife and her family. The other two families considered themselves as passive participants. They would contribute some money when asked to do so. But they do not actively participate in the rituals.

To the villagers, the significance of religious revivalism and the staging of communal religious fairs is as follows: First, these cultural traditions serve as a bridge between Chinese and village kin, helping them to unite. Second, the activities encourage the Chinese overseas to visit their ancestral home village on a regular basis, which is also instrumental in cementing social and kinship their ties with the *qiaoxiang*. Third, these are important social functions, which bring the villagers themselves together and help to create social solidarity. Fourth, they, as significant social events, create variations in village life and enliven it. Fifth, the religious events and accompanying production of religious paraphernalia and services are important for the local economy, supporting the small cottage industry catering for the dead, the living, and the gods.

Official Patronage and Religious Legitimacy

Village, district and county cadres were more subtle in their support of large-scale communal religious fairs and ritual activities. The village cadres were the most open in their support, while the county level cadres were the least open. The degree of openness is thus tied closely to the needs of persons in varying official positions to display political correctness in their treatment of social events and activities.

As in their support of ancestor-worship activities, cadre support was rationalised. At the village and district levels, the 1978 reform is seen as a watershed for both economic and socio-religious liberalisation. The relaxation of policies pertaining to institutional religion by central government is seen as a positive move to revive religion, which has resulted in a more liberal interpretation and support of village religious practices by the cadres. To a large degree, ancestor worship and communal religious fairs are now interpreted to be support for Confucianism, Buddhism and Daoism; with communal village fairs interpreted specifically as part of the Buddhist and Daoist systems of rituals and rites.

Village and district cadres are much more liberal in their interpretation of these communal rites than are county cadres, for two reasons. First, some are genuine believers. Secondly, there is the instrumental consideration: they feel that, with tolerance and support for the ritual activities, they will be able encourage regular visits by the Chinese overseas. Such visit will eventually lead to contributions and investment into the region.

Cadres supported the reconstruction of Qing-Shui Temple for three reasons. First, they see the temple as having historical value and worthy of preservation, as it is over eight hundred years old, its history stretching back to the Sung Dynasty. The central government has officially named the Qing-Shui-Yuan-Shi as a national historical monument - obviously, the cadres find it necessary to preserve it. Secondly, the temple seen as providing for the religious needs of villagers and Chinese from Southeast Asia and Taiwan, who have visited the temple in great numbers in recent years, supported the temple reconstruction, and staged the massive religious fairs for the deity. Support for the temple and its related functions are thus crucial concessions to Southeast Asian Chinese made to encourage them to invest in the region. Thirdly, the temple is seen as a tourist site and hence significant for the development of the tourist trade in Anxi. The reconstruction has led to an increase in the number of Chinese overseas visiting it, who have brought substantial revenues to Peng Lai District. Indirect benefits also filter down to the people and to the district and county governments.

However, village and district cadres have expressed the need to maintain a balance in the celebrations, the scale of which must be justified by substantial capital investment and aid to the region. The majority of them do not favour large scale, ostentatious celebrations, citing waste of resources as the main reason. However, they do not attempt to interfere in the functions. This non-intervention can be seen as tacit support. Although most village and district cadres do not participate in the ritual performances, they nevertheless oblige the organisers and attend the fair and feast, giving the functions legitimacy. Whatever feelings they have regarding these events, they keep to themselves. Some, who may feel the events are superstitious, nevertheless feel that it would be unwise to stop or boycott them. Others, however, see these as important cultural events that would alleviate the drudgery of village life. Irrespective of the reasons, these cadres want to be seen openly in support of the village cultural and religious activities as they need the support of the villagers to be successful cadres and they need the Singapore Chinese to help develop the *qiaoxiang*.

The county cadres were less supportive of religious activities; 85 per cent of those interviewed expressing disapproval. These felt that such activities are not in line with the ideological orientation of central policies. Their official line of argument is that the functions are superstitious and thus should not be encouraged. They also felt that such activities are a waste of precious resources that could be put to better social and economic use, but they conceded that, given the present socio-economic situation they could not and would not eliminate them. Some were willing to attend the fair's associated feast, to give face to the Chinese overseas who issued the invitation. Thus they too are flexible, wanting to maintain good relationships with the overseas Chinese, who have contributed much financially to the development of Anxi County. County cadres too see religious activity as a part of village cultural tradition that continues to have a profound impact on the life of its adherents. They see that communal spirit has increased with the staging of these religious fairs and the coming of the Chinese overseas and that the villagers are generally happier and less dull.

Thus, among the cadres at each level of the political bureaucracy, there continues to be a tension between support and disapproval of the communal religious fairs. To maintain a balance between pure social and religious functions and the economic interests of the region is a major consideration for the cadres. Overall, however, the communal religious fairs pass muster, and are now an entrenched part of the village social landscape.

Religion as Socio-Economic Capital

When villagers support communal religious celebrations, it is not necessarily a reflection of personal belief or religiosity, but is often a means to an end. Irrespective of age group, religion is seen as socio-economic capital. For example, after the reconstruction of Qing-Shui Temple, the village economy benefited from an annual income of 2-3 Rmb million from contributions for incense and oil by the Chinese overseas. Part of this income goes to the village treasury and is used for social and economic projects.

The pragmatics of treating religion as socio-economic capital are expressed in the following comments:

> We used religion and religious celebrations as the starting point to tap into the sentiments of the Chinese overseas and their contributions. So, we will support and facilitate their religious needs.

> Since these overseas Chinese are so superstitious and have instructed us to perform these religious activities, we should obey their instructions and perform to their satisfaction. If it were not for the sake of their money, then we would not go all out for them. We would put in our minimum for such activities.

> We also hope these religious functions and Qing-Shui Temple will attract the younger Chinese overseas so that they would understand the history of the village, love the ancestral village and help us with our social and economic development.

Conclusion

Religious revivalism has brought about much change in the life of the villagers and the *qiaoxiang*. To a certain degree, the religious communal fairs have revitalised the religiosity of the villagers, especially the older ones, whose formerly suppressed religiosity can now come out in the open. Socially, this revivalism has provided Singapore Chinese and villagers with a common ideology which allows for a renewal of kinship ties and social networks. It has provided the villagers with a new set of activities to liven the village atmosphere. It has also led to the emergence of a cottage industry geared to the production of religious paraphernalia and other related religious services.

Photo 4 Welcoming Overseas Chinese to the Ancestral Village

Photo 5 The Lineage Ancestral House

Photo 6 Rite of Gratification

Photo 7 Religious Offerings during Rite of Gratification

Photo 8 Communal Ancestor Worship

Photo 9 Villagers' Offerings to Ancestors and Gods

8 Rewriting Genealogy and Reclaiming One's Cultural Roots

Introduction

To members of the Ke Lineage, inclusion in the lineage genealogy constitutes the ultimate goal in reclaiming one's cultural roots. The final task is thus the addition and rewriting of the genealogy, *xiu-pu* (修譜) (literally mending the genealogy) as this completes the quest for cultural identity and establishes membership, one's position, social status and expounds on one's achievements within the lineage, thereby fragrancing the lineage.

Genealogy: Historical Significance

Chinese genealogies are commonly called *pu*, of which there are several widely recognised types: family registers, *jia-pu* (家譜), lineage registers, *zu-pu* (族譜), clan registers, *zong-pu* (宗譜), and locality registers, *fang-zhi* (方志).

It is generally agreed that the composition of Chinese genealogies began in the early Zhou period (1111-256 B.C.). However, it was only during the Chun Qiu period (770-477 B.C.) that the practice became fully developed (Lo, 1972b: 38). Though developed at such an early date, the fate of the genealogical records was highly dependent on the regime that succeeded in controlling China at different historical epochs. Throughout history, there have been several phases when large-scale destruction of records occurred. Records showed that the first phase of destruction occurred when Qin Shi Fan Di came into power and ordered the wholesale burning of maps, census registers and other works, among which were genealogies of some important families.

There were also periods where preservation of genealogies was encouraged by the imperial order. From the Han Dynasty through the Sui Dynasty (206 B.C. to A.D. 220), most royal houses, aristocratic families and clans of good standing kept genealogical records, some establishing offices solely for the purpose of keeping records and framing new genealogies (ibid: 38-39). The significance of genealogy was elevated to a new height, as social background became an important factor in gaining entry into the imperial bureaucracy and thereby achieving upward mobility and social success. Thus, during the Ming and Qing epochs, the gentry class focused their attention upon framing, printing and preserving their genealogies. After the founding of the Republic of China in 1911, many big clans and families all over China had taken a keener interest in the making of a genealogy. Lesser clans and lineages did so as well.

When the Chinese Communist Party took power, it engaged in a massive effort to destroy all existing records that were considered bourgeois in origin. Many family, clan and lineage genealogies and locality registers were destroyed in this "cleansing" campaign. Most were destroyed on a voluntary basis for fear of persecution, but others were destroyed forcibly by communist cadres. The result was a massive loss of some of the most important records for shedding light on the social history of China during previous historical epochs (Lo, 1972b: 38-55).

1950s and 1960s

According to Professor Akigoro Taga, who conducted a comprehensive search for them in the 1950s and 1960s, Chinese genealogies at the time numbered only some three thousand copies, which were found scattered in different university libraries throughout the world. According to his estimates, in Japan there were 818 genealogies housed in the Tokyo Bunko library; the Congress Library in Tokyo had 440; Tokyo University's Institute for Oriental Culture had 236 and its Institute of Oriental History Research had 6; Kyoto University's Research Institute of Humanistic Science had 4; the Cabinet Library had 3; Seika Do Bunko's Commission for Research in Modern China and Keio University's Research Institute of Chinese Literature had one each. The total number, minus overlapping genealogies, is 1,228. In the United States, Columbia University's East Asian Library had 926 genealogies while the Harvard-Yenching Institute's Chinese-Japanese Library had a collection of 125.

Within China, Beijing University had a collection of 348; the provincial library of Guangdong had 208 (primarily of clan genealogies); the National Sun Yat Sun Library had 59 genealogies; Nanking library housed 43; and the Chinese Academy of Science had 20. Almost all of these genealogies were framed during the Qing and Republican years. In Hong Kong, the Fung Ping Shan Library at the University of Hong Kong had a collection of 94 genealogies, also of the Qing and Republican years, but these were mostly of clan genealogies of those living in the New Territories (Lo, 1972b: 49).

These collections represented only a sample of what used to exist prior to the massive destruction by the Communist regime. Although the sample is sufficient to draw some broad conclusions about the various issues that are interesting to social historians and anthropologists, care must be taken in evaluating it. Many of these genealogies came from only a few Chinese provinces and hence are not representative of the whole country. For example, Akigoro Taga's catalogue of the 1,197 genealogies housed in Japan came primarily from three main provinces: Jiangsu (433 genealogies), Zhejiang (378) and Anhui (118). In other words, more than 75 per cent of the genealogical records that are available came from the three provinces around the Yangzi Delta region. It is also disturbing to note that in areas where kinship structures were important and strong, such as in Fujian and Sichuan provinces, few genealogical records were found (van der Sprenkel, 1973: 86).

Composition of a Genealogy

The existing genealogical records are usually composed of various sections that provide a wide range of information. There is usually a section on the descent pattern of the lineage and the branches of the family. The five-generation tabular form created by scholar-politician Ou-yang Hsiu (A.D. 1800-1072) of the Sung Dynasty, is most commonly used to record the lineage and branches of genealogical records (van der Sprenkel, 1973: 14)

The Ou-yang style records the family tree, beginning with the primogenitor where he first settled in a place and raised his family there, and ending with the contemporary generation that recorded the genealogy. Those in between are elaborated upon. The primogenitor and his great-great grandsons constitute five generations and are tabulated in one line, with the offspring listed laterally. There are descriptions of each generation, often very short narration, which include names and aliases of each ancestor, dates of birth and death, academic degrees, official ranks, location of graves; names, dates of birth and death of wife (wives) and location of graves; and the names of sons and daughters. This style is used for both the main lineage and the branches (van der Sprenkel, 1973: 14).

Other important information included in the tabulation is the existence of ancestral halls and graveyards. Ancestral halls were not built until the Ming epoch, where Emperor Shih Tsung (A.D. 1552-1556), decreed that the people of the nation made regular sacrificial offerings to their ancestors (van der Sprenkel, 1973: 14), after which families of some social standing built them for the purpose. Often, there was also detailed information regarding the *feng-shui* and sites of ancestral tombs. At times, wealthy families assigned portions of farmland to ancestors' tombs as ritual land, so that sacrifices could be held regularly and in style (van der Sprenkel, 1973: 15).

The academic degrees and official ranks of individual members were recorded in genealogies in great detail. This was important during the later regimes, for it provided the social background of family members who sought entry into the Mandarin bureaucracy. Often a candidate taking the imperial examination was expected to be from a family of good standing. In practice, once a person had launched himself in the Mandarinate, there would be great attempts to record his position and that of other members of his lineage, thus adding prestige to the lineage. It was a common practice for lineages to record the positions of *chu-ren, zhi-shi* and *han-lin* attained by their scholarly members (van der Sprenkel, 1973: 16).

Records of educational activities conducted by the clans and lineages are also found in the genealogy. As education was the most prized commodity and attaining the literati status a dream desired by all, clans and lineages organised classes, established schools and provided scholarship for bright young boys to pursue literary skills. During the Republican era, many ancestral halls were converted to schools for this purpose. There were also records on the teaching of Confucian moral values to the members (van der Sprenkel, 1973: 16).

Included in the genealogy was also information regarding the contribution, wealth and occupation of individual members. Members who engaged in philanthropic and charity works or provided great services to the lineage or clan were listed for their contributions. Likewise, morally upright clan elders and leaders were also given special mention in the genealogy.

Literary works of family or clan members, of both poetry and prose, were also documented in the genealogy. Many genealogies also include a "miscellaneous" section where additional information was offered. Included here were the mythological origin of the lineage and new skills and inventions by members (van der Sprenkel, 1973: 17).

Genealogy as a Resource Base

The types of information found in a genealogy provide clues to the social history of a specific family or lineage. Needless to say, the longer the historical depth of the genealogy, the greater the amount of information.

Some genealogies have a depth of over three or four hundred years of documentation. If sufficient genealogies could be assembled and studied in their entirety, the wealth of information would allow for a macro-societal analysis of the social morphology of Chinese society. At a more generalised level, specific functions of the genealogies can be listed as follows:

(1) Family and Kinship Patterns

One important source of information in the genealogical registers was the detailed records of births and death of all male members and their wives. This kind of information provides clues to kinship and marriage patterns of the family, lineage and clan as well as the demography of the wider society. At the individual level, genealogies tell us about the marriage links between or among families. Through examining members with different surnames who marry in and out of the families, it is possible for us to ascertain the extent to which marriage served as an alliance system, upon which families asserted their social influence, raised their social status and consolidated their power base. It also provides us with clues to the extent of reciprocity between the families. The details of births and death allow for deduction concerning birth rates and fertility patterns, as well as life expectancies.

However, some scholars have argued that the information given in the genealogies fails to provide an accurate picture of the actual demography of the family or lineage. This is especially so for the early genealogical registers with selective entries. To begin with, the practice of not including the daughters in the genealogy provides a biased picture. However, this was rectified in later genealogies where not only daughters, but (at times) sons-in-law, were also mentioned. There was also the problem of infant mortality rates. Only those children that survived were recorded, which meant that we could build a picture of the living but not the actual birth rate. This is compounded by the fact that those children who did not survive more than a few years were not included either. Likewise, genealogies do not provide accurate pictures of the sex ratio of infants. Female infanticide was widely practised, but there was no way of finding this out from the genealogies. Eberhard argued that the gross imbalance in the sex ratio (in favour of the male members) could be regarded as testimony to the practice of female infanticide. While plausible, this remains at best speculative (Eberhard, 1972: 33). It was also a common practice in Chinese families and lineages to exclude those members who had committed serious crimes or had behaved immorally, further distorting the picture found in the genealogies.

The entry of birth and death dates of sons in the genealogy makes it possible to study the life expectancy of the Chinese males who had survived childhood. It is also possible to deduce the length of fertility of couples by comparing the dates of birth of children with those of their parents. Eberhard found that there was a progressive drop, over time, in the age of the parents with a first born. Around A.D. 1200, parents were over twenty-five years of age when they had their first born; by 1800 A.D., the age had dropped to twenty-two. At the same time, life expectancy had also dropped progressively through the years, until the mid-nineteenth century. From this information, he concluded that there must have been a lowering of the marriage age, pointing to difficult living conditions and poor economic conditions. We may also calculate age differences between husbands and wives from the birth dates and horoscopes that were recorded. Under normal circumstances, the age of the husband was usually a few years more than that of his wife. If the wife's age was much greater than her husband's, it meant that the family was poor and had taken a girl into the house as future wife for the son. Such a girl (童養媳) would provide free labour when the boy was still young (Eberhard, 1972: 31).

The economic might of certain families was also reflected in the marriage pattern. Only wealthy families could afford to have secondary wives and concubines. In the genealogy, there were usually records of the status of women, either as principal wife or as concubines, and of their respective offspring. These reflect the extent to which polygamy was closely linked to the economic wealth of the family. As a general rule, the principal wife usually bore more children than the concubines, who usually came from a lower social class. Sometimes, these children might enjoy similar status as the offspring of the principal wife. However, it was usually the first born son of the principal wife who would be the successor, and it was he who would perform the last rites to the father upon his death. These families at times devised methods to differentiate between the offspring of the principal and secondary wives. One method was for the principal and subsequent wives to use different naming systems. It was a common practice to have one word in the two-word given name - usually the second one - common to all names of the same generation. In cases where children were born to both the principal wife and concubines, this second word might differ between the children of the principal wife and those of the concubines. Thus, by looking at the name, it was possible to establish the identity of the children (Eberhard, 1972: 31-32).

A second wife could also be taken into the family upon the death of the first or when the first was divorced. As divorce was very rare in China, it was more frequent that a second wife, *tian-fang* (添房) was taken as a substitute, after the death of the principal wife, to mend the household and take care of the children left behind by her.

Genealogies also inform us of the extent of adoption within the lineage. It was a common practice for families to adopt brother's sons, particularly when the adopting brother had no son. Such an adoption would enable the adopted son to carry out the last rites. At times, "ritual adoption" was conducted where the adopted son continued to share two sets of parents and lived with his biological parents but performed the last rites for the adopted parents. In most cases, adoption outside the family was frowned upon, but there were cases of this being practised (Eberhard, 1972: 32). The diverse methods of adoption allow us to estimate the fertility and infertility of couples, as well as to investigate changes within the family structure over time. This is possible through comparisons among existing genealogies and biographies of well-known individuals (Eberhard, 1972: 33).

Genealogies also inform us of the practice of uxorilocal marriage and residence. Often, wealthy families with only daughters would invite the sons-in-law into the family, whereupon the first born son of the couple would usually take on the surname of the girl's family. The second and other sons would then resume the man's surname. This often took place when the man was from a poor family Eberhard, 1972: 32).

Another sociological significance of the genealogy is that it allows us to calculate the rate of upward mobility through the centuries. The elaborate details on members who succeeded in imperial examinations and received appointments in the bureaucracy often signify elevations in a family's social status and the beginning of its upward mobility, or its ability to maintain and upgrade its status through the centuries. It is estimated that during the earlier centuries, many families tried to get their eldest sons into the examination and obtain civil appointment. However, in later centuries, families tried to get the most able son into it, reflecting the progressive difficulties in passing the examination (Eberhard, 1972: 35).

(2) Migration and Establishment

The genealogies also showed great details on movements of families and lineages, often detailing the migration of the first member of a family to a different region, either voluntarily or by coercion. Throughout Chinese history, it was not uncommon for criminals and those who fell foul of the administration and their families to be exiled to different regions. There were also veterans who were relocated by the government to newly opened lands in South China. Though there is no mention of criminal records, the genealogies nevertheless provide information on the social movements and inter-marriages between these families. Other persons migrated in search of greener pastures. This form of migration followed well-established routes, following the rivers and the lines of communication (Eberhard, 1972: 36).

The genealogies also show the diffusion process of the family structure. Once settled and having acquired some wealth, families began to acquire new lands. The original family often continued to reside in the same location, while their sons were sent out to manage new fields at a distance. Through time, new branches were set up, creating a "family colony" (Eberhard, 1972: 36). The branch families continued to pay allegiance to the main family, which continued to be an important ritual and economic centre for the extended family. Important ritual events were held within the main family household. It provided economic assistance to those branches that needed aid; likewise, the branches sent money to the main family if they were able to. It was this form of social obligation and reciprocity that bound the main family and its branches together; and this also explains why the overseas Chinese have continued to be bound to their main families for generations (Eberhard, 1972: 36).

It was also not uncommon for government officials, sent to administer distant places, to acquire lands of the region under their administrations. At a later stage, these officials retired into the regions and assumed high status in the district. Often these families would separate from their main families and establish themselves as main families (Eberhard, 1972: 36).

At times, deviant sons, who did not follow in the scholarly footsteps expected of them would leave the family. Some ended up as merchants and amassed great wealth. While some contributed gifts and money to the main family, others acquired property in distant lands, establishing permanent settlements and finally acquiring independent identities (Eberhard, 1972: 36). This was especially true of those who emigrated and settled in Southeast Asia.

Rewriting Genealogy and its Contemporary Relevance

After the Communist victory in 1949, any kind of major lineage activity, including the compiling of genealogies, came to a complete halt. Indeed, many of the genealogies have been destroyed during the Cultural Revolution. However, among the lineages of Fujian, attempts to conceal them have been successful. It is only in recent years members are made aware of the existence of the lineage genealogies.

There is a resurgence of interest in genealogy among Singapore Chinese. Those who have continued to maintain strong ties with lineage members in their *qiaoxiang* are now busily engaged in the process of re-compiling their genealogies (*xiu-pu*), as many elderly members feel an urgent need to make new entries before their generation dies out. To them, it is important that a new genealogy be compiled so that their descendants living in the overseas environment can be included, as the incorporation of overseas members will allow for lineage continuity. Thus, in rewriting genealogies, Chinese overseas seek to incorporate not only the members of the lineage in China, but also themselves.

The writing of genealogies, which can document the existence of individuals and their success, wealth and contributions, is important, as thereby successful and ambitious individuals can reassert their identities and assert their dominance within the lineage. For Singapore Chinese, this is an assertion of power and wealth made possible as a result of their emigration to the Nanyang region during earlier years. Genealogy thereby helps to establish or re-establish a hierarchy of dominance and power amidst complex social relationships. Such a hierarchy of power is now based not so much on seniority and wisdom, as it would be according to Confucian tradition, but on wealth and *guanxi* with wealthy and politically powerful elite.

In a sense, genealogy serves as a cultural idiom, reinforcing the traditional social divide between insiders and outsiders. Now, however, the divide is deeper and wider. Those who have the wealth to perform philanthropic and charity works, who are politically prominent or who are scholarly-oriented are given prominence in the genealogy. In this regard, the genealogy reflects the present-day reality of the inversion of the traditional class order, where businessmen and entrepreneurs are given disproportionate attention. It also reflects on the predominance of Chinese overseas entrepreneurs and businessmen and their contributions to home villages, to their countries of domicile and to their communities. While blood ties remain an important criterion for one's inclusion in a genealogy, the actual boundary of the lineage becomes slightly negotiable in favour of those with wealth and status, as every lineage wants a share of members with wealth, knowledge, status and power. Thus, Chinese without a lineage can buy their way by becoming an adopted son of a lineage member as adopted sons are counted as part of the lineage structure. Biological or blood ties thus continue to be only one criterion for admission. This flexibility of the lineage boundary allows the Chinese overseas to gain significant inroads into the inner circles of lineage committees. The situation is not unlike during the nineteenth century when the Qing government, with a bankrupt coffer, sold imperial titles to overseas Chinese.

Genealogy serves as a symbolic representation of kinship relations, cutting out those who are at the margins. The social deviants, non-conformists and political radicals can, theoretically, become excluded. However, included in the genealogy will be those sons that are not recognised officially by the Communist regime (those families who failed to adhere to the one-child policy and thus did not report the birth of subsequent children to the authority). As such, such children have no official status or identity, but they are recorded in the genealogy, thereby providing us with much information on the demography and the success or failure of the centrally administered family planning policies.

Recompiling the Chinese genealogy, which incorporates both the mainland and Chinese overseas as part of a single lineage, is, to a certain extent, an attempt by the Chinese to rewrite their own history and cultural identity in a rapidly changing environment. This is particularly so for Chinese overseas who have found that their cultural identity has been increasingly subjected to challenges by forces of ethnic pluralism, corporatism and homogenisation; as well as by those of modernity and social liberalism. To them, the only way to arrest this is by looking back to their source of origin and understanding their position within the wider lineage structure. Exploring the genealogy is one main way of identifying oneself and giving oneself a cultural identity.

Re-compiling Ke Lineage Genealogy

It was the Singapore Ke lineage elders who first mooted the idea of compiling and updating the genealogy in the 1989 when they visited their ancestral village. In 1990, a year later, several Singapore Chinese, after a subsequent meeting with the Singapore elders, returned to the village to gather support and do preparation for launching this project. It was only in 1994, when during the first meeting of the World Anxi Association, held in Anxi, that the idea of recompiling the Ke Lineage Genealogy became finalised. Upon returning to Singapore, a group of elders voted in support of the recompilation. During the spring of 1995, a Singapore elder returned to Peng Lai Kui-Tou Village and invited every Ke household to a meeting to discuss recompilation of the genealogy. During the meeting, it was agreed that a recompilation was necessary. At the same meeting, it was agreed that there would be two committees formed for this project. An executive committee of 11 Singapore elders would be based in Singapore. A second managing committee of 7 village elders would be based in Anxi. The managing committee would be divided into 4 sections mainly editorial, compilation, treasury and management.

The committee had selected an auspicious date to stage the "opening of lineage genealogy" ceremony, *kai-pu-yi-shi* on the 8th day of the 2nd lunar month in 1995 to inform the ancestors of the start of the lineage recompilation. A chief compiler was appointed to do the entry of new names and amend any mistakes and omissions found in the earlier versions. The project was given one and a half years to complete. It was scheduled that the recompilation should complete and the new genealogy made available to all members by the 3rd day of the 10th lunar month of 1996 where the "closing of lineage genealogy", *xie-pu-yi-shi* ceremony was planned. This was to be followed by the "celebration of descendants", *zu-ding* ritual ceremony a few days later on the 8th day of the 10th lunar month.

The reason for compiling and updating the genealogy was a simple one. It had been over half a decade since the last entry was made. A whole new generation of Chinese had not been included, and the time had come to make the new entries. This need to re-compile the genealogy was made more urgent by the fact that the Singapore branch of the Ke lineage has moved in a separate direction, especially the younger generation of Singapore Ke members, who have less emotional attachment and hence, less concern for their ancestral home. Their disinterest also means that they are less likely to be interested in tracing their genealogical roots, let alone re-compiling the genealogy. For elderly Ke members, inscribing the present generation in a recompiled genealogy had become part of their moral responsibility. They hoped that by doing so, the future generation would have reference to their forebears.

There had been two to three generations since the last compilation. By bringing together the names of all members, the recompilation would allow lineage members to know the expansion of their members, including those overseas. A search for lineage members globally was then conducted as, while the majority of Ke emigrants went to Singapore and Malaysia, others went to Indonesia, Burma, Thailand or the Philippines, as well as to western countries such as Australia and America. However, the immediate concern of elderly Ke lineage members was to allow their own children, grandchildren and great-grandchildren to know their own origin and source, to prevent a permanent break in the genealogical record, arguing that their basic responsibility was not to allow such a break during their own generation. If the younger members have no interest in maintaining lineage continuity, it will be the problem of the younger generation and they will have to face the consequence of answering for the break to their descendants. The conscience of the elderly Ke members thus required that they do their part to ensure the genealogical continuity of their lineage, and so perform their filial duty to their ancestors and carry out their moral responsibility to their descendants.

An added factor in this urgency was the relatively relaxed political climate in Communist China and the amicable attitude of the Communist cadres towards cultural events and items. In the emigrant villages, official cadres not only supported the process of re-compilation, but some became involved in it. To them too, it was important for all members to "recognise the ancestors", *ren-zu* (認祖), and particularly the babaised Singapore Chinese. They felt that by supporting the compilation of the genealogy, they were indirectly encouraging and fostering good will and winning the trust of the Chinese overseas, and hoped that this would encourage the Singapore Chinese to become culturally involved in village activities and contribute to village reconstruction and development. Many cadres too, therefore, had felt that the time had come to embark on re-compiling the genealogy.

Who should be included?

The main consideration during the recompiling was who should be included and who should be excluded? The inclusion and exclusion of members in a genealogy requires a difficult and delicate decision-making process. Ideally, all members should and would be incorporated. However, it turned out that not all members wanted to be included; and there were others who wanted to be included but were refused entry, as they were not considered part of the lineage. Discussion concerning the entry of new members was thus a lengthy process.

The main target was for total inclusion of all living members of the Ke lineage of Anxi ancestry scattered throughout the world. In China, about one-third of the members continue to live in Anxi, although a small number live in other cities in China. About two-thirds of the lineage members reside in Singapore, Malaysia, Taiwan, and other Southeast Asian countries. Others live in America and Australia. They originally went to United States and Australia for their studies in the 1970s and remained behind after their education. Who were these people and how could they be included in the genealogy? What was the possibility of total inclusion? Or would there be an incomplete genealogical update?

Inclusive Strategy

As mentioned, the committee had adopted an all-inclusive strategy for this new compilation, aiming to include every known person into the genealogy. In the emigrant villages, 95 per cent of lineage members were eager and excited over the re-compilation of the genealogy and expected to be included, so there was no problem with them. The territorial confines of the villages and the relatively low mobility of the members enabled a complete list of the members to be drawn up with relative ease. This had been especially important for sons who had not been recorded as part of the household system as a result of the One Child Policy.[1] Such sons are important, as they will eventually assume the headship of households and continue their immediate family lines. The genealogy thus provides these families with a legitimate means of recording and proving their existence in the lineage.

On the other hand, including every member who had emigrated overseas proved to be a more difficult task than anticipated. There are three recognisable categories of overseas members. First, there are those who have, through the years, maintained some kind of contact with the home village or with other kin known to the lineage in their adopted countries. They are thus part of the lineage network, and there was no difficulty in contacting them and including them and their families in the genealogy. Many of these are also members of the Ke Surname Association in Singapore, Malaysia or other parts of Southeast Asia. Fortunately, this category forms the majority.

The second category are those who have not maintained any contact and are not known to other kin, either inside or outside the ancestral village. There was no way of knowing and contacting them, and so they could not be included in the genealogy.

A third category of lineage members consists of those who are known to the kin inside and outside the ancestral village but had chosen not to acknowledge their status within the lineage and did not wish to be included in the genealogy. There is currently a handful of these. The elders told me that one main reason why they were not included was that these members had openly refused the invitation of the committee to be included in the genealogy. These members argued that they no longer had any contact or desire for contact with their home village, and so they felt that it would be futile for them to have their names and that of their children to be written into the genealogy. According to the committee members, they told me that if members insisted on having their names omitted then they would not be included in the genealogy. But that the committee would explain to them that their family tree would thus stop with their immediate forebears and that once the compilation was completed, no addition could be made. This would be to prevent any conflicts that may arise as a result of non-entry. Often, such members then agreed to entry, even though some had only nominal interest in the lineage and its activities, partly because they desired not to break the family tree. In my survey, some Singapore Ke members told me that while they might not be very active or keen in lineage activities, they would certainly put the names of their ancestors and families in the genealogy, arguing that it is important for the younger generations to know their ancestral origins. So far, there are only two families who refuse to have their names entered into the genealogy.

Existing Genealogies

The first genealogical compilation of *Gui-Tou Ke Si Zu Pu* -the Ke Lineage of the Gui-Tou Village - was completed in the spring of 1541, 211 years after the first arrival of Ban-Shan-Gong. He was widely recognised as the first ancestor of the Ke lineage who resided in the village of Gui-Tou in Peng Lai District in 1330. Today, a tomb within the village is maintained in honour of him. This first complete genealogy recorded the sixth ancestor, Mu-Gan-Gong, through to the eighth ancestor, Peng-Chun-Gong; both were considered pioneers who had settled permanently in the Gui-Tou village and were known for their opening of their lands and the expansion of the Ke Lineage.

There had previously been seven amendments to the genealogy. The second compilation recorded new names from 1541 through to 1717 during the Kang-Xi era. This compilation was organised by Guang-Shen-Gong, and had a depth of 176 years of entry. The third compilation gave new entries from 1717 through to 1755 during the Qian-Long period, and included seventeen significant names. The fourth compilation covered the period 1755 through to 1835, during the reign of Dao-Guang, and had two significant entries. The fifth and sixth amendments were carried out during Guang-Xu era and covered 1835 to 1877 and 1877 to 1907, respectively; the fifth being initiated by Zhong-Lin and the sixth by Da-Zhong; each had 13 significant new names. The seventh amendment covered the period 1907-1948, again with 13 significant entries. The present compilation will be the eight compilation and the generational entries will include those born between 1948 and 1995. During the various compilations, the wealthy villagers, scholars and imperial officials and their achievements were recorded.

However, the lineage had, in its possession, only three earlier compilations: the genealogies of 1835-1877, 1877-1907 and 1907-1948. All earlier versions had been lost and could not be recovered. These three versions had been kept in the possession of the lineage elders in their ancestral house and were consulted when the eighth *xiu-pu* was in process.

Compiling Lineage Genealogy

When the lineage decided to recompile its genealogy, they engaged one main *xiu-pu* master, a retired teacher with the requisite experience, and two assistants to do the entry of names and to look at inconsistent entries and omissions. The retired teacher was also good in Chinese calligraphy - an important attribute, since he would be the person to write all the entries into the genealogy. Two lineage elders helped to verify and authenticate the existing names of lineage members and family branches, make decisions, and weed out inconsistencies found in the various versions. The three of them had to go through the minute details found within the three existent versions and make entries for the new generations. To assist in the task of recompiling, they consulted the Lau lineage genealogy, another one that had recently been recompiled.

Genealogical Content

The new version of the genealogy consists of two volumes. The first volume consists of the primary stems and branches, *zhi* (枝). Here, kinship links were traced from original ancestors downwards, showing the progression from the first generation through the present twenty-ninth generation. In the chronological progression the individual branches spread further and wider, encompassing all male members. The Ou-yang style is used in this genealogy, whereby those of the same generation are linked together in a black horizontal line while those across generations are linked with a red line. The genealogy shows only the male descendants within the family, together with their wives. Daughters, however, were not shown in this stem-and-branch genealogy, unlike some other genealogical styles. When asked about this omission, the elders told me that this was a tradition. There had been no record of female members in previous versions of the genealogy, so they found it inappropriate to add the females in the first volume of this one, which also only shows the stems and branches, arguing that female members are recorded in the second volume. From the stems and branches, all male members are able to trace their ancestral origins from their generation up to the first ancestor, Ban-Shan-Gong.

Along the stems and branches are annotations of the positioning of the sons, so that it is possible to tell who are the first-born sons, who the youngest, etc. There are also annotations indicating those who are deceased and sons that were adopted. The latter were together with the names of the adopting parents. There have been numerous cases where a son was adopted by a newly married couple who subsequently had several biological sons. However, such an adopted son, being the eldest, would assume the role of first-born and, upon the death of the father, would become the head of the household. Adopted sons, in the Chinese society are legitimate sons of the family with the rights and power of biological sons, and are also expected to perform duties upon the death of their foster parents.

Volume 2 consists of annotations and descriptions of each family and generation member, *ye* (葉), including the names of the female members within each family. This is a new entry and was insisted upon by the Singapore Ke members, who feel that daughters are an important part of the family structure. A large part of this volume is devoted to describing the achievements and contributions of its members. Those who have attained wealth, scholarly achievement, successful businesses, and technical skills are described in this volume. Likewise, members who have contributed significantly to public office, home village development and development in their adopted countries are commented upon. Here, a substantial portion has been devoted to the contributions of the overseas members, especially those from Singapore, both to their home village and to Singapore.

Members who have contributed to home village development feature prominently in this volume. This volume gives details of the Singapore members who left their ancestral home, the year they left Anxi, their age, their village background, their family members in Singapore, the types of occupations they were and are presently engaged in, their business enterprises and empires, and their contributions to village infrastructure and to the development of Singapore. Many have contributed to the building of village schools, bridges, roads, hospitals, ancestral houses and residential buildings. Those who have contributed to the construction of the power plant, village cottage factories, tea processing plants and other economic institutions have also been recorded.

In this second volume, the entries and achievements of daughters become significant. Daughters are not part of the stems-and-branches and hence, theoretically, not part of the lineage structure. Traditionally, daughters have been considered temporary members who, after marriage, belong to their husbands' families. The change of surname, and sometimes name, was thus more than symbolic - it ushered in a new phase in the life of women, as daughters-in-law, wives and mothers of their husbands' families. However, in contemporary context, while the lineage continues to be patrilineal and patrilocal, the status of daughters has changed considerably, especially for the Singapore members whose social and politico-economic experience have led them to view women and daughters in quite a different light from that of their village counterparts. To start with, the strict family planning policy of the Singapore government in the 1960s and 1970s has led to many families with two or less children. By the 1980s, women in Singapore are better educated and many choose voluntarily to have no more than two children. Even as the policy of encouraging more children has been implemented in the 1990s, many women continued to choose to have two or less children. The result is that today, the average size of the Chinese family is no more than 4-5 members. Correspondingly, there is also a change in the attitude of the parents towards their children; both sons and daughters tend to have more or less equal treatment, especially in terms of education.

A second factor is the fact that as women have become better educated and economically independent and have attained high office, their voices cannot be excluded. Their very success has made them visible even among conservative Singapore members. They not only are daughters-in-law, wives and mothers of their husbands' families, but also daughters of the agnatic family. Thus, being a daughter is now an independent status not linked to affinal identity. Such a change in attitude towards the female members of the family has implications for the treatment of women in general. It is thus to the advantage of Ke lineage members in Singapore to have daughters included in the genealogy, as many of these daughters have attained high status and achievement in society which are viewed highly, adding prestige to the immediate family and bringing glory to the lineage. The genealogy shows a proportionately high number of daughters of the Singapore branch with a high level of education, many with university degrees, in contrast to a modest number of sons with higher education. Their number compares favourably too with that of the village daughters, the majority of whom have received no more than ten years of education and a large number of who have received only nominal education or none at all.

In conversations with the Singapore members, I discovered that an important reason for the difference in educational attainment between sons and daughters in Singapore has been the desire of their parents, especially those with businesses, to introduce their sons into the businesses at a young age; and this in turn reflects attitudes towards family business, where the sons are expected to help out and succeed their fathers. Daughters, on the other hand, are not burdened with such expectations, and so have the freedom to pursue education without being pressurised to stop in order to help out with the family business. This attitude has been that of Ke lineage members in the 40-50 age group. On the other hand, those in the 20-30 age group have a great desire for both sons and daughters to complete university education. The easy access to education in Singapore has made it possible for the third and subsequent generations of Singapore Chinese to pursue higher education. There has also been an increase in the number of younger lineage members receiving education in a western country, and the ability to send children to a western university reflects the growing wealth, affluence and importance placed on such an education.

Incorporating daughters into the genealogy was a subject of negotiation between the Singapore and Anxi members. The Singapore members expressed their desire to incorporate their daughters, arguing that they, like the sons, are their offspring and so should not be ignored and left out of the lineage system. Because of their power and the wealth that they had contributed to the village economy and because of the fact that the making of the genealogy was funded wholly by the Chinese overseas, primarily those from Singapore, they were able to assert their influence in this matter. However, they would have upset the whole community if they had insisted on the incorporation of the daughters into the volume that records the stems and branches of the family tree.

Significance of Genealogy

(1) Views of the Villagers

In our survey of the Anxi villager, 95 per cent of the villagers had been aware of the genealogy and had felt that it was important for a lineage to have a record of its members. As mentioned above, they were also aware that the lineage was recompiling a new genealogy, had a favourable impression of the project, and felt that they should be included in it. They cited the need to include all members into it, arguing the need to know their ancestors and the ability to trace their ancestral roots. Many villagers said that after Communism and especially after the Cultural Revolution, they were very uncertain as to whether the other branches of the lineage, i.e. the Singapore, Taiwan, Malaysia, etc branches would continue to recognise their Anxi ancestors. They were also under the impression that the younger ones and some older ones had bad opinions of the Anxi villagers. They thought that these overseas members would want a break with the ancestral home. They were very surprised that this was not the case as the elderly members started visiting the ancestral village especially after the 1978 Reform. Furthermore, they continued to bring the younger members to visit the ancestral village. Thus, when asked of the importance of including the Singapore members in the genealogy, they argued that the genealogy is important for lineage continuity among Singapore and Anxi members. The Singapore Chinese, according to the Anxi villagers, had to be included in the genealogy for the following reasons:

(a) The search for roots and a recognition of the ancestral origin

Eighty-five per cent of the villagers surveyed viewed the position of the Singapore Chinese in a positive light, arguing that "since they have recognised that our [i.e., all Ke lineage members'] ancestors were from here, they [the Singaporeans] should be included". Kinship relations are one important way of recognising roots. Thus, "my cousins are Singapore-born and they should be included in the genealogy. It is important that they know Anxi because this is their ancestral home". "They bear the same surname. It is therefore important for overseas Chinese to understand us so that they will be interested in us. Eighty-two per cent of the villagers said that this [inclusion in the genealogy] will ensured that the contacts and relationship will continued. Otherwise, it would be broken. As relatives, we would not know one another if there was no contact and no record of them". Others claimed that "we share the same ancestors", "they are from Anxi", and "it is natural that they be included". Anxi is a source of origin in so far as the villagers are concerned. Thus, "this is their ancestral land even though the younger ones rarely visit here" and "this is their *jia-zu* and it is important for the young ones to recognise their ancestral home". They further stated that "because the roots and the source are located here, this is why the overseas Chinese come back to search for their roots and inquire about their ancestors", and that genealogical records would help them in their validation of their ancestral origin. Another reason given for the inclusion of Singapore Chinese in the genealogy is "so that they know that they are Anxi people and to help them deepen their sentiments towards their home village. As Chinese people, they and we should like our home village".

(b) For future generations

Eighty-seven per cent of the villagers also echoed the view that genealogy is important "so that the young ones would know of Anxi as their ancestral land". They would also understand that "they are descendants of Anxi. This is their origin". It is therefore important for "the descendants to recognise Anxi" as "they are part of the lineage and they should remember their ancestral home". To be included in the genealogy also means "they do not oppose the ancestors". Their ability to trace themselves in the genealogy as Anxi people mean "the descendants will get to know Anxi in order that they do not forget their ancestral home and home village". It is important for the future generations as "they are the children and grandchildren of this place. They only went overseas to seek a livelihood. They should return to their roots, *luo-ye-gui-gen*. They are the leaves and we are the roots. So, it is natural that they be included". "This [genealogy] is important to them when they want to search their roots and their relatives in future" as "it provides a written record for future generations. It is thus important that they are all included". To be included is "important so that we know who they are and if the younger generation did not recognise our ancestry, then they would become *fan*". The "overseas Chinese need to know their roots. That is why re-writing the genealogy is so important - it is important for the young ones to know their roots" as "this is for future generations". "If the lineage is broken, then it is impossible for them to locate their ancestors".

Furthermore, "they are an offshoot from here and it is especially important for the younger generations to come back and get to know the village members. Otherwise, they would not know us. They should come back and understand their village".

(c) Pragmatic considerations

To be included in the genealogy and be seen as a member is an important asset, as membership brings along a certain amount of social obligation to the villagers on the part of the Singapore members. Sixty-four per cent of the villagers argued that as lineage members, the Singapore Chinese should feel obligated to make important contributions to village reconstruction. Furthermore, their contributions should be acknowledged in their genealogy. "They [my Singapore relatives] should be included in the genealogy. They have contributed much to schools, their ancestral house and other public infrastructures. We should record their achievement and contribution in the genealogy". "He [a Singapore kinsman] has always thought of home and contributed to all public projects - ancestral home, hospital, etc. He was also very enthusiastic to become a pu-tau and contributed to this", argued an emotional villager. He further stated that "they should be included in the genealogy. After all, the cost of rewriting the genealogy comes from them (about 70,000 Rmb)". Another said, "they are members of this lineage and village and have contributed millions to village development. By incorporating them into the genealogy, it is a way of letting them know that Anxi is their ancestral home. Hopefully, once included, they will be aroused to become more interested in village affairs and their relationship with the village would be further enhanced".

(d) Cultural tradition

To 69 per cent of the villagers, "it is important, because it is a village tradition that the genealogy is a record of remembrance of its members". As the Singapore Chinese organised the rewriting, the villagers took this to be that "they [Singapore members] considered themselves as Chinese and as lineage members". As a cultural tradition, it is therefore important that "its members, both the Singapore and village members, understand the generational and genealogical order among us" so that they can accord us the necessarily respect befitting our elderly status.

(e) Historical record

According to 52 per cent of the villagers, "this is a record of our history and is meant for our future descendants. It is very important that the future generations know and recognise Anxi so that we will know one another" since "it is a historical tradition, its records need to be preserved. If there is no record, then, there will be no way that they or we could trace our roots, especially when we are separated and have no contacts". Thus, "inclusion is important because it is our roots and a record of our historical ancestors and families". Here, "genealogy records our lineage history. The younger ones should know Anxi so that the ties will not be broken. If they know their ancestors are from here, they can then find their ancestors". "Members residing overseas should be included so that we know who are our descendants and know of their success in other countries". Also, "It is important to know of their contributions to the home village and their adopted country". Genealogy should be seen as "a record of our contributions and achievements in both to our home village and the adopted countries".

(f) Including the "uncivilised guests" fan-ke [M], fan-ke [H] (番客).

The village members were also aware that some of the Singapore Chinese did not wish to be included in the genealogy. Ninety-three per cent felt that this was not right, for these Singapore members were depriving the lineage of a complete record of their descendants. Despite their dissatisfaction, there was little they could do but to accept this. They saw these Singapore members as becoming uncivilised and babaised. A 79-year old village female elder said, "some of them, especially the English-educated, do not want to be included in the genealogy because they do not the members in the Anxi villages". Despite this, the Anxi kin continued to feel that the reluctant members should be included in the genealogy "so that the future generations have a record of their roots, their ancestors and their home village, as this is not for their personal interests but for the whole lineage". "Those who are English educated", said this 79-year old village elder, "have become *fan* and do not understand the significance of the genealogy. But it does not mean that they should be deliberately excluded". A young villager, 26-year old male, had this to say: "my aunt told me that her children have expressed disinterest in the village and do not want to be included in the genealogy. We told them that if they do not want to recognise the ancestors, if the future generations could not find their roots, they should not blame us for the exclusion. Furthermore, there is nothing we can do even if they regretted their actions". Despite the fact that the villagers regarded these people as having turned *fan*, they were apprehensive at their being excluded. Thus, a 63 year-old village man said, "though some who have been there for 40 years or more have turned *fan,* their descendants might want to search for their roots in the future. A record in the genealogy is important for it allows my nephews and grandnephews to come back and search for their relatives".

(g) Initiatives from the Singapore members

The Singapore Chinese actively initiated the rewriting of the genealogy. One village male elder said:

> *xiu-pu* is very important. They [Singapore Chinese] are very enthusiastic about *xiu-pu* because they recognise their ancestors. These activities are being promoted by the overseas Chinese. It is therefore very important for them to be incorporated into the genealogy so that their achievements can be recorded and their future generations will know of their ancestral origins and of their ancestors. Such initiatives on the part of the Singapore members have allowed for continuity of generations and of the different member groups coming together. We should also understand that. During the earlier years, they took initiatives and went out because of economic difficulties. Now that they are successful and have taken initiatives to recompile the genealogy, we should support such a move and include them wholeheartedly. What they want is also what we want - to ensure that our lineage relationship is not broken.

(h) Strengthening of kinship ties

Genealogy is important because "it is good for the home village and would strengthen our traditional ties". It is the members that make up the lineage collective. Thus, a 69-year old village male said, "we should send people out to search for all members and ask them to provide information on themselves and their families so that we can record them. They are our people, our children and grandchildren". Such a move is important because re-compilation is only done every few decades. By having all members together, "we would know our strength and hopefully each member would play a role in strengthening the lineage ties".

(2) Views of the Singapore members

The importance of inclusion in the genealogy is also articulated by the Singapore Chinese.

(a) Reminder of one's cultural roots

The Singapore members see genealogy as a reminder of one's cultural roots

- especially important for the younger generations, as older Singaporeans are concerned to prevent the eventual loss of cultural roots and self-identity by the younger generations of the Singapore-born. The genealogy is an important source in which they record the continuity of their ancestors and of their present whereabouts. A 52-year old Singapore male said, "if there is someone writing the genealogy, it is good to be included so that we know who our ancestors are. It is also very important for our descendants to know Anxi because of the need to understand our roots from a historical point of view. Although we have been naturalised [as citizens] in another country, we should not forget our roots and should know more of our origin. This is important. They [descendants] should know more about their ancestors and their achievements".

(b) Recalling their roots

Another 45-year old woman said, "it is important to be included in order to understand our generational tree and to recall all names". She continued, "it is important for my family and I to be included in the genealogy so that each generation is passed down to the other (sic). We need to know that we are Chinese. It is important for the younger Singapore Chinese to know their home village so that they know their roots. This is a Chinese tradition". Another 70-year old male said, "Anxi is our root. We must prepare the next generation and help them to understand their cultural and ancestral roots. We should not break the relationship". An 84-year old Singapore male elder said that "our Singapore ancestors are from Anxi and the roots should not be broken".

(c) Understanding generational hierarchical structure

Eighty-four per cent of the Singapore informants said that genealogy is also important in "informing one of generational ranking". A 79-year old male informant stated that "[Genealogy] is to record blood ties. It is important to record our family in it and to know whether our family stands in relation to others. This is for the future generations to search for their roots. This is a Chinese traditional way of thinking. If it is possible, there is a need for complete recording of all members, but this is not easy". As already mentioned, a few families refused to have their present names recorded in the genealogy, so there will always be a gap of entry in the genealogy.

(d) A social history

Eighty-two per cent of the Singapore informants agreed about the importance of being included in the genealogy as "it is a record of your social history, how we developed and how our ancestors developed and their achievements". It is "...important to be included because we still have sentiments towards our home village". Many of the older members said that it is important "to let the future generations know where we came from and to continue the tradition and prevent it from breaking". Another stressed its importance in this way: "this is a Chinese tradition and it allows us to know of our ancestors' movements. It is a record of our origin and movement and of our ancestors too".

Why Some Choose Not to be Included in the Genealogy?

There are others who do not see inclusion in the genealogy as important. In our survey, only two families choose not to want to have their names entered into the genealogy. One said, "I do not think that it is necessary or important for us to be included in the genealogy except for the sake of knowing our roots and where our ancestors were from". In this case, he finally submitted his name and the names of members of his family as he did not want to be blamed for leaving a gap in the family tree. A second man said, "inclusion in the genealogy depends on individuals. Most of us are more westernised are less concerned about it".

Cost

Compiling a genealogy is an expensive project. The cost of compiling the genealogy was estimated to amount to 700,000 Rmb. This includes the cost of hiring the *xiu-pu* master and his two assistants for a year, printing costs and the cost of the ritual ceremonies that mark the opening and completion of the genealogy (*kai-pu* and *xie-pu-yi-shi*, respectively).

Funding came primarily from the Singapore members. 4 of the 11 initiators of the project contributed S$10,000 each. At an exchange of around S$1 to 5Rmb, it came up to about 200,000 Rmb. The others contributed S$1,000 - 5,000 each. The committee in charge of the genealogy project agreed among themselves a charge a sum of S$1,000 from the well-to-do Singapore members for an entry of all family names. These members would be given a genealogical register. Others could contribute whatever sum they can afford. The Anxi villagers had the names of their families included without the need to pay. Those who wanted neither to contribute nor to have their names included had to make known their objections. According to the Singapore elders, "there are very few who do not want to be included. Almost all want to have the names of their families recorded in the genealogy. When we tell them of this project and of the need to contribute, they sign a cheque and come forward with a list of names of their family members". These names were then collected and given to three compilers who make the entries.

A breakdown of the cost included the following. The genealogy master was paid 3000 Rmb per month plus food and housing as he is not a Ke member and lived in another part of Anxi. The cost of production that included employing a company to input the 2-volume genealogy into a computer cost 150,000 Rmb and the printing of 200 copies cost 100,000 Rmb. The rest of the money collected was used for the "closing of the genealogy" ceremony which came up to over 400,000 Rmb.

The Process of Compilation

The process of *xiu-pu* was a methodical one. From conception of the idea through the collection of new names, the entry of names (hand-written by the genealogy master), the entry into the computer, the printing of the genealogy and the final closing of genealogy ceremony, this project took about three years.

(1) Conception of the genealogy project

In 1994, talks about the need to recompile the lineage genealogy began among several active Singapore and Anxi members, who felt that the time had come, as some two to three generations had not been recorded since the last recompilation. The older generation felt that the compilation should be done while the elders were still alive so that they could provide missing information on their immediate forebears and help chart the family tree, stems and branches. They worried that, otherwise, vital information might be lost forever after the elders passed away.

(2) Format of the new genealogy

The most important consideration for the recompilation of the genealogy was the format. They could have followed the traditional style or have adopted new ones. Before they decided on the format, the compilers together with the committee had decided on the amount of information to be included in the genealogy and had opted for a two-volume genealogy. In deciding on this format, they consulted recently compiled genealogies of other lineages and adopted the format used in the Lau Surname Genealogy.

(3) Collection of names of members from each household

Collection of names of members from each household was done systematically by committee members. The Anxi elders were responsible for informing all households of the project. Each household then submitted a list of members within the household, including the daughters (married and unmarried). For those who were illiterate, the village elders compiled the list for them using the birth documents and oral information from the household concerned. In Singapore the same method was employed, except that, there, local elders also asked for contributions.

Heads of households were required to submit a list of all living members from all generations, including parents, sons and daughters, grandchildren and great grandchildren. They were also required to submit their achievements and contributions to their present homes and to the ancestral home, and the achievements of their children and grandchildren. Selected members with recognisable achievements and/or who had made significant contributions were asked to provide additional information on their successes.

(4) Examining existing genealogies and filling gaps

To start with, there was a need to ensure that there was a continuity of the names belonging to the various stems and branches of earlier generations. This was done by comparing the three versions of the genealogy that they had. Missing names and gaps in the earlier generations were filled after consultations among the committee members to ensure the accuracy of the names. Amendments were made when names were added to earlier generations, and information on the status of sons (such as whether they were eldest, youngest, adopted, etc.) was added if it had been omitted in the earlier versions. Through cross-referencing, the compilers were able to fill some of the gaps in earlier generations.

Going through the various versions was a tedious exercise. The compilers read each version several times and made notes, comparing places where inconsistencies and gaps occurred, searching for reasons for omissions and establishing reasons for reincorporation. They had to interpret information provided in the genealogy, ascertain its accuracy, and then add, subtract or amend it. They made notes on the page wherever this was done.

In filling the gaps and amending the wrong entries, this is how it was done. There were three versions available. The three versions were cross-referenced and checked. The newest of the three versions was copied in its entirety. Any omission found would be added on to the new copy of the old version, with the corrections and amendments written in with writing brush in the same calligraphic style but with annotation so that future genealogy would know that amendments and addition had been made. After cross checking and completing the omission, it was then written formally on the genealogy papers with a Chinese brush. Having completed this, the new generations of names would be then written on to the genealogy paper to complete the full entry of names of the present genealogy. Two more copies of this genealogy would be hand-written, making a total of three hand-written genealogies. This would be bounded in the traditional style. One copy would be send to the typesetting company to produce it in a modern form. The other two would be kept in its original form for future reference.

(5) Entry of new names

When the names of all members of the households had been collected, the three member team collated them and assembled them according to the stems and branches that each belonged to. The next step would be to trace the immediate ancestor/line of descent for each household. Having traced the name of the ancestor, the names of the present members were then added to each household. The search for the right tree and branch was an enormous task. Once the right tree was found, the names of the recent descendants were added; the trees were then linked together by the branches. After all had been carefully laid out and checked for accuracy, the names were entered into the genealogical register.

(6) Inclusion of daughters

It had been decided that names of all daughters would be entered into the annotations, the so-called "leaves" volume of the genealogy, but would remain left out of the tree-and-stem section. I was told that, if they had been included in the latter section, the Chinese patrilineal structure would have been undermined. Another reason for leaving them out of it was that it would have created too great an inconsistency to begin entry of daughters from the present generations onward, as traditionally this had not been done, and the compilers had not wanted to change the whole format of the genealogy. As volume two provided detailed annotations of individuals and families, women could easily be included in it.

The inclusion of the names of all daughters was the result of much negotiation and insistence on the part of the Singapore Chinese, but the Singapore elders were willing to depart from tradition and include them, not only because many of them are highly educated and hold high positions and contribute much to family prestige and status, but also because the success of family planning policies in Singapore had resulted in smaller family sizes and some families did not have sons. Given the change in family structure and the change in ideology towards the importance of sons in Singapore, it is not surprising to see the demand for change in this area. While among present-day Singapore Chinese, having a son to carry on the family name continues to be an important consideration, daughters are now seen as important members of the family as well, although they do not continue the family name. The filial-ness of daughters and their willingness to care for elderly parents are considered important qualities in contemporary Singapore society, and shrinking family size in Singapore has made both sons and daughters more important to many Chinese parents. Besides, "who would not like to include a millionaire CEO daughter, a daughter who is a politician or one with a Ph.D. in the genealogy", I was told "for they add much prestige, 'face' and glory to the family and lineage".

In Anxi, during one of my research trips, an elder, who was also a cadre, told me that it was good to have daughters like myself to help change the way the villagers look at their own daughters, and that it helped him to feel more comfortable, as he had only one daughter and no son and would not feel so guilty for not having a son to carry on the family name or to carry the incense stick upon his death.

(7) Final product - the Ke Shi Zu Pu

Having completed the entries, the committee decided that a total of two hundred copies would be printed and distributed to all those who had contributed financially to the project. It was also decided that the genealogy would be typeset into a computer database for easy retrieval, amendment and future addition, although they would retain the hand-written copy as the original version of the genealogy.

Genealogy: Cosmic Rite of Renewal

The recompilation and updating of a genealogy is a dignified and solemn ritual process, as the genealogy is seen as a sacred book. Before the entry of names takes place and after the compilation, elaborate ritual processes are conducted in order to call upon the local gods and deities to witness the recompilation and completion. At the start, there is the ritual pertaining to the opening of the genealogy, *kai-pu-yi-shi* (開譜儀式). When the genealogy is completed, there is the thanking ritual, *xie-pu-yi-shi*

(謝譜儀式) and the closing ritual, *guan-pu-yi-shi* (關譜儀式).

(1) Opening the genealogy (kai-pu-yi-shi)

Before beginning the recompilation of the genealogy, the Singapore and village elders consulted the almanac and sought the advice of monks in selecting the most auspicious date for the "opening of the genealogy". A separate altar within the ancestral house was created for the King of the Netherworld, *Da-shi-ye* (大士爺), who is the overseer of the founding ancestors' soul, who would be invoked during this period to witness the recompilation. On this day, the monks performed a ritual ceremony and invited *Da-shi-ye* and ancestors as witnesses. Offerings of incense, paper money and food were offered to them. During the ceremony, the three existing compilations of the genealogy were brought forward (two earlier versions had been lost during the early part of the Twentieth Century and two had been destroyed during the Cultural Revolution). The main genealogical compiler or genealogy master was introduced to the ancestors. After the ritual, the genealogy master started the task of recompiling the genealogy.

This was a relatively simple ritual and involved few people. The main function of this ritual was to invite the ancestors, overseen by *Da-shi-ye,* to witness that only members of the lineage were entered into the genealogy.

(2) Thanking ritual (xie-pu-yi-shi) and closing ritual (guan-pu-yi-shi)

When names and annotations had been entered, the *pu* was considered to have been completed: there was a master copy of the hand-written genealogy, written in Chinese calligraphic style, which was reproduced[2] by entering it onto a computer disk and then printing the two volumes (the villagers were very excited about this new technology).

The auspicious date was chosen one year ahead for the thanking and closing rituals, which were held together and in conjunction with the "rite of gratitude for the flow of descendants", lasting three days of the total of five days for the combined events. The ritual celebration involved a religious procession in which the genealogy, *pu* was carried from the Zhou-Yue Miao to the ancestral house where, earlier on, the thirteen local gods and deities had been invited to witness the closing ritual ceremony. After the necessary rituals, the *pu* was placed in a box and padlocked, the monks then sealing the lock with a religious amulet. The wooden box is now kept in the ancestral house and is not to be opened until the next recompilation.

In this ritual, all the thirteen village gods and deities, all past ancestors and members of the lineage were called upon to witness the completion of the new version of the genealogical register. It was a time of cosmic renewal, where past ancestors and living lineage present members were brought together to celebrate the birth and continuation of the lineage. The past ancestors were revered and their presence was essential for this occasion. The ancestors were not only present as witnesses to the growth and achievement of their lineage, however: their early sacrifices, achievements and contributions were highlighted to firmly entrench their roles in everyone's minds. Members alluded, in Confucian ritual fashion, to the source of origin, the fountain of life and the birth of the lineage. Here, early lineage history was being re-recorded and new entries made, in order that descendants might understand the difficulties and endurance of their ancestors in building the lineage. These events are all written as annotations in the second volume of the genealogical register.

The celebration was also a time of renewal of kinship ties among members and the renewal of the lineage, and a celebration of the coming together of the two branches of the Ke lineage. The physical separation of the two branches as a result of migration, followed by little contact during political upheaval in China, has impacted greatly on the relations between the two groups. Although kinship ties had remained relatively strong among some members, others had witnessed a dilution of ties, and a sizeable number had severed ties altogether. Even among those with strong ties, relationships had been somewhat strained as a result of differences in perception and attitudes. In this rite, then, the coming together of the various generations of members from overseas (notably those of Singapore and Malaysia) and Anxi branches, was to help re-cement lost ties and reawaken sentiments. Over a hundred members from the overseas communities attended the celebration. About two-thirds of whom were elderly and middle aged and one third were young adults and children, on whom the celebration made a great impact as, apart from the grandeur of the celebration, it was the first time many of them had come into contact with their ancestral village and village kin. Unlike those during the earlier years who were repelled by the "greed" and "laziness" of the villagers, these visitors were impressed with both the organisation and the generally friendly atmosphere of the festival. This friendly atmosphere created a generally good feeling among the visitors, and many said they were prepared to return for subsequent visits.

To the village elders, too, such an atmosphere was conducive to the renewal of kinship ties between overseas and village members. They provided new visitors with some insights into village life by bringing the younger Singapore and Malaysian members around the village, explaining to them about the religious rites and showing them around the farm and explaining to them what farming life is all about. They hoped that by explaining to their life style, they would be able to arouse their interest in the ancestral village. To a large degree, this celebration has kindled interests among the younger generations - like other communal religious fairs, it provided the opportunity for younger members to get to know their ancestral village a little.

Conclusion

The genealogy serves to inform Singapore lineage members of their common social history and to record the existence of the immediate family and its membership in the Singapore branch of a wider lineage structure. It is a record of their ancestral roots and allows them to search for their cultural and social history. It also allows them to come to grips with their emigration background, to resolve their tensions with their village kin, and to mark their ethnicity and their cultural identity within the wider Singapore polity. They thereby become part of the wider lineage structure, with continuity to village China, from which they derive aspects of their cultural understanding and practices. The Anxi village is seen as an ancestral home, to which they have kinship ties, although their orientation and national identity remains firmly with Singapore.

Notes

1   During my research, I discovered that many village households have more than one child. Indeed some have several, especially those with daughters, as many women will continue to reproduce till they finally have a son. Under the one-child policy, they dare not risk registering all their children, so that many daughters and sons were not formally registered with the Bureau of Birth. Such children are called "Japanese sons" by the locals to differentiate them from those who have registration papers issued by the village government. Only after they have given birth to a son or have the desired number of children would the family bring all the children for registration and pay the required fines.

2   Early versions had all been hand-written and then printed. A later version had been produced on a Chinese typewriter. The present version is typed using a word processor.

9 Chinese Lineage as a Cultural Network

Introduction

When the Singapore Ke visit their ancestral home in search of ancestral and cultural roots, they are inevitably confronted with a renewed sense of lineage identity. They are also forced, whether they like it or not, to acknowledge the existence of the other branches of the same lineage. This is the case of the younger generation Singapore-born Ke members as the various degrees of kinship relations unfold in front of their eyes. They are, involuntarily, asked to acknowledge the extended kinship and lineage circle. Some are completely taken by surprise, while others have some knowledge prior to their visit. Coming to grips with their kinship and lineage structures are emotional affairs for many. Some are delighted by it but many express much resistance to it.

Whether they like it or not, the Singapore members inevitably establish a web of social relationship that further lock them into linked socio-cultural and socio-economic networks. These networks enable the moral economy to become operationalised, thereby enabling the *qiaoxiang* to tap into moral and social capital as a result of the new meanings attached to the lineage structure. The operation of such a moral economy can be understood as an attempt by the Singapore Chinese to recompense for their inattention to their ancestral homes and villages, to allay their guilt over their failure to discharge social and economic duties to their immediate kin and to the lineage in general. At the same time, the ability of the village kin to extract social capital out of their Singapore counterparts demonstrates the intricate nature of the production of social capital.

Why does the operation of the lineage structure continue to be of primary significance among the Ke lineage in Singapore? To what extent is this an aberration from the wider Chinese community? How does the lineage structure operate in contemporary Chinese societies? To what extent has the nature and operation of the lineage structure changed in contemporary situations? How do various groups of Chinese, of the same ancestry but separated by history and geography, perceive the lineage structure? How do they attempt to reintegrate themselves into a common ancestral lineage structure? What is the modern lineage structure like? How can we best conceptualise the modern lineage structure? Should it be viewed as a social institution or a system of networks? What is its structure and membership composition, and what are the roles and linkages among its members?

This chapter argues that the actions of the Ke Lineage is not an aberration but are commonly practised by other lineages in Singapore and Southeast Asia where there continues to be strong ties with their ancestral villages. In so doing, it argues for a need to reconceptualise the Chinese lineage as a cultural network in contemporary society.

Lineage Formation

The term "lineage" has been interpreted by various scholars in their attempts to understand wider kinship organisation. The social anthropologists Evans-Pritchard and Fortes (1970) focused much of their scholarly work on understanding lineage as an important social organisation, basing their understandings on studies of African tribal societies; other studies followed.

Maurice Freedman was the first anthropologist to focus on the study of Chinese lineage structure, when he conducted studies on the social organisations of the two Southeastern provinces of Fujian and Guangdong. In his study, he described land as the most important element motivating the formation of a single lineage group in a village. "The centrality of the ownership of land is so important that where there is enough land, a nucleus of agnates strive to build themselves up to form a large homogeneous settlement. If to begin with they must share a territory with members of one or more lineages, they will await their opportunity to dominate and eventually drive out their neighbours. Land, which constitutes the most important material focus of any agnatically constituted group" determines the status of a lineage within a village vis-à-vis lineage in other villages (Freedman, 1966:8). Thus, the powerful and wealthy lineages were those that occupied the most fertile stretches of land (Freedman, 1966: 12). Freedman further argued that what constitutes a lineage is that the people form corporate groups of agnates living in one settlement or tight clusters of settlements. He terms this a "localised lineage" (Freeman 1966: 20). The grouping of a localised lineage with other local lineages was often based on an agnatically defined common ancestor. The central focus of this whole unit was on the ancestral hall or other pieces of property (Freeman 1966: 21).

The connection between the status of individuals within a lineage and the enlargement of a lineage was directly connected to the possession of landed property, more specifically ritual land. As pointed out by Freedman (1966), there was great desire among Chinese who accumulate substantial wealth to purchase ritual land and construct ancestral halls. Landed property, in this sense, was used to differentiate between groups within a lineage and thereby created status and class differentiation and corresponding differences in power distribution among the various groups. It was also wealth in the form of land that allowed a segment or segments of a lineage to construct its own ancestral hall, thereby establishing its separate identity from the rest and resulting eventually in the formation of sub-lineages, often of an asymmetrical kind.

Watson extends Freedman's definition of lineage to include other features. He wrote that a lineage is a corporation in the sense that members derive benefits from jointly owned property and shared resources. They also join in corporate activities on a regular basis. Furthermore, members of a lineage are highly conscious of themselves as a group in relation to others whom they define as outsiders. A lineage "is not, therefore, a loosely defined collection of individuals" (Watson, 1986: 5). It is a corporate group that celebrates ritual unity and is based on demonstrated descent from a common ancestor (Watson, 1982: 594). Lineage here is seen to be comprising three main components parts: namely, descent through patrilines from a common ancestor, ritual activities through which membership is collectively expressed, and the incorporation of membership through the joint possession of property, usually land. Like Freedman, Watson views a localised lineage as one whose members live in a well-defined area - usually a village or a set of neighbouring communities - which has a high degree of interaction among members of the localised group (Watson, 1986: 5-6). When several patrilineally related localised lineages combine, they form a higher-order lineage. The latter is usually well endowed with resources, as seen from their possession of ancestral halls and other properties located in the market town or county. Here, members of the higher-order lineage usually conduct regular ritual activities that serve to bind them together in a closely knitted fashion (Watson, 1986: 6).

Faure, on the other hand, sees lineage as corresponding to the *zu* or *fang* organised along the male line (Faure, 1989: 5). The formation of a lineage is closely linked to the access of resources by a group of people and their ability to produce a legitimate claim over such resources. Hence, Faure argues that "the right to exploit natural resources within what villagers consider to be their communal territories is so consciously recognised that it may be said the possession of them has demarcated villagers from outsiders. These rights include the right to build houses in or near the village, to gather fuel on hillsides, and to open for cultivation land that had not been privately claimed" (Faure, 1989: 6). To Faure, the formation and perpetuation of the lineage is a consequence of the broad agreement of lineage history. Thus, the ability of members to articulate their genealogical links with their ancestors and their fellow members is a basic criterion for acceptance of membership in the village, in territorial alliances and in ancestor worship (Faure, 1989: 6). Cultural and religious activities (such as religious sacrifices), together with other welfare facilities, are therefore organised in the territorial boundary of the group and are meant for the benefits of its members only.

In recent years, social historians have joined in the study of Chinese lineage from the Sung dynastic era onwards. Historically, they have argued, most kinship groups formed during the imperial eras did not conform to the definition postulated by Freedman (Ebrey and Watson, 1986). Rawski argued that while land played an important role in enhancing the prestige of individuals, such estates did not play a determining role in promoting kinship solidarity or dependence.

Most studies agree that a lineage is formed when a group of people demonstrates to themselves and others that they are of the same decent line. It is demonstrated descent that serves the core of all descent groups. While descent on its own points to biological links, the primary concern here is demonstrated descent, a product based on social construction by its people (Watson, 1982: 594). In traditional Chinese society, the standard device for demonstrating descent has been the written genealogies. However, among the peasantry, where illiteracy prevailed, it was the oral recollection of the genealogical links that proved to be the most important source of information for the group concerned. While the genealogy at times was used to stimulate the formation of lineage, at other times it signalled the completion of lineage formation.

Hymes sees the formation of a lineage as a kind of localist strategy "for the elite-gentry class where a member of the elite is seen carving out from the local population an agnatic pool of potential allies and clients" (Hymes, 1986: 122). Here, genealogy writing is "a strategic act" by which members of the local elite seek to strengthen their position in local society. At times, it was an important method for positioning the local elite for their social interaction with the regional elite.

Yet another view suggests that the existence of written genealogical records among the local elite is a step forward in further entrenching their power and creating a stable socio-political order at a localised level. The result is a kind of patron-client relationship between the elite-gentry and the rest of the lineage members. Despite this social differentiation, or perhaps because of it, argues Hazelton, an environment conducive in social interaction is created among lineage members.

As the common descent group developed and was stabilised by its genealogical record, it became possible for a dominant lineage to incorporate segments of lineages with the same surname into its fold, thereby extending its territorial claim. Here, "higher-order lineage" and "lower order lineage" are used to contrast those with power from the subservient groups. Dominant lineages could thus project their elitist images and further consolidate their positions through a series of political alliances with members of the local elite. In so doing, they created a large network of kinship relations (Hazelton, 1986: 137-169).

Another important aspect of the lineage is the role of ritual. In an article written by Ebrey about kinship life during the pre-Song and Song epochs, rituals, especially the worship of ancestors at graveside, are viewed as a key organisational element. From a functionalist viewpoint, Ebrey sees the various ritual elements as important pre-requisites for the establishment of various interaction patterns among groups of agnates. Such ritual elements reinforce and strengthen the kinship solidarity and group consciousness that will ultimately lead to the formation of a lineage (Ebrey and Watson, 1986: 16-61). Watson, on the other hand, argues that such a view neglects other aspects of social organisation. Brook, on this issue, argues that kinship and ritual systems have exercised considerable influence on the structures of many precapitalist societies (Brook, 1988: 75). Kinship has, under certain circumstances throughout history, assumed an important role in structuring relations of production and especially in fostering specific forms of domination. To ignore non-economic factors such as kinship organisation and political overlordship is to ignore their profound influence on the structure of society (Brook, 1988: 75).

Another important feature of lineage is the role of the elite-gentry class in shaping the communal social life of peasants. Fei Hsiao-tung, in his various works, has illustrated this point (Fei, 1939, 1953). Likewise, Hazelton treats the elite as engaging in a localist strategy that pursues a mission to translate "transitory achievements of individual degree winners and office-holders into an enduring elevation of the status of their line and segment" (Hazelton, 1986: 149). What intensified agnatic interaction from the level of casual groupings to that of organised lineages was the elite - even at its highest bureaucratic levels - in their promotion, celebration, and in some sense, creation of such structures (Hazelton, 1986: 131). By the Qing Era, the lineage and the panoply of rituals attached to it were seen as part and parcel of the gentry's strategy for success. Those with gentry as their leaders were able to compete better than those without.

In assessing Freedman's paradigm, Ebrey and Watson suggest that the word "lineage" be avoided when dealing with agnatic groups that do not fulfil all elements of the definition, especially the joint ownership of property. Anything less than a full lineage is a "descent group", that is, a group (by contrast to a loose collection of agnates) whose members are aware of their kinship connections, but whose corporate behaviour may be limited to activities such as ancestral rites or the compilation of genealogies. A descent group becomes a lineage when "it provides material benefits for members". They argue that this distinction "will affect not only how individuals look on membership but also the internal dynamics of the group and the power of the group can exert in society" (Ebrey and Watson, 1986: 5).

Brook rejects both Freedman's and Watson's definitions. He argues that leading members of a lineage sought to build reliable networks of ties of dominance and dependence that placed their own patrilines in advantageous positions. Corporate property was used to achieve such ends. The institutions did not create the lineages. Rather, they served to formalise and extend kinship ties that created the lineages. It is for this reason that Brook argues that the concept of lineage may be better analysed in terms of networks than institutions. He argues that lineages should be perceived as structured networks of agnatic kinship ties, and that institutional arrangements that matured out of what Hymes called the "lineage orientation" were in secondary position to, though powerfully supportive of, the primary function of the lineage. Its main role was to tie individuals and families together systematically within the structure of local society. The lineage also provided them with an organisational context within which to mobilise potential ties with lesser agnates in order to gain, consolidate and perpetuate the lineage's elite status and to maintain advantageous relationship vis-à-vis outsiders. In this way it produced a ready- made set of accessible clients, identifying patrons and allies and placing them in a hierarchy of power. As to its possession of corporate property, this is highly dependent on the socio-economy of the wider region (Brook, 1988: 78). In Brook's view, a lineage can exist when a group of agnates or, more particularly, certain families within the group, are conscious of their ties to each other and have created institutional formats to reinforce the consciousness and maintain the visibility of those ties.

Chinese Lineage: A Cultural Network Model

The views offered above help us to understand the socio-economic base for the formation of lineage in early Chinese society. They identify various factors that are instrumental in the consolidation and expansion of a lineage structure, the inter-relationships among various lineages and the interactions among their members. Lineage, to all these scholars, is an important social institution of traditional Chinese society.

How should Chinese lineage be viewed in contemporary situations? What is its present structure? What are its contemporary roles and functions? To what extent is Chinese lineage an integrative force for Chinese culture? How can we reconceptualise the lineage in light of its changing structure and the players involved? We will explore the changing nature of Chinese lineages at two levels: first, Chinese lineage as a chain of cultural networks; second, at the macro-level, Chinese lineage as part of the global socio-economic *guanxi* networks in the restructuring of *qiaoxiang*.

Subcultures and Microcultures

Culture is subject to varying interpretations. In the *Mirror of Man*, Kluckhohn defines it as the following: "the total way of life of a people", "the social legacy the individual acquires from his group", "a way of thinking, feeling and believing", "an abstraction from behaviour", "storehouse of pooled learning", "a set of standardised orientations to recurrent problems", "learned behaviour", a "mechanism for the normative regulation of behaviour", "a set of techniques for adjusting both to the external environment and to other men" and a "precipitate of history" (Kluckhohn, 1960; Geertz, 1973: 4-5). Geertz, on the other hand, views culture as "the webs of significance he [man] himself has spun" where the search is not so much for meanings but rather interpretations of these actions (Geertz, 1973: 5).

Hannerz looks at culture as a social organisation of meaning where it is made up of a set of complex interlinkages (Hannerz: 1992: 68). At any one time, the individuals within the culture are subjected to a set of culturally shaped meanings which influences his ordering of experiences and intentions. At the same time, the individuals are capable of interpreting the set of culturally given phenomenon. This individual interpretation can differ from that of the culturally sanctioned one. These differing modes of interpretation result in a tension zone between culture and social structure (Hannerz, 1992: 65). He terms it a network of perspectives because of the variations and diversities found within a culture. Within the wider culture, there exist subcultures, microcultures and countercultures. (Hannerz, 1992: 69-81). Such subcultures are collective phenomenon and belong to a particular set of social relationships. Within the subculture or microculture, there exist only aspects of the flow of meaning that are directly relevant to the subcultures or microcultures. These subcultures and microcultures are therefore distinctive in their own right and contrast with the flow of meanings of the wider culture.

The Chinese lineage structure is an important part of Chinese culture. It is widely conceptualised as a social institution within which the reproduction of Chinese culture takes place, as described in previous chapters of this book. Today some Chinese lineages have branches scattered throughout China and the world, each branch having developed its own subcultures and microcultures. Within the broad lineage framework, there continue to be shared cultural elements and collective memories; but within the subcultures and microcultures, there are distinctive elements that belong uniquely to particular branches. This has been demonstrated clearly in our example, where the attitudes of the Singapore Ke differ considerably from those of their village counterparts.

Within the wider lineage structure, there exist shared collective memories and attitudes that serve as integrative forces which bring together the various branches. The converging of its members at the lineage ancestral house is a testimony to these shared beliefs, values and memories. The religious and ritual reproductions have served to unify and allow for expression of this cultural identity (in being Anxi Chinese, speaking the Fujianese dialect, etc.). This sense of cultural identity serves as a habitus that contains members and rejects outsiders.

The subcultures and microcultures are clearly displayed when various branches of a lineage gather together for communal ancestor worship or religious celebrations. This is where Singaporean, Malaysian, Hong Kong and other Chinese appear distinct in attitudes, dress, social habits and social etiquette. At such times there exists a high level of tension among them, with individuals from the different branches attempting to outdo each other in their displays of wealth, power and social status and thereby challenging each other's level of social existence. But at the wider level, they share common characteristics that identify them as members of a shared culture.

Nodal Links

Given the varieties of subcultures and microcultures among the various branches that are separated in geographical and spatial distances from one another, the Chinese lineage can no longer be seen as a locality-bound social institution. Emigration has led to the formation of separate Chinese overseas communities. The various branches of the lineage created by migrants residing permanently in their adopted countries cater to their needs and those of their local born descendants. While these branches are distinctively Chinese in orientation, many of their activities have taken on a contemporary look to suit the needs of the members located in a different country with a political allegiance to that country.

These Chinese overseas communities set up social institutions such as surname and territorial groupings, which are known respectively as *zong-qing* and *tong-xiang hui guan* to cater to their needs. Such groups have grown powerful and functioned independently of it in providing much of the cultural activity of their members. They have also, on their own accord, established informal social relationships with similar local institutions. Their roles within their communities have been largely cultural and ritualistic in nature. They continue to play the role of cultural identity marker, although their ability to do so is increasingly being dwarfed by that of professional groupings in recent years. They can be found in many Chinese communities throughout the world.

At the same time, recent migrations of the Chinese from Southeast Asia to the United States, Australia and other English speaking countries have also witnessed a renewed awareness of a further spreading out effect of the members from the lineage point of view. Correspondingly, some of these Chinese will establish the traditional form of social institutions to cater for their quest for a Chinese cultural identity. The emergence of sub-branches of a lineage in various parts of the world has meant that the lineage structure is no longer confined to one locality. It is thus no longer a social institution, as in Freedman's sense, with a distinctive geographic boundary.

As the Chinese outside China have established their political, economic and social allegiance to their country of domicile and as their descendants, born and raised in those countries, they become part of the Chinese overseas communities. Today, many of these Chinese overseas communities are beginning the process of searching for their ancestral roots and cultural identity. As they traced their ancestry back to China, they also acknowledge that part of their roots is in their present country that they live in today.

Given the global spread of members of a lineage in various countries throughout the world, it becomes inevitable that the lineage structure should now be seen as a cultural network with chains of links connecting various *nodes* as represented by Chinese overseas communities scattered throughout the world. Each node is an encapsulation of Chinese culture, but its representation differs among the nodes. The nodal links can be strong or weak and expanded or contracted depending on the needs and views of the group concerned, and can function independently as well. Each node is linked to others in a socially horizontal manner, as each node is a branch of the main lineage structure and enjoys equal social status, irrespective of their other attributes. Here, power, wealth and social status, while playing an important role in determining the strength and dominance of the branch, theoretically have very little impact on the social relationships among the nodes: the nodes are *theoretically* among social equals.

A Web of Lineage Culture

Within the lineage network, there are two sets of relationship. The first is the relationship between the source, represented by the ancestral village in China and the second is the relationship between the nodes, represented by the Chinese overseas communities. The nodes are also the transmitter of Chinese culture and hence are known as regional cultural centres.

The relationship between the source of the Chinese lineage and the nodes is qualitatively different from the relationship among the various nodes, as it is based on a different set of dynamics, the source conveying the primordial origin of the branches that are its offshoots. Theoretically, the primordial centre should have power and dominance because of its status as source. However, in the *qiaoxiang* relationship, the traditional social stratification system has been replaced by a contemporary utilitarian system within which wealth has become an important marker of social status. In this system, the nodes with their wealthy members have become the dominant players in the trans-national relationship between the source and the nodes.

At the same time, members both at the source and in the nodes share a collective memory and a real and/or an imagined sense of history based on their common knowledge of the ancestral home and their understanding of their cultural roots. Yet the nature of their relationship is again subject to the effects of the variety of life experiences and socio-political changes that they have undergone. Those who left the source and migrated during the early years experienced great upheavals, but their livelihoods have now stabilised and the majority has been able to progress up the economic and social ladder and has achieved a relatively comfortable standard of living, while some have become wealthy. This is again different from the second and younger generations Chinese who have been born in an overseas environment and whose political and social experiences differed from those of their parents and grandparents.

Members at the source, on the other hand, have experienced great political upheavals and uncertainty, and even with the doors open to reform many continue to be apprehensive of political change. Only until recently has life returned to stability and normalcy. It was also only in the last two decades that there is renewed kinship ties between them and their overseas kin.

Socially, members of the nodes have been able to carry out, reproduce and develop their socio-cultural and religious activities, the customs and rituals which they had knowledge of, without much hindrance. However, those who remained at the source have been forced to curb their socio-cultural and religious activities as a result of political pressure. This has resulted in a very uneven development of Chinese culture between the source and the nodes. Thus, the "residual Chinese communities", a term used by Freedman to describe Chinese overseas communities, have become, to a large extent, guardians and proponents of Chinese culture. Many of these nodes have been able to recreate aspects of Chinese culture in Chinese overseas communities and at the same time modify it and add new elements to it, thereby carrying it away from the village culture in an urban, foreign-based direction. When the source and the nodes have interacted in recent years, the mix of village and Chinese overseas cultural elements have begun to produce a wider synthetic Chinese culture. It is the ability of Chinese culture to receive and yet to retain an essentially Chinese character that challenges the static idea of cultural authenticity. Cultural authenticity here is represented by the overall image of the wider culture as it is recognised by its adherents. Yet certain core elements are retained - the additions and changes do not disqualify it as "Chinese culture" in the eyes of its adherents, who acknowledge its changing aspects. To them, cultural authenticity is what they are familiar with and are able to practise in their country of residence and in their ancestral village.

This relationship between the source and the nodes forms a web. The complexity of which is determined by the relationships between the source and the numbers of nodes found both in China and in the Chinese communities overseas. The operation of this network is seen as follows:

First, there is the membership consideration within the lineage web. Lineage members can be divided into two main groups, those within China and those overseas. Within China there are: (a) the source, (b) nodes that remain within the village polity; and (c) nodes formed in Chinese cities when members have relocated. Overseas lineage members could be geographically scattered throughout the world, but not every Chinese overseas community forms a node. The greatest concentration of nodes is found in Southeast Asia.

In the case of the Ke lineage, nodes have formed in Singapore, Malaysia, Indonesia, Thailand and the Philippines. There are also several nodes in Taiwan and a small one in Hong Kong because of the small number of lineage members there. These members reside permanently overseas, function within their respective Chinese communities, and are citizens of the local nation states.

In the example of the Ke lineage, the relationship between the source and the nodes can be seen as follows:

1. The Source

For Singapore Ke lineage members, the source has different components. At the broadest level, the source is the locality their ancestors came from. It can be divided into outer and inner sources. The outer source is Anxi county, often regarded as the ancestral land. The inner source, on the other hand, is Peng Lai District which is regarded as the place of origin, *qi-yuan-di* (起源地), the place where the first ancestor planted his roots in the region. It is the place where the grave of the first ancestor, Ban-Shan-Gong and the ancestral house, *zu-zhai* are sited. To travel to the source is to locate the inner source, pay homage to the ancestors and reconnect oneself with one's ancestral roots.

Village members live within the Peng Lai and other districts in Anxi County and are in connection with the source all the time. They thus experience no break in their relationship with their ancestors. Though they experienced political upheavals during the Cultural Revolution and were forced not to acknowledge or worship their ancestors, they nevertheless continued to reside there and thus remained connected to the place of origin. This physical presence at the source serves as a powerful reminder of their origin; whether they consider it good to reside at the source is not the concern here. Since reform, they, together with their overseas kin, have reconstructed their links with their ancestors through individual and communal rituals.

In identifying with the source, one is confronted with the issue of allegiance. The relationship between the individual and both the inner source and outer sources is determined by the social distance between them. The relationship with the inner source is an intimate one, members being inter-connected through the web of agnatic and affinal kinship ties. Members are able to recognise the immediate ancestors, locate the ancestral house, *zu-zhai* and trace the genealogical links with all other members within the lineage structure; and it is these ties that are instrumental in establishing and operationalising the moral economy. Embedded in the various ideological constructs such as the moral reasoning of Confucianism and the Buddhist understanding of karma, the moral economy ensures that the players within it discharge their social and moral obligations to the source and to the members within it.

For the Singapore members who visit their inner source, an additional set of social relationships unfolds in front of them. Members become part of the extended kinship and lineage, with kinship and social relations based on the shared surname - in our case, the surname "Ke". In an involuntary manner, they have to acknowledge the existence of kin of all the different grades found in the lineage, both socially close and socially distant; and there is great social expectation that they acknowledge their kin and recognise their ancestors. Visiting the ancestral village is thus not just a visit to a physical place, but also an entering into the social relations bounded within that space; and it is this that some Singapore Chinese find difficult to cope with.

In the ancestral village, the Singaporeans are introduced to agnatic and affinal kin. Within the village, they assume the identity of brothers or sisters, uncles or aunts, nephews or nieces, and cousins of village lineage members - identities bestowed upon them by their village kin. Similarly, the villagers are uncles, aunts, nephews, nieces, etc. to the Singaporeans. Other individual identities are no longer important: the reference point is the family (usually the extended family) and the lineage.

As members of the moral economy, the Singapore Chinese are culturally bound by a sense of moral obligation and duty to give assistance to their immediate family, lineage and ancestral village, and to others extending outwards into the "outer source" area. Within the inner source, personalised gifts, in the form of money or material goods, are given to blood and affinal kin. The amount and type of gifts are dependent on the individuals themselves. One main characteristic of the moral economy is the varied and personalised nature of gifts given and the amount of money given, which vary according to the needs of village kin and the ability of the Singaporeans to provide for them.

Within the inner source, there are also moral obligations to the ancestral village. Apart from contributions to individual kin, members overseas are also expected to contribute to the communal well-being of the ancestral village as a whole - perhaps by assisting with village reconstruction, raising the material standard of the villagers, providing for infrastructure for education or medical facilities or road transportation. The basic obligation is to help improve the life of the villagers. This attempt to restructure the village life and economy has led to a distinctive identity for these villages in contrast to the surrounding ones: they become the wealthy emigrant villages, the *qiaoxiang*.

In regard to the outer source, the moral economy operates in a less personalised fashion, focused not so much on primordial ties with individual lineage members as on affiliation with the region as a whole, with the ancestral village or ancestral home as the key reference point. Many Singapore Chinese recognise that Anxi is the county where their ancestors came from - most of them are, in fact, more familiar with the wider territorial district than with the village of their ancestors, and "Anxi County" is a more familiar term than "Peng Lai District". It is not uncommon for members to search for the outer source when they do not know the inner source: a small group of Singapore Chinese have said that, although they do not know the village of their ancestors, they feel that by knowing the outer source, they at least have the opportunity to locate the inner source if they wish: by visiting the outer source, they can begin to search for their cultural roots.

Within the outer source, social relationships are not closely bound to the kinship ties that one is expected to acknowledge. As social relations here are not based on shared surnames but on territorial affiliation, the ties between individuals and the outer source are generally less intimate, with social expectations less personalised and fewer obligations to specific kin members. Instead, the operation of the moral economy is involved with the general welfare of the district and county. Here, the overseas Chinese are asked to look at the overall development of the county. According to governmental reports, Anxi is still one of the poorest regions in China; the aim is to encourage the Chinese overseas to contribute and alleviate this poverty. Contributions are not made to individuals but to the district and county governments, for investment in large infrastructure projects. From such development, benefits attained can flow throughout the outer source area and into the inner source.

Some overseas lineage members find it more satisfying interacting with the outer source than with the inner source, as within the outer source there is less moral obligation to immediate village kin and little or no allusion to village kin or lineage ties, so that they are better able to control the operation of the moral economy. They also feel that their contributions are put to better use and can benefit the whole region. When dealing with immediate village kin, many find themselves unable to stop from becoming part of the kin-based moral economy within which they must share control; whereas vis-à-vis the outer source they can more easily control their contribution agendas and choose those village, district or county projects to which they wish to contribute. As we have seen in Chapter 5, the Singapore Ke lineage members have favoured making contributions to district-level education and, at the county level, to the construction of the main arterial road. In making these contributions, the feelings of their immediate village kin members are of lesser concern to them; and so they have changed the nature of the moral economy by focusing their participation on philanthropy and charity.

Within both inner and outer source areas, the dominance of a shared communal identity works to undermine individual identity. This shared communal identity forms part of the wider cultural identity, both Singapore and village members assuming a common Fujian Anxi Chinese identity. For the Singapore Chinese, there are the added layers of being

Singapore Fujian Anxi Chinese, *Xinjiapo Fujian Anxi Huaren* (新 加 坡 福 建 安 溪 華 人).

2. Nodes: Overseas Regional Chinese Cultural Centres

The nodes are made up of two components: the lineage and its members (at times, represented by the lineage/surname association, *zong-qing-hui* (宗親會) and at other times, independent of the association) and the territorial associations, *tong-xiang-hui*. The two taken together are overseas regional Chinese cultural centres.

Although these social institutions have attracted varying degrees of support from their members since the war and have become less popular in recent years, they continue to be important conduits for the expression of Chinese culture in present-day Chinese communities throughout the world, and especially in Southeast Asia. They can be found in Singapore, Malaysia, Indonesia, Thailand, the Philippines, Vietnam and elsewhere. During the nineteenth and the first half of the Twentieth Century, they performed important social and economic functions (Yen, 1986). During the early post-colonial days, in post-independence nation-states, their roles were greatly reduced because they were considered seats for Chinese nationalism and chauvinism, and today, in countries like Indonesia and Malaysia, they continue to be viewed with suspicion. In Indonesia they are not permitted to function; in Malaysia they may function only at a low level; in Singapore earlier roles played by these social institutions have been taken over by government-led institutions.

In recent years, the recognition of Chinese social institutions as seats of Chinese culture and tradition by the Singapore State has led to a revival of these social institutions. They have now taken on a more active role in the promotion of Chinese culture and cultural activities, thereby carving for themselves a specific niche as custodial guardians and promoters of Chinese culture. In Singapore, they promote: the "Speak Mandarin" campaign; Chinese cultural activities such as Chinese opera, folk dance and traditional Chinese music; education, by allowing their premises to be used for after-class tuition for members' children; and various Chinese religious and cultural activities. They also include "modern" popular activities such as sports and karaoke-singing as part of their programmes, aimed at encouraging the participation of younger members.

Relations between these nodes and the sources have vacillated with the political atmosphere of the times. They were very weak from the 1960s through to the mid-1970s: formal institutional contacts were occasionally made, but most contacts were those informally made by individual members. Links have been strengthened since the late 1970s, with increased institutional exchanges and visits of official cadres from Anxi County in recent years. One main reason for these visits has been to promote Anxi and the emigrant village phenomenon to the Singapore Chinese, and to encourage Singapore Chinese to visit and contribute to the development of their ancestral villages and to Anxi County. The Singapore Chinese visit their ancestral villages for sentimental reasons; visits to the outer source and the establishment of ties with cadres tend to lock them into *guanxi* networks.

From the 1980s onwards, with the relaxation of the political atmosphere, interaction between the regional centres and the sources intensified, with the key focus on cultural reproduction and economic revival. Relationship between overseas centres and the source are of two types. The first type consists of relationships of individuals who visit and make contributions to their ancestral villages, engaging in religious reproduction and assisting in the setting-up of small retail businesses for the benefit of immediate village kin. Contributions to infrastructure development of ancestral villages are also made, the object being to raise the standard of living of village kin. This type of relationship is focused on the *qiaoxiang*; at this level, the flow of financial and material benefits is unidirectionally towards Anxi. The second type consists of the relations of Chinese social institutions and corporate groups whose members claim ancestry from the district. Here, contributions are in the form of aid or joint business ventures, the primary aim being to help the district and county to develop economically and to obtain small investment returns. These overseas institutions and corporate groups combine sentiment with business interest in their economic ventures with the district and county governments. One example of this type of involvement is the development of power plants in the county to provide electricity to the region.

Social relationships between the inner source and the nodes are now characterised by movement in both directions. Relationships between members in the nodes and their *qiaoxiang* are intense. Previously, interaction was unidirectional, the flow being from the nodes to the inner source, to the ancestral village. In recent years, however, the flow has been in both directions, with Anxi villagers making social visits to Singapore. The recent relaxation of policies pertaining to the employment of mainland Chinese workers in Singapore has resulted in the recruitment of workers from the inner and outer sources, and there is now much pressure exerted on Singapore Chinese to help their village kin to find employment. This has raised the level of tension between the two groups and resulted in much misunderstanding and dissatisfaction between them.

The flow of social and economic interaction between the source and the nodes has fostered greater emotional ties between them, but some of these "ties" have been negative ones, and feelings among Singapore Chinese are often mixed. The older generation want to establish closer links with village kin but are constantly frustrated by lack of villager understanding of the Singapore situation, as they are pressurised by demands to arrange employment in Singapore for the younger villagers. The younger generation of Singapore Chinese often choose to be emotionally less engaged, maintaining a social distance from their village kin and thereby attaining a comfort zone for themselves.

In diagram 1, the inner source, represented by the ancestral village, is linked to the nodes and overseas regional cultural centres through the members and the associations (surname and territorial). The link between the source and the nodes can either be strong or weak. In our case, the physical source of the Ke lineage is the Peng Lai District but is most represented by the existence of the ancestral house, *zu-zai*. It has strong links with the Singapore Ke members and the Ke Association and Anxi Association in Singapore. There is also strong links with the Malaysian and Indonesian counterparts. There is a weak link with United States via the Singapore node.

At the institutional level, the links were weak and for many years, while there was some interaction among the lineage members, there was very little institutional interaction between the source and the Anxi association. Only in recent years have the links been revived and strengthened through various activities, one of the most important being the International Conference of World Anxi Associations in 1992, which was organised by the Singapore Anxi Association and held in its premise, with the participation of members world-wide, including numerous members from Anxi County itself. In November 1997, the source, Anxi County Government in conjunction with the Anxi Chinese overseas held the international conference in Xian-Chen, the county town.

The Anxi Association is a mixed-surname association based on locality. In recent years, village, district and county reconstruction, particularly the building of public infrastructure such as roads, bridges and hospitals, has become of major concern to the Anxi Chinese in Singapore and elsewhere in Southeast Asia, who have contributed much to such projects. Members from various lineages including the Ke lineage members also contributed substantially to these infrastructure projects, as territoriality has become an important marker of identity and Anxi has become transformed into an outer source. At the same time, the Anxi Ke have assisted projects related directly to their lineage, especially as individuals, doing so through organising those within their own social networks. At the same time, the lineage members have also provided large contributions and funded many public work projects in the inner source.

Chinese lineage is an important cultural network and it provides the individual, the family and social groups with various guanxi networks where they could seek information and assistance.

3. Guanxi networks

There are several types of intra-lineage social networks in operation in the *qiaoxiang*. All are informal. First there are the primordial *guanxi* networks. There are two types of *qing-qing guanxi wang-luo* (親情關系網絡): the first operates among the lineage members in the regional cultural centres, the second involves cross-regional relationships between Singaporeans and villagers. For these two types of primordial networks, membership is exclusive; the ties are based on shared common experiences, and shared outlooks on, and attitudes towards, the outside world.

The Singapore regional cultural network consciously attempts to exclude those that are not from the region including Anxi villagers. Several factors account for the creation of this Singapore-based *guanxi* network. First, there is the issue of Singapore national identity, which serves as a marker to distinguish between insiders and outsiders. Second, there is the issue of class. Among the Singapore Chinese, many consider their village kin to be of low social status, and therefore consciously exclude them.

A second type of network involves lineage members from both Singapore and the village, lineage guanri network, *zong-qing guanxi wang-luo* (宗情關系網絡). It can be viewed as the moral economy network, *dao-de jin-ji wang-luo* (道德經濟網絡). Social expectations exist and interactions occur at varying degrees of intimacy depending on the individual members involved, but attitudes and actions are governed by a set of moral values and a sense of duty and responsibility. Participation within this network is both voluntary and persuasive. Numerous members have been persuaded and inducted into the network in a semi-coercive fashion. Some enter because their parents are in it and they often represent their parents. Others are inducted by their kin to help out. This is especially the case for the younger Singapore Chinese. Once in it, they become permanent members unless they declare otherwise. Many are more likely to choose to be within it and perhaps become inactive members rather than to be seen as rejecting the network. Often, however, they are not left alone but are pushed into activity through obligatory ritual duties.

This *guanxi wang* has been created as a shared common ground for members, particularly for purposes of ritual reproduction and village reconstruction. Members find this common ground as they engage in, for example, ancestor worship and communal religious functions, or the recompilation of the lineage genealogy. Throughout, there is the desire to revive the lineage structure and to bring together the various branches of the lineage. In addition, members share a similar objective to develop the emigrant ancestral village. The network provides a ready pool of people to help organise ritual activities and to help with village reconstruction and economic development in the areas of education, village health care, the construction of roads and bridges, and through retail businesses and cottage industries.

Within this network, male members often involve themselves in the social and economic aspects of village life while women group themselves for socio-religious activities. The number of men and women involved is about equal. Most are village and Singapore elders with strong emotional ties to the ancestral village. These are the main proponents of communal activities. Members also see themselves as being in the vanguard for the advancement of the economic interests of the villages.

Unlike the formal institutions, these *guanxi* networks are not burdened by formal rules. Most activities are *ad hoc*, and participation is voluntary and elicited through informal recruitment. The extent of participation is dependent on personal interest and on the effectiveness of persuasion by kin. Because of the informality of the network structure, movement in and out of the network is a fluid one, and involvement in any particular activity is dependent on time and interest. It is possible to distinguish several categories of participating members: there are the very active members who form the core of the *guanxi wang*, the passive ones who need persuasion, and the inactive ones whose participation is infrequent. However, most can be depended on to support major events in the ancestral village. This is represented by diagram 2.

4. *Inter-lineage* guanxi-wang

Communication among branches or sub-lineages of the same lineage is a common occurrence. These inter-lineage *guanxi* networks are also informal and fluid. Members from various lineages routinely exchange news and provide information about activities and developments in their mutual *qiaoxiang*. They also provide advice to those who need it.

In Anxi, there is much communication among members of the nine surname groups. In Singapore, there has been also increased communication among members of different lineages and surname associations both at formal and informal levels since the 1980s. At the formal level, these social institutions have increased their co-operation in social, cultural and educational activities. These inter-lineage *guanxi* networks are important in raising the profile of Chinese culture and Chinese activities within Singapore society. They are also important in elevating the status of not only the lineage but also the territorial associations, tongxianghui such as the Anxi Association in Singapore and transforming them into custodial institutions of Chinese culture and identity.

These *guanxi* networks have important socio-economic functions, which involve three distinct sets of players: members of different emigrant villages; Singapore Chinese members with different surnames; and official village, district and county cadre members. The Chinese overseas are consciously courted by village elders to help with cultural reproduction, village reconstruction and the rekindling of kinship sentiments. Official cadres network with Chinese overseas and village elders in the hope of encouraging the Chinese overseas to invest in the region. Like their village counterparts, the cadres transform ancestral and kinship affiliation into social capital to attract overseas Chinese into their network. The latter allow themselves to be inducted into the network in the hope of establishing good guanxi for prospective economic investments in the region.

This three-way courtship permits certain observations. First, it enables large capital flow into the villages and, to a certain extent, into other parts of the county. Rapid development has thus been made possible resulting in the social and economic betterment of the *qiaoxiang* villages. Many villagers are now more sophisticated due to their travels overseas. Secondly, by courting overseas Chinese, the latter are given the social status and self-esteem by the three levels of cadres. They are treated as important VIPs who have contributed philanthropically and charitably. While many of these persons are successful in Singapore, they are not recognised for their contributions to the community as, in many cases, they do not have a sufficiently large pool of resources to make a mark in Singapore society; but in the villages in Anxi Province they are honoured for their contributions. Such recognition is especially important to these members: they are "somebody" in their home village. (See diagram 3).

Global Lineage Flows

In recent years the regional cultural centres have taken on extended roles and have globalised their outlook, using their institutional structures to provide bases for their members to form new networks and springboard into new areas of activity, while reaching out to lineage members and members of the same surname groups world-wide.

The Ke lineage in Singapore has established linkages with their ancestral village and has become active in village and county cultural and economic reconstruction. It next recompiled the genealogy, searching for members scattered throughout the world. Then the formal Ke institution in Singapore, the Ke Association began to organise business tours for the Singapore members to visit China; later this was expanded to encompass visits to other Southeast Asian countries.

One method of reaching out to scattered members was the recent exercise in rewriting the genealogy. In order to ensure that all members would be included, the world-wide search for lineage members, by newspaper advertisement and word of mouth, was launched. Most members residing in the west are in fact offshoots of families in Southeast Asia (especially in Singapore and Malaysia), and continue to have strong ties with kin in Singapore. Through these ties they have been brought into contact with relatives in Anxi, albeit obliquely, and have thus come to know of the rewriting of the genealogy and have had their names included in it. It will be interesting to see the extent to which these ties are maintained by the younger generations born and brought up in the west.

The Ke Association serves as a natural setting for members to network among themselves and with their counterparts in other countries. It lends its name to help its members explore economic links and joint ventures with the governments of Vietnam, Cambodia and Burma, and has proven to be important for establishing contacts with foreign governments, thereby once again establishing itself as an important socio-economic institution. Today, Ke Association provides information and support for members to carry out their own economic ventures.

Relevance of Network Analysis

In this chapter, I have attempted a network analysis of the reformulation of the lineage structure. I argue that the Chinese lineage has undergone various phases of structural development; unlike in the Nineteenth and early Twentieth centuries, it is no longer a social organisation, as Freedman and other scholars have argued.

In the reconceptualisation of the Chinese lineage structure, there are various considerations. First, there is a need to take into consideration its spread through geographical space. It is no longer confined to one geographic area but has developed various nodes and regional cultural centres that operate both formally and informally. Second, there is a need to take into consideration the power and influence of various sets of players within the lineage. Power is no longer derived from the Anxi source, nor is the source an influential player: in the contemporary context, the regional centres are just as, if not more, powerful. It is they that set the agenda with regard to the ancestral village. Third, the lineage has set up the formal bureaucratic institutions of *hui-guan* and *tong-xiang-hui* to help with the implementation of socio-cultural activities, and these institutions have taken on important roles in recent years, networking among themselves in attempting to globalise and providing bases for members to network with each other. Increasingly, they also allow themselves to be used by their members to network with government bodies and other corporate groups for economic purposes. Fourth, they are also important social institutions within the country they live in today and play an important role in defining the Chinese community within the wider polity.

In analysing the Chinese lineage as a cultural network, this analysis also allows us to give due recognition to the continuity and diversity between the source and the regional centres. The source - primarily, the ancestral village - functions as the place where lineage members can trace their ancestral roots and engage in Chinese culture on a large communal scale, where lineage members from overseas can gather to perform communal ancestor and religious worship and acknowledge their common origin. But it is not necessary a seat of power or influence.

This analysis also provides an understanding of the diversities found within the Chinese overseas communities. Each Chinese overseas community develops a distinct identity. Thus, the Singapore Chinese identity is different from that of the Chinese community in Malaysia, Indonesia, the Philippines, Australia or the United States. The varying social experiences in the adopted countries have led to changes and modifications in the village culture that migrating ancestors brought with them. Today, the processes of adaptation and localisation to suit the local needs is continuing in the respective Chinese overseas communities. In this sense, these are independent communities with distinctive identities. What ties them together is the concept of "being Chinese".

This analysis allows for cultural continuity between the source and the regional centres by characterising their mutual relationships as neither dominant nor subservient, but as that of a sense of nostalgia and collective memory. The flows of nostalgia and collective memory are important factors that help to rekindle lost sentiments of the members of the regional cultural centres and force members to look again at their source. This sentimentality and nostalgia is instrumental in pushing the members to visit their ancestral village and to participate in cultural reproduction and village reconstruction; all of which has enabled the process of cultural networking to take place, finally leading to the creation of a lineage network incorporating the various branches.

Within the cultural network, the strength of individual nodes and links can be analysed separately. Some nodes and links are more active than others, and each can be studied on its own and compared to others. Network links between nodes can be strong or weak, depending on the interests of their members. It is generally true to say that the nodal links between the source and the cultural centres in Southeast Asian countries are strong, with much flow between them; and among the cultural centres in Southeast Asia there are also strong links. Nodal links between the source and the centres in North America, Europe and those parts of Asia not in Southeast Asia are weaker than those between the source and Southeast Asia.

Several factors affect this state of affairs. One consists of political considerations. Another consists of the attitudes of the regional centres themselves. Today, the right political climate in Singapore and the desire of the Singapore Chinese to recreate links with the source have allowed for the establishment of strong relationships between the nodes and the source. The example of the Ke lineage has demonstrated that lineage, seen as a cultural network, has enabled us to understand the continuity and diversity between the ancestral village and the Chinese overseas communities. Although there is desire by the Malaysian Chinese to recreate links with the source, the political climate in Malaysia continues to restrain their action.

Conclusion

In late modernity, it is possible to argue that the study of lineage structure continues to be an important feature in the understanding of the organisation of a society. In Chinese society, lineage structure continues to play an important role in the Chinese overseas communities and in China today. However, the usefulness of this structure can be further enhanced through a reconceptualisation of its structure. As discussed above, contemporary Chinese lineages can be best understood if they are reconceptualised as a cultural network in order that we can understand the dynamics of relationship between the various branches and the source of a lineage and among the various branches themselves, taking into account the process of world migration and the formation of permanent Chinese communities in various parts of the world today.

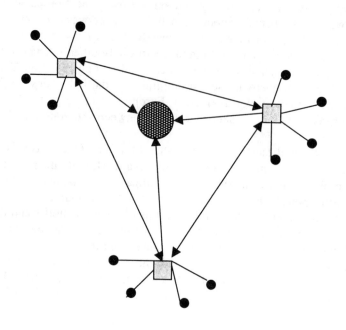

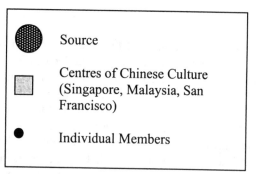

Diagram 1 Lineage Network
(Relationship between the source and centres of Chinese culture is weak and unidirectional while the relationship between the centres of Chinese culture and the individual members is strong)

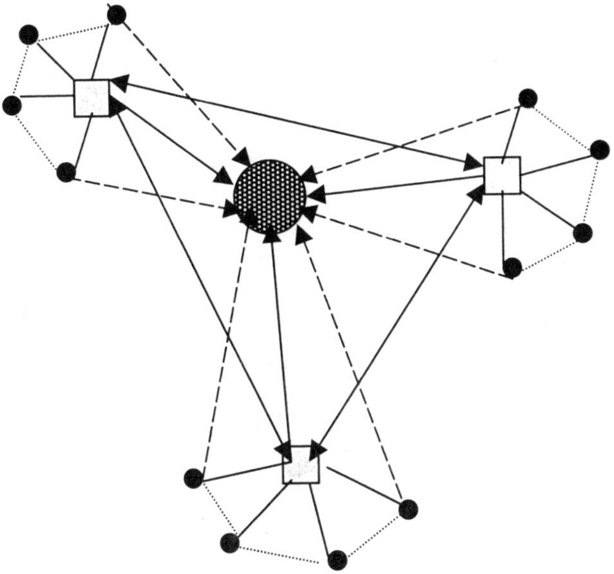

Diagram 2 Intra-Lineage Networking
(Strong interaction between individuals and the source, and between individuals)

Lineage A

Lineage B

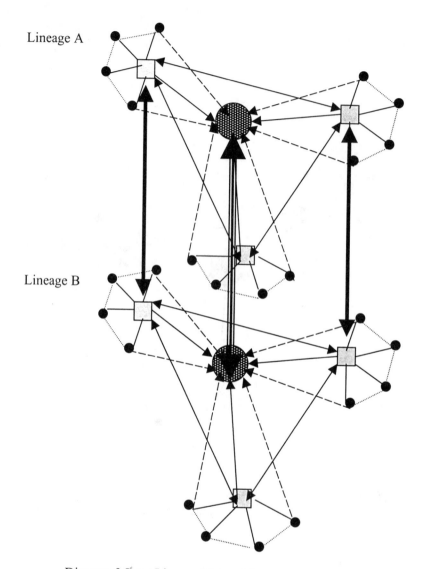

Diagram 3 Inter-Lineage Networking
(There is some interaction between the sources and strong interaction among the regional centres of Chinese culture of Lineages A and B)

10 Conclusion: From Lineage to Transnational Chinese Network

From Nostalgia to Cultural Reproduction

In this study, I have explored the relationship between the Singapore Chinese and their *qiaoxiang*. For the Singapore Chinese, visiting the *qiaoxiang* is a journey in search of ancestral and cultural roots. This search is facilitated by the fact that there continues to be a sizeable number of elderly first-generation Chinese migrants in Singapore, who have played a large part in encouraging the younger Singapore-born Chinese to visit the *qiaoxiang*. It is this unique group of Singapore Chinese and their quest for kinship and lineage continuity that set in motion the search for cultural and ancestral roots.

The search for these cultural and ancestral roots has been very much influenced by feelings of nostalgia and by collective memory. This older group of Chinese often recalled, with much emotion and sentiment, their childhood experiences in the villages, their migrant journeys to Singapore, and their village kin; a small number also experienced life in the villages during the various phases of Communist rule, and maintained contacts with the villages and/or experienced village life during the Cultural Revolution years. Some, of course, immigrated before Communist rule and therefore never experienced it. They were able to relate to their village kin and to empathise with them concerning their political plight and material poverty; and they found themselves with mixed feelings concerning their own situations: on the one hand, they felt fortunate to escape the Communist regime; on the other, they felt guilty for leaving kin behind or being unable to rescue them. Sending remittances and money during the early years was the most they could do; but as the political tension eased and reforms were introduced after 1978, the guilt feeling gradually gave way to a renewed sense of wanting to do something for their ancestral villages.

The period since 1978 witnessed an increasing number of Singapore-born Chinese making their way to their ancestral villages. They relate to the *qiaoxiang* differently than do their parents or grandparents, as

259

they had no social experiences pushing them to empathise with the recent plight of their village kin. For them, the *qiaoxiang* was an illusive ancestral home. Many neither liked nor appreciated their village kin, and there was much tension between this group and their parents and grandparents because of differing perceptions and expectations. Such tension remains today, although it is more muted than before.

There is also tension between the Singapore Chinese and their villager kin. The tension between them and the villagers is most clearly felt within the moral economy. Confucian morality, kinship obligations and parental demands dictate that the Singapore Chinese, being financially and materially bettered endowed, should assist and provide for their poor village kin. The early requests for material goods, perceived as the insatiable demands of the village kin, led the Singapore Chinese to experience "*qiaoxiang* fatigue", as they became wary of these constant demands. To say that they feared receiving *tang-shan* letters was, for some, no overstatement, and was reinforced by a lack of understanding of the village economic structure, especially by the younger generations of Singapore Chinese.

Despite these apprehensions, the Singapore Chinese participated in the operation of the moral economy. As the saying goes, "blood is thicker than water" - the kinship ties and the call of duty from the ancestral home became socio-moral bonds which pushed many Singapore Chinese to contribute to village reconstruction and to provide material and financial assistance to members of their extended kinship groups.

The success of the moral economy is closely related to the relatively large-scale cultural and religious reproduction in the *qiaoxiang*. In attempting to widen the moral-economic networks, the village elders, cadres and the villagers have all supported the reinvention and reproduction of cultural and religious elements - the main preoccupations of the Singapore Chinese when they visit their *qiaoxiang*. In a way, it is this attitude of give and take that creates goodwill and reciprocity between the two groups.

From Lineage to Transnational Networks

At the social structural level, the Chinese lineage has gone through various stages, transforming itself from a parochial social institution into a transnational network. From the source of origin, the lineage has spread outwards and, at present, there are numerous branches throughout China and overseas, especially in Southeast Asian cities.

The source of the Ke lineage remains Peng Lai in Anxi, where it is represented by the physical presence of the ancestral house, which has been reconstructed in recent years to cater for revived communal worship and which serves as a physical reminder and a testimony to the origin of the lineage and to the works of the ancestors. Its existence reminds lineage members to perform their rightful duties to their ancestors. Lineage members, from within the village and from overseas, have come together to acknowledge the ancestors and the ancestral roots through communal ancestor worship and a series of related rituals. In this context, lineage members acknowledge each other as such. The relationship between the source and the overseas branches is governed by this ancestral bond based on assumed blood ties. Kinship intimacy, however, is often confined to those within immediate and/or extended family structures.

As the Chinese overseas settled in their adopted countries and established their own communities, they came to accept roles within them as elders and leaders of these overseas branches, which remain independent and/or autonomous of their source. They organised their own socio-cultural activities and provided economic and welfare facilities for their members. These social institutions then also became important organisations for the transmission of Chinese culture and identity.

The relationship between source and branches is characterised as follows. First, there is the centrality-satellite pattern of relationship, with the source, represented by the ancestral house, remaining the central focus for lineage members. However, this centre-satellite relationship is not one of domination and subordination: although, theoretically, the centre should dominate, in fact the social status of the members of the branches is much higher due to their financial and material wealth. Secondly, each branch is a separate entity - with its own individual functioning, dynamics, membership and institutional base - and functions solely for its members, imparting a knowledge of Chinese culture to its members. Thirdly, the relationship between source and branches is imbued with tension arising from mutual demands and expectations, and there is a high level of rivalry between the two. They are, however, bound together by the common ancestral bond, and they influence each other in the areas of cultural and religious reproduction. The result is that neither group can claim to be the dispenser of authentic Chinese culture. To a large degree, it is the synthesis of their relationship that has created the unique Anxi culture that we witness today.

In understanding the relationship between the source and the branches overseas, the lineage structure must be seen as a cultural network allowing for multidirectional integration among its members, with connectional flows among the branches scattered throughout the world, branches within each of which individuals have established ties with one another and created a personalised level of interactive flow among themselves. Formally, the branches are represented by their organisational bases, which have strong links to one another for co-operation in cultural, religious and other activities.

The various forms of social interaction with the various members, either at individual or collective levels, are instrumental in our understanding of the Singapore Chinese and their *qiaoxiang* connections. The various sets of relationship are important to the operation of this cultural network. Within the cultural network, relationships are characterised by informality and fluidity, with members free to communicate with each other individually or collectively. They are not bound together by strict rules or regulations.

The local cultural network can draw upon the support of other branches scattered throughout the world when the need arises. As the lineage sheds its parochial identity and embarks on the process of globalisation, more of its members throughout the world might form their own branches and join the network. As the lineage network adds its function of generalised communications medium for its branches and diversifies the roles, which it plays beyond those of a strictly social, welfare and/or economic nature, it becomes increasingly advantageous for the different branches to take part. The ability of the lineage structure to serve this modern need is imperative for its survival, and it is to this end that the Ke lineage is working towards to transform its image as part of this wider cultural network structure.

Re-inventing a Chinese Cultural Identity

The level of negotiation between the Singapore Chinese and the villagers on cultural issues shows the extent to which each group must compromise its understanding of what the culture should be like. What we see is thus a *negotiated* Chinese culture being created to suit the needs of these two groups of Chinese. This negotiated Chinese culture comprises the socio-cultural and religious elements of village China, the early migrant society and the contemporary Singapore Chinese community. It is the coming together of these three bodies of cultural practice that constitutes Chinese culture for the Ke lineage. The Singaporeans' simultaneous acknowledgement of both their ancestral roots and their Singaporean identity allows them to formulate this particular Singaporean style of Chinese identity and yet maintain a sense of historical and cultural continuity with the past.

As for the identity of the Anxi villagers, it is now bound to that of their overseas kin. This relationship thrusts them into the global sphere. Their territorial identification is no longer confined to the village, for they now move beyond it into a global space. Their cultural identity has been subject to external influences since the reform years, when the numbers of Singapore Chinese visiting and engaging in cultural and religious reproduction began to increase. They now have to reassess their cultural identities. The fact that the Singapore Chinese have been influential in dictating the types of cultural and religious practices that they have wanted to conduct in the village environment has impacted on how these village Chinese look at themselves and their cultural identity.

Since the reform years, both the Singaporeans and the villagers have been active proponents of village cultural and religious activities, which are now carried out at regular intervals (two to three times a year) and have become important aspects of village culture. This return to religiosity and spiritualism among the Chinese villagers has strong influences on their cultural identity. The elaborate communal religious functions has resuscitated their understanding of their own culture. The village cultural identity is one marked by a plethora of cultural events that affect the whole village, links it with overseas kin and maintains a continuity with the past in which the ancestors are once again given centrestage.

Future Directions: Chinese Overseas Communities and Their Identity

How can we conceptualise the Chinese overseas communities and their identity? This work has demonstrated and argued that the Chinese overseas are constantly searching for their own identity. This is especially so in new nation states with multi-ethnic populations.

Singapore is one example of a society within which Chinese are subjected to various types of identity. First, there is the Singapore national identity, which is tied to the status of the polity, where citizens are required to declare their allegiance to the nation-state. Thus, an imagined sense of identity and community becomes essential for the collective well being of the state and its population. The Singapore Chinese being subjected to this call of duty have declared their commitment to the state and have displayed their sense of Singapore national identity.

Second, there is the Singapore Chinese identity. This is an identity that is constructed through a negotiated process between the Singapore State and the Chinese community. It is an identity that portrays the Singapore Chinese as a homogenised group to outsiders, who use Mandarin as the lingua franca, and are economically successful, urbane, sophisticated and obedient. Culturally, this Singapore Chinese identity is represented to a large degree by its food and religious practices both at communal and individual levels. Other aspects of traditional Chinese culture (e.g. art, traditional music and dance, calligraphy, etc.) are less significant for modern Singapore Chinese.

Third, there is the narrower regional and dialect-based identity that many Singapore Chinese continue to subscribe to. This is an insider's identity, within which the Chinese differentiate among themselves. Important internal differences are marked by dialect, slight variation in religious practice, mannerisms and food culture.

It is thus possible to portray Chinese identity in three concentric circles. At the centre is the primordial cultural identity, followed by the Singapore Chinese ethnic identity and at the outermost, the Singapore national identity. Where the different types of identity overlap, their common foundational base increases. At the outermost layer, identity is shared with other ethnic groups. At this level, there are integrating factors that allow the citizens to proclaim themselves as Singaporeans. The state attempts to shape this identity with a set of shared values. At the second level, all Chinese in Singapore share selected values with one another, based on ethnicity and shared cultural elements. At the third level, the social base is narrower. Chinese from the same region, who speak the same dialect, identify with each other here. The Ke lineage falls within the very narrow social base.

In their quest for a cultural identity, the Singapore Chinese have looked for their ancestral roots and have striven for historical and cultural continuity. In this search, they have been confronted with a renewed sense of "Chineseness". How the Chinese look at the issue of "Chineseness" and "Chinese cultural identity" is important for their identity as Singapore Chinese. To a large degree, the Singapore Chinese use the three identities in different social contexts to represent themselves to different groups of people, be they of other nationalities, ethnicities, dialect groups, etc. The three identities form a total cultural baggage, which make them Singaporeans. Their expression of the different identities is only displayed in relation to the groups and people they are dealing with, that is, their identity is context- and situation-bound, and represents the social distance with the people they come into contact with. Because of the fluidity of movement from one identity to the next, most Singapore Chinese tend to be relatively comfortable and at home with these three identities.

Singapore has moved away from its main preoccupation with economic and political stability and is now focussing on the cultural and social values of its citizenry. In the next century to come, the urgency of the quest for a national identity will be less pronounced, as new generations of

Singaporeans will have known no other home than Singapore with the policies of multi-ethnicity and multiculturalism fully entrenched. Given such a situation, individual ethnic and sub-ethnic groups will probably be given greater room for cultural expression, thereby further entrenching their cultural identities. In this sense, greater cultural autonomy allowed by the state will foster greater dynamism on the cultural fronts for the ethnic groups, enabling the reflowering of cultural activity and cultural identity.

For the Chinese, this is already underway. The encouragement by the state and the active roles taken by the various Chinese social institutions have enabled the Chinese to undertake initiatives and embark on a cultural renaissance where the focus on art, literature, music, philosophy and aesthetics become possible. The result of this reflowering remains to be seen in the future.

Glossary

an-we (安位) - positioning

Anxi Hui Guan [M], Ann Kway Hui Guan [H] (安溪會館) - Anxi Association

bai-tian-gong (拜天公) - praying to Heaven

Bei-shan wan-shui (背山望水) - literally backing the hills and facing the waters. This phrase is used to explain a good location with a good view. In the case of the Chinese, it is used to explain a location with good geomancy

biao-jie-mei (表姐妹) - cross-cousins (female) of second degree, mother's sisters and brother's daughters

biao-wen (表文) - a religious rite. The priest makes a submission to the deities on behalf of the supplicant

biao-xiong-di (表兄弟) - cross-cousins (male) of second degree, mother's sisters and brothers' sons

bi-shan-bu-zu, bi-xia-you-yu (比上不足比下有餘) - literally below the above and above the below. In this case, it is taken to mean that one is comfortable in life

bo-fu (伯父) - paternal uncle, father's elder brothers

bo-mu (伯母) - paternal aunt, father's elder sisters

bo-shi (博士) - a person with a Ph.D

bu-hui-zuo-ren (不會做人) - literally does not how to be a person. In this case, it means one does not know how to behave properly in a given social situation

chang-shou-deng (長壽橙) - longevity lanterns

cho-yuan (湊文) - petition to the deities/gods

ci-tang (祠堂) - lineage ancestral hall

Da zhonghua (大中華) - Great China Thesis

dao-de jin-ji wang-luo (道德經濟網絡) - Moral Economic Network

Da-shi-ye (大士爺) - A deity, proctector of the Netherworld

da-tin (大廳) - first hall

da-wu (大屋) - literally grand house. In this case, it means spirit or soul house

dian-xie (點謝) - offering of libation to the deities or dead

Di-Chang-Wang-Jing, (地藏王經) - Kistargabha Bodhisattva

di-fang-zhi (地方志) - locality register

er-tin (二廳) - second hall

fan [M], and huang [H] (番) - ie, uncivilised and detribalised

fan ren (番人) - uncivilised and /or detribalised person

fang (房) - room. In this case, it means a stem family

fangyan gonghui (方言公會) - dialect associations

fan-ke [M], huang-ke [H] (番客) - uncivilised guest

fa-shi (法事) - religious activities

feiqiao (肥僑)- literally fat overseas Chinese. Here, it means wealthy Chinese overseas

feng-shui (風水) - geomancy

feng-shui-di (風水地) - burial sites chosen according to geomancy

fo-dan (佛誕) - birthday of Buddha

fo-tou [M] or puo-tau [H] (佛頭) - literally buddha head. Also known as stove master who is in charge of a religious celebration

fu (符) - amulet

fu-gu-bu-li-zu (富貴不離祖) - wealth does not divorce from the ancestors

gan-qing (感情) - sentiments

gen (根) - roots

gen-yuan (根源) - source of origin

getihu (個體户) - private individual/household enterprise

gong-de (公德) - meritorious deeds. It is a religious ceremony to transfer merits to the dead and to increase the dead's store of good karma

guanxi (關系)- social connection

guanxi wang (關系網) - social network

hong-bao (紅包) - a small sum of money placed in a red envelope

hua-qiao (華僑) - overseas Chinese

huaren hua (華人化) - becoming Chinese; also becoming sinicised

hui-tou (匯頭) - head of the credit rotation system

hun (魂) - soul

jia (家) - family

jia-gen (家根) - family roots

jia-pu (家譜) - family genealogy

jie-yuan-qian (結緣餞)

ji-nian [M]; ki-liem [H], (紀念) - in remembrance, in memory, memorialise

Jin-Kang-Jing (金鋼經) - Diamond Sutra

ji-zu (祭祖) - in remembrance of the ancestors

juan-ding (涓丁) - continuous flow of descendants

junzi (君子) - gentleman

kai-pu (開譜) - opening the genealogy

kai-pu-yi-shi (開譜儀式) - the opening of the genealogy ceremony

kai-zu-zhai men (開祖宅門) - opening the doors of the ancestral house

ku-hun (孤魂) - lonely soul

Kui-tou Ke-Shi Zu-pu (魁頭柯氏族譜) - Kui-tou village Ke's Genealogy

kui-tou-zu-zhai [M] or kway-tau zhor chu [H] (魁頭祖宅) - Kui-Tou Ancestral House

kui-xing-gong (M) or kway-sin-gong (H) (魁星公) - Peng Lai district guardian deity

lao-jia (老家) - old home

li (禮) - properity

Lien-Hua-Jing (蓮華經) - Lotus Sutra

ling (靈) - spiritually effacicious

ling-wu (靈屋) - soul/spirit house. See da-wu

liu-lien (留念) - have fond memories

luo-di-shen-gen (落地生根) - planting one's roots in the foreign soil

luo-pi-zu (落脾祖) - drooping nose ancestor

luo-ye-gui-gen (落葉歸根) - the leaves returning to the roots

mao-wu (茅屋)- communal latrine made of planks and thatched roof

Ma-Zu (媽祖) - Heavenly Empress, also known as Tien-Hou (天后)

mingyun (命運) - life fate

mi-xin-de (迷信的) - superstitious

mu-bei (木杯) - a religious item. Small boat shaped wood 8-10 cm long and 4 cm wide with one side in concave shape and the other flat surface.

mu-yi (母姨) - maternal aunt, mother's sister

nei-jiu (內疚) - remorseful

nian-shou (念壽) - chanting of prayers for the dead

O-mi-to-jing, (阿彌陀經) - Amitabha Buddha

Peng Lai Shi (蓬來寺) - Peng Lai Temple

po (魄) - spirit

pu (譜) - genealogy

Pu-Du (普渡) - religious rituals to provide good merits to the dead

qiao-bao (僑胞) - overseas comrades

Qiao-Lian-Suo (僑聯所) - Guest House for Overseas Chinese

qiao-qin (僑親)- overseas relatives

qiaoxiang (僑鄉) - emigrant villages

Qing-Ming Jie (清明節) - Festival for Sweeping of the Tomb

qing-qing guanxi wang-luo (親情關系網絡) - kinship social network

Qing-Shui-Yan (清水岩) - Clearwater Deified Ancestor Temple

Qing-shui-zu-shi-gong (清水祖師) - Clearwater Deified Ancestor

qin-qing (親情) - kinship sentiments

qi-pao (旗袍) - traditional high collared gown

qi-yuan-di (起源地) - place of origin

ren (仁) - human-ness, humanity

re-nao (熱鬧) - heat and noise. It means noisy and exciting atmosphere

ren-jian (人間) - humanly plane of existence

ren-zu (認祖) - recognise or acknowledge the ancestors

sang-li (喪禮) - mourning rites

shan-qu (山區) - mountainous district

she-hui wang luo (社會網絡) - social networks

shu shu (叔叔) - paternal uncle, father's younger brothers

shu-bo (叔伯) - father's older brothers

Shui-Chan-Fa-Jing, (水懺法經) - Water Sutra

si-fang-qian (私房錢) - private room money. It means women's private saving

si-shu (私塾) - private tuition during the nineteenth century. This was usually for girls who did not go to schools

souqiao (瘦僑) - literally thin overseas relatives. It means not wealthy overseas relatives

tang-shan (唐山) - China

tang-shan xin (唐山信) - China letter

tang-shan-ke (唐山客) - China guests

tang-shu (唐叔) - father's younger brothers

tang-xie-mei (唐姐妹) - paternal first degree cousin (female), father's sisters' and brothers' daughters

tang-xiong-di (唐兄弟) - paternal first degree cousin (male), father's brothers' and sisters' sons

tian-fang (添房) - adding a room. In this case, it means a concubine

tongxiang (同鄉) - same village

tong-xiang-hui (同鄉會) - same village or territorial based associations

tong-xiang-hui-guan (同鄉會館) - territorial based associations

tu-di-gong (土地公) - Earth God

wenhua qu (文化區) - cultural district

wenhua zhongguo (文化中國) - Cultural China Thesis

wu-ke (五穀) - mourning rites according to the 5-grain categorisation

wu-mian zu-shi gong (烏面祖師公) - Black-faced Deified Ancestor

xian (縣) - county

Xian Chen (縣城) - county town

xiang-lu (香爐) - incense urn

xiang-you (香油) - incense and oil

xiao (孝) - filial

Xiaojing (孝 經) - the Book of Filial Piety

xia-shu-wei [M], ae-chiu-ber [H] (下樹尾) -below the tree

xie-pu-yi-shi (謝譜儀式) - The Rite of Thanking the Genealogy

xie-zu (謝祖) - giving thanks to the ancestors

xie-zu-juan-ding (謝祖涓丁) - The Rite of Gratification to the Ancestors for the Continuous Flow of Descendants

xin (心) - heart, spirit

xin-jia (新家) - new house

Xinjiapo fujian anxi huaren (新加坡福建安溪人) - Singapore Fujian Anxi Chinese

Xinjiapo huaren (新加坡華人) - Singapore Chinese

Xin-Jing (心經) - Heart Sutra

xin-lao-jia (新老家) - rennovated old house

xinshi gonghui (姓氏公會) - Surname association

xin-yong (信用) - trust

xi-tou [M], kway-tou [H] (溪頭) - source of a river

xiu-pu (修譜) - literally mending the genealogy

xiuxin (修心) - spiritual cultivation of the heart

xi-wei [M], kway-ber [H] (溪尾) - downstream of a river

xue-tong-guan-xi (血統關系) - blood ties

yang-jian (陽間) - heavenly plane of existence

yang-qi (陽氣) - yang energies

ye (葉) - leaves

yi (儀) - rites

yi-mu (姨母) - mother's sisters

yin qi (陰氣) - yin energies

ying zu-shi (迎祖師) - Rite for the welcoming of the deified ancestor

ying-qing shui-zu-shi (迎清水祖師) - Rite for welcoming the Clearwater Ancestor

ying-shen-ying-huo (迎神迎火) - Rite for welcoming the deities and fire

yin-hun (引魂) - Rite for guiding the soul of the dead

yin-jian (陰間) - netherworld

yin-qian (銀錢) - paper money for the dead, spirits and gods

yin-shui-si-yuan (飲水思源) - literally when drinking the water think of the source

yi-xiong-di (儀兄弟)

you lu wu wu (有路無屋) - there is a road but no home. In this case, it means a Chinese overseas is able to make it to the ancestral village but has no home to go to

you-hun (游魂) - sad spirit

zhang-cheng (章程) - petition

zhi (枝) - stems and branches

zhong (忠) - loyalty

Zhong-Yuan Festival (中元節) - Festival of the Hungry Ghosts

Zhou-Yue-Miao (州月廟) -Zhou Yue Temple

zi-ji-ren (自己人) - member of one's group

zong (宗) - ancestor

zong-ci (宗祠) - ancestral hall

zong-miao (宗廟) - ancestor shrine

zong-pu (宗譜) - genealogy
zong-qing (宗親) - lineage members
zong-qin guanxi wang-luo (宗情關系網) -lineage guanxi network
zong-tang (宗堂) - lineage shrine
zong-xiang hui (宗鄉會) - lineage association
zou-jin (做勁) - religious service, chanting of sutras
zu (祖) - ancestor
zu-jia (祖家) - ancestral family/home
zu-miao (祖廟) - ancestral temple
zu-pu (族譜) - lineage genealogy
Zu-Shi-Dian (祖師殿) - Shrine hall devoted to the Deified Ancestor
Zu-Shi-Gong-Dan (祖師公誕) - Birthday of Deified Ancestor
zuxiang (祖鄉) - ancestral village
zu-zai [M], (祖宅) or zhor-chu [H] (祖厝)

Bibliography

Anderson, B. (1986), *Imagined Communities: Reflections on the Origin and Spread of Nationalism*, London: Verso Pub., 3rd edition.

Anxi Xian Zhi (1994), Fujiansheng anxixian difangzhi bianzuan weiyuanhui bian: *Zhonghua renmin gongheguo difangzhi: Anxi xianzhi* (福 建 省 安溪縣地方志編委員會編:《中華人民共和國地方志:安溪縣》), Beijing: Xinhua chubanshe (北京新華出版社), vols 1 and 2.

Bourdieu, P. (1993), *The Field of Cultural Production*, New York: Columbia University Press.

Brook, T. (1988), "Must Lineages Own Land?" in *Bulletin of Concerned Asian Scholars*, vol. 20, no. 4, pp. 72-79.

Cai Wen (1990), "Qingshan zushi shi yingxiong shen" (蔡 文 :"清 山 祖 師 是 英雄神"), *Guanxi wo* (《關 系 我》) vol. 37, pp. 75-77.

Castells, M. (1976), "Theory and Ideology in Urban Sociology" in Pickvance, C.G. (ed.), *Urban Sociology: Critical Essays*, London: Tavistock.

Chen Jintian, (1989), "Zuxian shenzhu ji jisi" (陳 金 田 :"祖 先 神 主 及祭祀"), *Taiwan fengwu* (《臺 灣 風 物》) vol. 39, no.1, pp. 99-106.

Chen Kezhen (ed) (1994), *Anxi huaqiao zhi* (陈克晨主编:《安溪华侨志》) Xiamen: Xiamen University Press.

Chen Luxi (1980), *Jizu wenti* (陳 璐 兮 :《祭 祖 問 題》), Taipei: Xiaoyuan shufang (臺 北 校 園 書 房).

Chen Xiangshui (1978), "Zhongguo shehui jiegou yu zuxian chongbai" (陳 祥 水 :"中 國 社 會 結 構 與 祖 先 崇 拜"), *Zhonghua wenhua fuxing yuekan* (《中 華 文 化 復 興 月 刊》) vol. 11, no. 6, pp. 32-39.

Chen Zhongmin (1969), "Jinjiangcuo de zuxian chongbai yu shizu zuzhi" (陳 中 民 : "晉 江 厝 的 祖 先 崇 拜 與 氏 族 組 織"), *Minzuxue yanjiusuo jijkan* (《民 族 學 研 究 所 集 刊》 vol. 23, pp.167-193.

Chen Zi-Ping (1991), Wubai nian de Fujian zongzu yu wenhua, (陳 志 平:《五 百 年 的 福 建 宗 族 與 文 化》) Shanghai: San Lian shuju (上 海 三 聯 書 局).

Chua, B. H. (1995), *Communitarian Ideology and Democracy in Singapore*, London: Routledge.

Daye, D.D. (1978), "Cosmology" in Prebish, C.S. (ed), *Buddhism: A New Perspective*, University Park: Pennsylvania State University Press, pp. 123-126.

De Groot, J.J.M. (1964), *The Religion of the Chinese*, vols 1 to 6, Taipei: Literature House, reprint.

Dun Jue (1980), "You yige anjing de difang gen zuxian shuohua" (頓 覺 :"有 一 個 安 靜 的 地 方 跟 祖 先 説 話"), *Guanxi wo* (《關 系 我》), vol. 1, pp. 27-29.

Eberhard, W. (1972), "Chinese Genealogies as a Source for the Study of Chinese Society" in Palmer, J. (ed.), *Studies in Asian Genealogy*, Brigham Young

University Press, pp. 27-37.

Ebrey, P.B. and Watson, J.L. (1986), *Kinship Organisation in Late Imperial China*, 1000-1949, Berkeley: University of California Press.

Evans-Pritchard, E. and Fortes, M. (eds) (1970), *African Political Systems*, London: Oxford University Press.

Faure, D. (1989), "The Lineage as a Cultural Intervention", *Modern China*, vol. 15 no. 1, pp. 4-36.

Fei H.T. and Chang, C.T. (1953), *China's Gentry*, Chicago: Chicago University Press.

Fei, H.T. (1939), *Peasant Life in China*, London: RKP.

Fentress, J. and Wickham, C. (1992), *Social Memory*, Oxford: Blackwell.

Feuchtwang, S.D.R. (1974), *An Anthropological Analysis of Chinese Geomancy*, Vientiane: Vithagna.

Freedman, M. (1958), *Lineage Organisation in Southeast China*, London: LSE Monograph no. 18.

Freedman, M. (1966), *Chinese Lineage and Society: Fukien and Kwangtung*, London: LSE Monograph on Social Anthropology, no. 33.

Fujian jingji (1987, 1989, 1990) (《福 建 經 濟 》).

Fujian tongji ninajian (1992), (《福 建 統 計 年 鑒 》).

Fujiansheng tongjiju bian: *Lao shao bian dao diqu zhuyao tongji ziliao shouce*, (1992) (福 建 省 统 计 局 编：《老、少、边、岛 地 区 主 要 统 计 资 料 》).

Furnivall, J.S. (1980), "Plural Societies", in Evers, H-D (ed), *Sociology of Southeast Asia*, Kuala Lumpur: Oxford University Press, pp. 86-96.

Geary, P.J. (1994), *Phantoms of Remembrance*, New Jersey: Princeton University Press.

Geertz, C. (1973), *The Interpretation of Cultures*, New York: Basic Books.

Granet, M. (1975), *The Religion of the Chinese People*, Oxford: Oxford University Press.

Guo Zhenwu (1985), "Jizu Shangfen youzui ma" (郭 晨 武：" 祭 祖 上 墳 有 嗎 "), Taipei.

Halbwachs, M. (1992), *On Collective Memory*, Chicago: Chicago University Press.

Hannerz, U. (1992), *Cultural Complexity: Studies in the Social Organisation of Meaning*, New York: Columbia University Press.

Harding, H. (1993), "The Concept of 'Greater China': Themes, Variations and Reservations", in *The China Quarterly*, no. 136: 660-686, special Issue on Greater China.

Harvey, D. (1985), *Consciousness and the Urban Experience*, Oxford: Basil Blackwell.

Hazelton, K. (1986), "Patrilines and the development of localised lineages: the Wu of Hsiu-ning City, Hui-chou to 1528" in Ebrey, P. and Watson J. (eds), *Kinship Organization in in Late Imperial China 1000-1940*, pp. 137-169.

Hicks, G.L. (ed) (1990), *Overseas Chinese Remittances from Southeast Asia 1910 - 1940*, Singapore: Select Books.

Hobsbawn, E. and Ranger, T. (eds) (1983), *The Invention of Tradition*, Cambridge: Cambridge University Press.

Hsiao, K.C. (1966), *Rural China: Imperial Control in the Nineteenth Century*, Seattle: University of Washington Press.

Huang Shu-min, 1989, *The Spiral Road: Changes in a Chinese Village Through the Eyes of a Communist Party Leader*, Boulder: Westview Press.

Huang Youzhi (1988), "Zhongguo zuxian chongbai de yiyi tantao" (黃 有 志 : 中 國 祖 先 崇 拜 的 意 義 探 討 "), *Shijian xuebao* (《實 踐 學 報 》), vol. 19, pp. 1-24.

Hymes, R.P., 1986, "Marriage, Descent Groups, and the Localist Strategy in Sung and Yuan Fuchou", in Ebrey, P. and Watson, J. (eds), *Kinship Organization in in Late Imperial China 1000-1940*, pp. 95-136.

Kaye, B. (1960), *Upper Nankin Street: Singapore*, Singapore: University of Malaya Press.

Ke Si Zu-Pu, n.d., vols 1 and 2 (《柯氏族譜》), Genealogy of the Ke Lineage.

Kluckhohn, C. (1960), *Mirror of Man*, Greenwich: Fawcett Publications.

Kuah, Khun Eng (1999), "The Changing Moral Economy of Ancestor Worship in a Chinese Emigrant Village" in *Medicine, Culture and Psychiatry*, vol. 23, pp. 99-132.

Kuah, Khun Eng (1998a), "Maintaining Ethno-Religious Harmony in Singapore", *Journal of Contemporary Asia*, 28(1): 103-121.

Kuah, Khun Eng (1998b), "Rebuilding Their Ancestral Villages: The Moral Economy of the Singapore Chinese" in Wang, G.W. and Wong, J. (ed), *China's Political Economy*, Singapore: University of Singapore Press and World Scientific, pp. 249-276.

Kuah Khun Eng, 1998c,"Doing Anthropology within a Transnational Framework: Study of the Singapore Chinese and Emigrant Village Ties", in Cheung, S.C.H. (ed.), *On the South China Track*, Hong Kong: Hong Kong Institute of Asia-Pacific Studies, Chinese University of Hong Kong, pp. 81-109.

Kuah, Khun Eng (1990), "Confucian Ideology and Social Engineering in Singapore" in *Journal of Contemporary Asia*, vol. 20, no. 3, pp.371-383.

Kuchler, K. and Melion, G. (eds) (1991), *Images of Memory: On Remembering and Representation*, Washington: Smithsonian Institute Press.

Kuo, E.C.Y. (1996), "Confucianism as a Political Discourse in Singapore: The Case of an Incomplete Revitalization Movement" in Tu, Weiming (ed), *Confucian Traditions in East Asian Modernity*, Cambridge, Mass.: Harvard University Press.

La Fontaine, J.S. (1985), *Initiation*, Middlesex: Penguin Books.

Lang, O. (1946), *Chinese Family and Society*, New Haven: Yale University Press.

Lau, P.C. (trans) (1970), *Mencius*, London: Penguin.

Lau, P.C. (trans) (1979), *Confucius: The Analects*, Middlesex: Penguin.

Le Goff, S. (1992), *History and Memory*, translated by Rendall, S. and Claman, E., New York: Columbia University Press.

Lee, P.H. (1978), *Chinese Society in Nineteenth Century Singapore*, Singapore: Oxford University Press.

Leo, J.B. (1976-77), *Confucianism in Singapore*, Singapore: University of Singapore, Department of Sociology, Academic Exercise, unpub.

Liao Kuntian (1979), "Cong shenxue de guandian yanjiu dangqian taiwan hanren shehui zuxian chongbai zhi zongjiao benzhi" (廖昆田: "從神學的觀點研究當前臺灣漢人社會祖先崇拜之宗教本質") Yazhou jinxinhui shenxue yanjiuyuan shuoshi lunwen (《亞洲浸信會神學研究院神學碩士論文》).

Lim, J.H. (1967), "Chinese Female Immigration into the Straits Settlement, 1860-1901", Journal of the South Seas Society, vol. 22, pp. 58-95.

Lin Luo (1986), "Gen - Tan jizu de liyi ji qita" (林洛:"根 - 談祭祖的禮儀及其他"), Minsu yu Xinyang (《民俗與信仰》), vol. 102, pp. 82-85.

Lin Meirong (1990), "Zupu zhong youguan jizu de wenshu'"(林美容: "族譜中有關祭祖的文書"), Minzu yanjiusuo ziliao huibian (《民族研究所資料匯編》), vol. 3, pp. 181-194.

Lin Shuguang (1990), "Zushigong shi shidao erjiao zhi shen" (林曙光: "祖師公是釋道二教之神"), Guanxi wo (《關系我》), vol. 37, pp. 78-83.

Lin Wenlong, "Jiekai cankui zushi zhi mi" (林文龍:"揭開慚愧祖師之謎"), Taiwan shiji conglun (《臺灣史績衆論》), Taizhong: Guozhang (臺中:國彰), Part 1, pp. 1-15.

Lin, Y.H. (1947), The Golden Wing: A sociological study of Chinese Familism, London, Kegan Paul, Trench, Trubner.

Liu Guoguang (1973), "Taiwan minjian sizu zhi fengsu" (劉國光:"臺灣民間祀祖之風俗"), Taiwan funu yuekan (《臺灣婦女月刊》), vol. 202, pp. 3-5.

Lo, H. L. (1972a), 'The History and Arrangement of Chinese Genealogies', in Palmer, J. (ed), Studies in Asian Genealogy, Brigham Young University Press, pp. 13-26.

Lo, H.L. (1972b), "The Preservation of Genealogical Records in China", in Palmer, J. (ed), Studies in Asian Genealogy, Brigham Young University Press, pp. 38-55.

Lou Zikuang (1969), "Zushigong Chen Zhaoying" (婁子匡:"祖師公陳昭應"), Taibei wenxian (《臺北文獻(直)》) vols 6-8, pp. 1-3.

Lou Zikuang (1977), "Qingshui zushi de lailongqumai" (婁子匡:"清水祖師的來龍去脈"), Taiwan wenxian (《臺北文獻》), vol. 22, pp. 49-52.

Lyons, T.P. (1992), China's War on Poverty: A Case Study of Fujian Province, 1985-1990, Hong Kong: Chinese University of Hong Kong.

Lyons, T.P. (1994), Poverty and Growth in a South China County: Anxi, Fujian 1949 - 1992, Ithaca: Cornell University East Asia Series.

Mak, L.F. (1981), The Sociology of Secret Societies: A Study of Chinese Secret Societies in Singapore and Peninsular Malaysia, Kuala Lumpur: Oxford University Press.

Mei, J. (1975), "Socioeconomic Origin of Emigration: Guangdong to California, 1850-1882", Modern China, no.5, pp. 463-501.

Nosco, P. (1990), Remembering Paradise: Nativism and Nostalgia in 18th C Japan, Cambridge, Mass: Harvard-Yenching Monograph 31, Harvard University.

Nyce, R. (1969), "Chinese Folk Religion in Malaysia and Singapore", *The Southeast Asia Journal of Theology*, vol. 2, pp. 81-91.

Obeyeskere, G. (1968), "Theodicy, Sin and Salvation in a Sociology of Buddhism" in Leach, E. R. (ed), *Dialectic in Practical Religion*, Cambridge: Cambridge University Press, pp. 7-40.

Ong, A. and Nonini, D. (eds) (1997), *Ungrounded Empires: The Cultural Politics of Modern Chinese Transnationalism*, New York: Routledge.

Ong, T.C. (1979), *Report on Moral Education, 1979*, Singapore: Ministry of Education.

Palmer, J. (ed) (1972), *Studies in Asian Genealogy*, Brigham Young University Press.

Parish, W.L. and Whyte, M.K. (1978), *Village and Family in Contemporary China*, Chicago: Chicago University Press.

Peng Jingyuan (1977), "Tantan guanyu jingtian jizu de yiyi" (彭 敬 元 : "談 談 關 於 敬 天 祭 祖 的 意 義 "), *Hengyi* (《恒 毅 》) vol. 26, no. 8, pp. 2-3.

Perry, R.B. (1901), *The Moral Economy*, New York: Charles Scribner's Sons.

Png, P.H. (1969), "The Straits Chinese in Singapore: A Case Study of Local Identity and Socio-cultural Accomodation", *Journal of Southeast Asian History*, vol. 10, no. 1, p. 95-114.

Potter, S.H. and Potter, J.M. (1990), *China's Peasants: The Anthropology of a Revolution*, Cambridge: Cambridge University Press.

Purcell, V. (1951), *The Chinese in Southeast Asia*, London: Oxford University Press.

Purcell, V. (1967), *The Chinese in Malaya*, Kuala Lumpur: Oxford University Press.

Quah, J., Chan, H.C. and Seah C.M. (eds) (1985), *Government and Politics of Singapore*, Singapore: Oxford University Press.

Rawski, E.S. (1988), "A Historian's Approach to Chinese Death Ritual" in Watson, J.L. and Rawski, E.S. (eds), Death Rituals in Later Imperial and Modern China, Berkeley: University of California Press, pp. 20-36.

Reid, A. (ed) (1996), *Sojourners and Settlers: Histories of Southeast Asia and the Chinese*, St. Leonard, N.S.W.: Allen and Unwin and ASAA Southeast Asia Publication Series.

Rodan, G. (ed) (1993), *Singapore Changes Guards*, Melbourne: Longman Cheshire.

Scott, J. (1985), *Weapons of the Weak*, New Heaven: Yale University Press.

Simoniya, N.A. (1961), *Overseas Chinese in Southeast Asia: A Russian Study*, Ithaca: Cornell University Southeast Asia Programme.

Soothill, W.E. (1973), *The Three Religions of China*, London: Curzon Press, reprint.

Tamney, J. (1996), *The Struggle Over Singapore's Soul*, Berlin: Walter de Gruyter.

Tan, T.T.W. (1984), *Modernisation: A Study of Traditional Chinese Voluntary Associations in Social Change*, Ann Arbor: Microfilms International, University of Virginia Ph. D. dissertation, 1983.

Tan, T.T.W. (1986), *Your Chinese roots: The Overseas Chinese story*, Singapore: Times Books International.

The China Quarterly (1993), "Greater China", December issue.

Tong, C.K. (1982), *Funerals, Ancestral Halls and Graveyards: Changes and Continuities in Chinese Ancestor Worship in Singapore*, National University of Singapore, Department of Sociology, M.A. dissertation, unpub.

Topley, M. (1961), "The Emergence and Social Function of Chinese Religious Associations in Singapore", in *Comparative Studies in Society and History*, vol. 3., no. 3, pp. 289-314.

Tu W. M. (1985), *Confucian Thought*, Albany: State University of New York Press.

Tu W.M. (1994), "Cultural China: The Periphery as the Centre" in Tu, W.M. (ed), *The Living Tree: The Changing Meaning of Being Chinese Today*, Stanford: Stanford University Press, pp. 1-34.

Tu, W. M. (ed) (1994), *The Living Tree: The Changing Meaning of Being a Chinese Today*, Stanford: Stanford University Press.

Turnbull, C.M. (1972), *The Straits Settlement 1926-67*, London: The Athlone Press.

Turnbull, C.M. (1977), *A History of Singapore, 1819-1975*, Kuala Lumpur: Oxford University Press.

Turner, V. (1969), *The Ritual Process*, Ithaca: Cornell University Press.

van der Sprenkel (1973), "Genealogical Registers", in Leslie, D.D., Mackerras, C., and Wang, G.W. (eds), *Essays on the Sources for Chinese History*, Canberra: ANU, pp. 83-98.

Van der Veer, P. (ed) (1995), *Nation and Migration: The Politics of Space in the South Asian Diaspora*, Philadelphia: University of Philadelphia Press.

Van Gennep, A. (1960), *The Rites of Passage*, Chicago: Chicago University Press.

Vaughan, J.D. (1972), *The manners and customs of the Chinese of the Straits Settlements*, Kuala Lumpur: Oxford University Press, reprint.

Wang Jianzhu (1980), "Jizu yu baishen" (王 建 柱 : " 祭 祖 與 拜 神 "), *Guanxi wo* (《 關 系 我 》) vol 1, pp. 14-20.

Wang, G. W. (1996), "Sojourning: The Chinese Experience in Southeast Asia", in Reid, A. (ed), *Sojourners and Settlers: Histories of Southeast Asia and the Chinese*, St. Leonard, N.S.W.: Allen and Unwin and ASAA Southeast Asia Publication Series, pp. 1-14.

Wang, G.W. (1958), "The Chinese in Search of a Base in the Nanyang", *Journal of the South Seas Society*, vol. 14, pts 1 and 2, pp. 86-96.

Wang, G.W. (1981), *Community and Nation: Essays on Southeast Asia and the Chinese*, Singapore: Heinemann.

Wang, G.W. (1991), *China and the Chinese Overseas*, Singapore: Times Academic Press.

Wang, G.W. (1993a), "Greater China and the Chinese Overseas" in *The China Quarterly*, no. 136: 926-948, special issue on Greater China.

Wang, G.W. (1993b), "Migration and Its Enemies", in Mazlish, D. and Buultjens, R. (eds), *Conceptualizing Global History*, Boulder: Westview Press, pp. 131-151.

Wang-Liu, H.C. (1959), *The Traditional Chinese Clan rules*, New York: Locust Valley.

Watson, J.L. (1982), "Chinese Kinship Reconsidered: Anthropological Perspectives on Historical Research" in *The China Quarterly*, pp. 589-622.

Watson, J.L. (1986), "Anthropological Overview: the Development of Chinese Descent Groups", in Ebrey, P. and Watson, J. (eds), *Kinship Organization in in Late Imperial China 1000-1940*, pp. 247-292.

Watson, J.L. (1991), *The Renegotiation of Chinese Cultural Identity in Post-modern Era*, University of Hong Kong: Social Sciences Research Centre Occasional Paper, vol. 4, 27pp.

Watson, J.L. and Rawski, E.S. (eds) (1988), *Death Ritual in Late Imperial and Modern China*, Berkeley: California University Press.

Watson, R. (ed) (1994), *Memory, History and Opposition*, Santa Fe, New Mexico: School of American Research Press.

Weber, M. (1951), *The Religion of China*, New York: Free Press.

Weber, M. (1966), *The Sociology of Religion*, London: Associated Book.

Whyte, M.K. and Parish, W.L (1984), *Urban Life in Contemporary China*, Chicago: Chicago University Press.

Whyte, M.K. (1988), "Death in the People's Republic of China" in Watson, J.L. and Rawski, E.S. (eds), *Death Rituals in Late Imperial and Modern China*, Berkeley: University of California Press.

Wickberg, E. (1985), "Chinese Organisations and Ethnicity in Southeast Asia and North America since 1945: A Comparative Analysis", Canberra: *Australian National University, symposium on 'Changing Identities of the Southeast Asian Chinese since World War Two*.

Willmott, W.E. (1964), "Chinese clan associations in Vancouver", *MAN*, vol. 94, no. 49, pp. 33-37.

Wilson, H. (1978), *Social Engineering in Singapore*, Singapore: Singapore University Press.

Wolf, A.P. (ed) (1974), *Religion and Ritual in Chinese Society*, California: Standford University Press.

Wong, J. (1996), "Promoting Confucianism for Socioeconomic Development: The Singapore Experience" in Tu, W.M. (ed), Confucian Traditions in East Asian Modernity, Cambridge, Mass.: Harvard University Press, pp. 277-293.

Xiamen jingji tequ nianjian (1990), (《厦門經濟特區年鑒》).

Xinjiapo Anxi huiguan (1988-1996), 《新加坡安溪會館》, 从 1988-1996.

Yang, C.K. (1961), *Religion in Chinese Society*, Berkeley: University of California Press.

Yang, M.M.H. (1994), *Gifts, Favours and Banquets*, Ithaca: Cornell University Press.

Yen, C.H. (1981), "Early Chinese Clan Organisations in Singapore and Malaya 1819-1911", in Yong, C.F. (ed.), *Ethnic Chinese in Southeast Asia, Journal of Southeast Asian Studies*, vol. 12, no. 1., pp. 62-87, independent issue.

Yen, C.H. (1986), *A Social History of the Chinese in Singapore and Malaya 1800-1911*, Singapore: Oxford University Press.

Yong, C.F. (1968), "A Preliminary Study of Chinese Leadership in Singapore 1900-1941", *Journal of Southeast Asian History*, vol. 9, no.2, pp.258-285.

Yong, C.F. (1977), "Leadership and Power in the Chinese Community of Singapore during the 1930s", *Journal of Southeast Asian Studies*, vol. 8, no.2, pp. 195-209.

Yong, C.F. (1977), "Pang, Pang Organisations and Leadership in the Chinese Community of Singapore during the 1930s", *Journal of the South Seas Society*, vol. 32, nos 1 and 2, pp. 31-52.

Yong, C.F. (1987), *Tan Kah Kee: The Making of an Overseas Chinese legend*, Singapore: Oxford University Press.

Yong, C.F. (ed.) (1981), Ethnic Chinese in Southeast Asia, *Journal of Southeast Asian Studies*, vol. 12, no.1, independent issue.

Yu Guanghong (1987), "Meiyou zuchan jiumeiyou zuzong paiwei - E. Ahern xinan ziliao de zai fenxi" (餘光弘: "沒有祖産就沒有祖宗牌位 - E.Ahern 溪南資料的再分析), *Minzuxue yanjiusuo jijkan* (《民族學研究所集刊》), vol. 62, pp. 115-177.

Zhenxiang zazhi bianjibu (1987), "Qingshui zushi de chuanqi yu lingji" (真相雜志編輯部 : "清水祖師的傳奇與靈績 "), *Zhenxiang zazhi* 《真相雜志》, vol. 40, pp. 57-59.

Zhongguo xiangzhen qiye nianjian bianji weiyuahui bian (1992), *Zhongguo xiangzhen qiye nianjian* (中國鄉鎮企業年鑒編輯委員會編 : 《中國鄉鎮企業年鑒》), Beijing: Nongye chebanshe (北京 : 農業出版社).

Zhou Fengjun (1978), "Shenzhong zhuiyuan de jizu yishi" (周豐君 : "慎終追遠的祭祖儀式 "), *Guohun* (《國魂》), vol. 387, pp. 26-27.

Index